Hoggin' The Page

Groundhogs
The Classic Years

AF754444

Martyn Hanson

SONICBOND

sonicbondpublishing.com

Sonicbond Publishing Limited
www.sonicbondpublishing.co.uk
Email: info@sonicbondpublishing.co.uk

First Published in the United Kingdom 2005
First Published in the United States 2005
This edition 2024

British Library Cataloguing in Publication Data:
A Catalogue record for this book is available from the British Library

Copyright Martyn Hanson 2005-2024

ISBN 978-1-78952-343-0

The right of Martyn Hanson to be identified as the author of this work
has been asserted by him in accordance with the
Copyright, Designs and Patents Act 1988.

All rights reserved. No part of this publication may be reproduced, stored in a retrieval system or transmitted in any form or by any means, electronic, mechanical, photocopying, recording or otherwise, without prior permission in writing from Sonicbond Publishing Limited

Typeset in ITC Garamond Std & ITC Avant Garde Gothic Pro
Printed and bound in England

Graphic design and typesetting: Full Moon Media

Follow us on social media:
Twitter: https://twitter.com/SonicbondP
Instagram: www.instagram.com/sonicbondpublishing_/
Facebook: www.facebook.com/SonicbondPublishing/

Linktree QR code:

Hoggin' The Page

Groundhogs
The Classic Years

Martyn Hanson

SONICBOND

sonicbondpublishing.com

Dedication

When you are one of life's weary foot soldiers, very few shining beacons appear on the horizon. Our granddaughter, Ellie-Anne, is certainly one of them. With the ebb and flow of life ever rolling relentlessly on, it was during the final stages of preparing this book that our mom left us. I dedicate this book to them both. (2005)

To the memory of my parents, Hazel and Bill. (2024)

Foreword By Joanna Deacon

Tony McPhee was proud of his music. Every single piece was his creative experience, and he would be hurt to hear any of his songs criticised. He only ever wrote one 'fill in' track, 'Cherry Red', which was his fun imitation of pop music – it became his most famous track. The irony was not lost on him.

For Tony and me, writing a book about his life and the Groundhogs was always a project for some time in the future, something on the back burner. When he was approached by Martyn Hanson, we put our faith in him to get something written, knowing that Tony (even with me and a pointy stick) would never get it finished on his own.

Martyn turned up at the door, sat down and produced a 1970s personal cassette recorder, a precise list of questions, a soft Brummie accent and a gentle, get-to-work attitude. Martyn wanted *detail*, and as he and Tony talked, I would be sent to search for diaries, calendars, old adverts, ticket stubs and reviews, trying to nail down dates, names and photos collected by Tony. He employed the Eric Morecombe method of filing: he had all the right pieces of paper, but not necessarily in the right order.

I don't know how many cassettes were filled over how many visits (I bet Martyn does), but then came the drafts in the post. Tony and I would settle down, I would read the chapters aloud and Tony would provide occasional outbursts of 'That's not right!' Martyn never seemed to get exasperated by our changes.

We were delighted by the finished book, with its wittily captioned photos, intricate detail and valuable annexes – including a selected discography and lists of gigs to 1976, the latter updated in this edition, thanks to records from Groundhogs fans. The book became a critical fount of information for us. Set the scene: just sitting down to dinner and we get a message, 'Me and my mate Dave are just having a beer and can't remember when we saw you in Brighton in the early 1970s. It was my birthday …' Easy!

Tony McPhee had direction to his life, and – despite his incredible talent as a guitarist, songwriter and singer – he was a jobbing musician, very down-to-earth about his commitments: write an album, do the gig, feed the family, buy the house. From the mid 1990s, a series of strokes progressively took his physical dexterity and eventually his voice, and yet he still insisted on getting out to play. Eventually in 2014, after a gig in Skegness, where he struggled to deal with amp problems and an obnoxious stage crew, followed by a terrible rehearsal for the next gig, I suggested that he could retire if he wanted. It was as if I had taken the weight of the world off his shoulders. The gig was cancelled and he never looked back.

After a contented retirement, Tony McPhee died at home on 6 June 2023, following a fall. He is still the nicest man I have ever met.

Joanna Deacon
23 October 2024

Foreword To The 2005 Edition By Captain Sensible

Tony McPhee was the British Hendrix. He could do soaring feedback solos and really took the whole guitar-playing thing as far as he could. And what he doesn't know about the blues isn't worth knowing, I mean, Clapton? Don't get me on that tosspot – he had one solo and bored us to death for 30 years with it. He's a turgid git. McPhee's the real thing. Every time he plays a song, he plays it differently. And that's a wonderful thing, not to repeat yourself.

Thank Christ For The Bomb is the most amazing album I've ever heard. I got it when it first came out in 1970 and I must have worn out about three vinyl copies over the years. I used to play it all the time. When I got into songwriting myself – I wouldn't have nicked from it, but I was grateful to be influenced by that stuff. I thought of it as psychedelic punk – The Hogs, Soft Machine and Syd Barrett.

The problem with the expression 'prog rock' is that it's been sullied by the likes of Yes, Genesis and ELP. So if you say you're into prog rock, everybody thinks you're into that (booming voice) 'Oh, I saw a wizard walking through the woods the other day. The pixies were running around...' Dum, dum, dum – 20-minute guitar solo. 'And then the wizard said...' I mean, fucking hell, what's that shit about?

But it's like classical music. There's great classical music. Rachmaninov – he's brilliant. Sibelius – fucking genius. And then there's crap like Mozart and Beethoven. Same with prog rock. There was some wonderful stuff, like all the Krautrock stuff with Neu! and Kraftwerk, and then there was the bombastic nonsense that Yes produced. The Groundhogs were probably the finest example of prog rock you can possibly get – a mixture of blues, psychedelia and pop that's never been bettered before or since.

Thank Christ... is a perfect album. There's not a filler track on it and the sequence is brilliant. Plus, McPhee produced it all himself. One minute, it's a full-on power trio playing this manic, almost punk rock – angrier, anti-establishment, anti-war stuff – and the next minute, it drops right down into this extremely quiet and subtle finger-picking stuff.

Tony McPhee is an absolute genius; I used to stand and watch him at the Croydon Greyhound. I'd stand right at the front and work out which chords he was playing. But he made most of them up himself. Read this book and try to work out some of his secrets.

With thanks to Scott Rowley, *Classic Rock*

Acknowledgements

After having written two books on completely different bands, I thought it would be interesting to do something on a band that came from the blues. It's clear that ELP and The Nice were inspired by European classical music, so it was a breath of fresh air to write from another perspective.

I can still recall the first time I heard 'Thank Christ For The Bomb' and it's a moment that's stayed with me. With this in mind, it proved to be memorable to interview the actors involved in the story. There were a few that couldn't be traced, but despite a lot of effort, they had to be filed as 'the ones that got away'.

First and foremost, I would like to thank Tony McPhee for an in-depth series of interviews. I would also like to thank Tony's partner, Joanna Deacon. It was thanks to her that his voluminous archive was catalogued and this, in retrospect, made the job much easier. Joanna also compiled the gig list and put a huge amount of other work in behind the scenes.

A million thanks to Michael Heatley for having faith in me and publishing this book.

I would also like to thank the following for their co-operation: Pete Cruickshank, Ken Pustelnik, Dave 'Jim' Wetton – who delved into his diaries with gusto and compiled an accurate order of events from Tony's early musical life – John 'Cakey' Weeks', John 'Oscar' Wild, John Cruickshank, Roy Fisher, Bob Hall, Terry Goldberg, Terry Slade, Clive Brooks, Wilf Pine, Simon Prager, Andrew Lauder, Mike Vernon, Dave Kelly, Mike Batt, Mick Hubbert, Jerry Gilbert, Chris Welch, Bob Glass, Denis Knowles and Len Tempan.

The fans came to my aid, too. I give special thanks to Tony Sherratt and Mick Stones because they provided me with a lot of material; their valuable insights were also very helpful. Tony also supplied the discography from his excellent 'Squealing Pups' Groundhogs website. I would also like to thank Steve Thompson. All three contributed 'I was there reports'. Garry Bodenham provided the Weeley photo and Paul Brears came up trumps with pictures of Tony's 'Two Sides' tour. Nick Moss deserves a mention in dispatches for ploughing through the first draft and making useful comments. My old friend David Flavell has proved to be a good sounding board for my projects over the years, too. Graham Vosper also deserves a mention. Jenny Seager and Linda Hardy did all the work in acquiring and setting up the computer I used to write the book.

Now, here's the backup team. My wife, Carole, has put up with my different projects over the years and certainly deserves a medal. Dale and Lee-Anne still provide me with plenty of inspiration. All had to put up with my gripes when things were not going well; I can tell you that, in the course of a book, there are many indeed!

Thank you to Stephen Lambe of Sonicbond for having enough faith in this book to reprint it.

Hoggin' The Page

Groundhogs ***The Classic Years***

Contents

Chapter 1 - Scratching The Surface

Don't you know you are wasting your time with that guitar?
A teacher to Tony McPhee

Mac was the electrical whiz kid, so we just did what he advised.
Seneschals bassist Dave Wetton

Anthony Charles McPhee was born on 23 March 1944 at 2 pm on a snowy Thursday afternoon to Eileen and Charles. The location was just outside the small Lincolnshire town of Humberston on the east coast of England. By dint of birth, he automatically fell under an astrological sign, but it was not something that bothered him in any way: 'I am definitely not hot-tempered or have any of the fiery attributes of the typical Aries male ... but I consider the astrology myths, along with religious ones, as being good stories and they make nice epic films, but are basically legends and half-truths which I don't need to live a moral life.'

The comings and goings in the house that day belied the fact that The Second World War was raging to its savage conclusion. This 'total' war spread its tentacles into all spheres of society. Every family was affected by it and the McPhee family was no exception. Tony's father was stationed at the nearby New Waltham wireless station, where he worked as a naval operator.

The house where he was born has long since been knocked down, but the McPhee family didn't stay at 'Redlands' for long after Tony's birth anyway. The war had just ended when they moved to Okeburn Road, Tooting, South London. They moved into a two up, two down. It was pretty basic in those days, and as hot water was in short supply, he shared baths with his elder brother Sam or his sister Olive. On the face of it, this corner of the world was no different to most. But fate had provided more than a helping hand, as he summed up: 'Moving to London was probably the luckiest thing that happened to me because when the blues came to England, a lot of r&b clubs proliferated and these were where bands like The Stones, The Yardbirds and Jeff Beck, who was in a band called the Tridents, first played.' Clubs like The Marquee, The Jazz Club (now the 100 Club) and The Crawdaddy were in easy reach via the London tube.

The young McPhee attended the local Ensham Infants School, which was next to a Girls' school that would harbour greater significance in the future. This was still the time of rationing and slates, and chalk instead of paper and pencil was the order of the day. One of Tony's earliest memories at school was the visit of the school photographer. He hated having his picture taken, as he didn't like his body: 'I have an inordinately large head which was on top of a fairly puny body, and when I foolishly showed the picture to Jo Ann Kelly about 20 years later, she exclaimed, 'Good God, The Mekon!'' (The Mekon was an alien featured in the *Eagle* comic and was the archenemy of Dan Dare, the hero spaceman).

In the 1950s, the radio was still the main source of entertainment and Tony's family would gather around it to hear shows like *The Goons* and *Journey Into Space*. The former moulded his sense of humour (he still loves that kind of slapstick) and the latter his interest in science fiction and fantasy. Tony's dad made certain that there was never a dull moment, even when the radio was switched off. He made sure that his children used their 'grey matter', imparting his general knowledge to them in the form of quiz nights. He taught Tony and Olive the Morse code and they would decode the messages he had sent them. There was no doubt that the young McPhee was a very inquisitive boy and the stimulus he received from his father was an important factor in developing it.

The McPhee family were a tight unit. His parents hardly ever went out, save for a couple of occasions; this went on until Tony was in his teens. His father was not a strict disciplinarian and it meant Tony never feared him, but this wasn't the case for many boys of his generation. He is the first one to admit his mother was a 'soft touch' and that he took advantage of her. In fact, he admitted in later life: 'I was a mummy's boy. I can't deny it, but it only made me more independent later on, so I don't regret it.' He was very close to his siblings. He shared a room with Olive and he hero-worshipped his elder brother Sam. Although he was a late child, family life was 'normal' and he was very close to his siblings, playing and falling out with both of them. One piece of retribution which still weighs heavy is the day his sister took his plasticine and mixed all the colours into a brown lump in front of his face – he still claims he was a golden child and didn't deserve it. They were both to play a major part in Tony's early musical development.

Later on, his father bought a television set – a Baird with a 9-inch screen – and young Tony's interest in science fiction was stimulated further. One of his favourite shows was *The Quatermass Experiment*. One memorable episode showed two astronauts disappearing into their spacesuits. By this time, he was hiding behind the sofa, not able to watch. Another of his favourite shows was *Three, Two, One, Zero*. Tony recalls a frightening aspect of the show: 'It was about the atomic bomb, and I have to admit that I found the footage of the explosions terrifying and yet exciting. These were dangerous days with the total paranoia of the Americans fuelling the arms race.' One thing was certain: there were a few markers being laid down that would surface later on.

The family home was very cold in the winter and they relied on an open fire to heat the living/dining room. Tony's mum would have to hold up a page from the *News Of The World* against the surround of the fire to draw the flames from the paper and wood under the coals. Sometimes, the newspaper would catch fire and she would be forced to take frantic action to put out the unwanted flames. Tony used the open fire in the front room to conduct chemical experiments. His party trick was to fart into a Smarties tube, put the cap on and throw it on the fire. It never blew up, but it did produce a few colours.

Occasionally, he'd visit his Auntie Olive and Uncle Tom in Teddington. He always got half a crown from his uncle, who worked at the National Physical Laboratory (which housed early computers) – he would sometimes take his young nephew there. It may have been these visits that started Tony's interest in things electrical and electronic, coupled with an inquisitive nature that drew him to gadgetry. These boyhood interests would be essential tools of the trade during his later career.

Tony's father got a job in the Civil Service and things got better for the family. Soon after, he bought a Bond motorised three-wheel car. They were basically bike engines with a body built around them and two seats side by side. Like all bikes, it was chain-driven and prone to coming off. One day, the inevitable happened. Tony remembers it very well: 'It was the only time I ever heard my dad swear. We were going up Franciscan Road, which is quite a steep hill, and suddenly, he spat out 'Shit'. We were going down the hill backwards, engine racing, as the chain came off the driving cog.'

At eight, Tony was quite well-developed regarding opinions in the ways of the world. One day, he heard his mother say, 'I don't like Atheists', but he had already come to the conclusion he didn't believe in God or any other deity. He had also firmly come to the conclusion that he was a socialist, so he was shocked and disappointed when he later found out that he was named after Anthony Eden, the Tory prime minister. He remains, to this day, firmly an atheistic lefty.

He took his 11-plus exam at Franciscan Junior. Things didn't bode well for the exam because it seemed he was never at school. He disliked it and was always ill or bunking off, though he did suffer a lot from recurring tonsillitis: 'My mom was a bit of a pushover on that score, telling me things like 'if you've got a sore throat, wrap a dirty sock round it.' So there were many times she would walk into my bedroom and I would have a sock wrapped around my throat; I was pretty sure that the rest of the day would be spent reading the Beano and eating sweets. It was even worth suffering Mum's cure-all: a small glass of whisky with hot water and sugar – YUK!' Eventually, the Health Authorities decided he needed a week of convalescing at a facility in Whitstable with 20 other 'serially' sick children. He hated the place and nicknamed it Stalag 13. They even made him eat things he didn't like and that never happened at home! The upshot was that he caught Adenitis there and had to have another two weeks off school when he returned home!

He managed to pass the 11-plus and it meant that he had a passport to a grammar school. He chose Tooting Bec, but only because it was the nearest to his home. The interview with the deputy head, Melhuish, at the school revealed things not just about the school but even more about the class system in Britain at that time: 'He asked me to read a text about Victorian England and then asked questions about it. It was fine until he found out that I had an older brother and asked me if I cleaned his boots! I stared at him incredulously – of course, I didn't! … Anyway, I was accepted and thus began the most influential and some of the most miserable years of my life.'

The first-year pupils at the Bec were called 'weeds' and the initiation ceremony involved having your head stuck down the toilet. Fortunately, Tony was quick enough to avoid this fate. Even though bullying exists in all schools, Tony was unfortunate in that the rituals of this grammar school were still in the Victorian age. It was still a predatory environment. Tony remembers one day that he was with a group of friends when one of them said, 'Who shall we get today?' Tony's reply was, 'Why do we have to get anyone?' He invited trouble for himself and it was clear he needed some new friends. He eventually made a fruitful friendship with three pupils in particular: David 'Jim' Wetton, John 'Oscar' Wild and John 'Cakey' Weeks. These were to make up Tony's first band. He had known them for a while but they were brought together, as firm friends, by the musical revolution that was the happening thing.

It was 1955 and the UK was a very austere place. This was still the time of the rag and bone man, the chimney sweep and the rent collector and even the last vestiges of rationing had only just finished the year before. Even some of the street lamps were still lit by gas! In amongst all the drabness, there was no separate youth/music culture. The music papers of the time featured jazz, folk and easy-listening pop music, of which Doris Day was a good example. Then along came Elvis Presley and things were never the same again.

Tony was very lucky that he had older siblings who were buying records. Olive used to buy 78s to play on their record player (not many people had them then). Initially, she bought Pat Boone and The Tanner Sisters records. Then, one day, she brought something different home: 'Rock Around The Clock' by Bill Haley & The Comets. The effect was devastating, as Tony made clear: 'I was intrigued by the strange instrument featured on the record and asked Olive what it was; 'I think it is an electric guitar', she replied – my mind was boggled. I sort of knew what a guitar was, but plugged into the mains?' It wasn't long before he knew he had to have one.

In those days, most of the artists in the charts were white. Black artists always had a bigger job to make it. In fact, it was Pat Boone's version of Fats Domino's 'Ain't That A Shame' which was a bigger hit. Tony loved Boone's version and didn't hear the original for quite a while, but when he did, he became, and still is, a big fan of Fats. By the summer of 1956, another classic had been and gone: Elvis Presley's 'Heartbreak Hotel'. However, it was Presley's next hit that made a massive impression on him. He heard some schoolmates talking about 'Hound Dog', which he thought was 'Two Hound Dogs', a Bill Haley flip side that he'd heard and didn't think was that hot. He was informed it was actually by Elvis Presley, and as luck would have it, Olive had bought a copy. As Tony recalls: 'I was totally mesmerised by the two Scotty Moore solos, even though I still wasn't sure how the electric guitar worked. I just knew they sounded damn good!'

To say that Tony and his friends were enamoured with this new music was an understatement. However, not all of his friends were that way inclined: 'I had another friend of mine who lived close by was John 'Pug' Wheaton, but I realised he was a musical philistine when he butted in on a conversation between Dave Wetton and me as we were discussing a new single. 'Pug' enquired what we were talking about, so we told him: 'Pat Boone's new single', 'Who's she?' he asked. We walked away scoffing.'

The first year at the Bec saw things going well for young Tony. He was fourth in his class overall. However, things were to go downhill rapidly the following year. A new headmaster was appointed at the school by the name of Wilfred W Hore; it didn't take long for the boys to ridicule his name. He had a line in religious zealotry and he delivered grace in Latin; this was typical of grammar schools in those days. It's no exaggeration to say that the young Tony McPhee loathed this man and everything he stood for. He unnerved the boy and Tony slowly plummeted down the class performance list. Tuesday morning was detention day (aka caning day) and Tony swore that he would never end up in his office under those circumstances; he never did! But plenty of buttocks were rendered black and blue by this arbitrary method of maintaining 'discipline'.

Back in the real world, Tony's brother, Sam was also bringing records home and providing his younger brother with another avenue from which to consider music. He was into Lonnie Donegan, who was spearheading the skiffle movement. Tony recalls a television performance of Donegan on *Six-Five Special* as 'one of the most exciting performances I have ever seen.' He soon realised his brother's tastes were well ahead of their time: 'He used to bring home Turkish music; it's what we would now call 'world music'. He used to get his records from *Imhofs* in Oxford Street, London.'

But there was one more thing that Sam was to initiate his younger sibling into and it changed his life: 'It was him who eventually got me into the blues!' The first blues that Tony heard had been recorded by the blues historian Alan Lomax in 1959 for the Library of Congress. These recordings were intended to document the folk music of the Southern States artists from a social perspective. They were later released as *The Blues Roll On* in the Southern folk heritage series.

However, all was not well with Tony. It was at school that he first started to experience occasional minor psychological troubles and would have panic attacks, as he related in an interview with *Penetration* magazine in 1973: 'It's the sort of thing I used to get when I was at school. I'd get this feeling of disembodiment somehow ... Lots of detachment. It's incredible to describe. Lots of people have had this sensation, and when I was young, I used to get over it by getting up and turning on the radio and forgetting about it.' He would still get these attacks occasionally into adulthood, culminating in an attack he was unable to forget about. It would provide the inspiration for the Groundhogs' finest musical hour.

Out of the emergence of this early youth culture came something else that had darker overtones: gang violence! Tony remembers this period very well: 'One day in the playground, I noticed a group of boys formed in a circle around 'Fud' Campbell, from 3G, who was demonstrating his latest acquisition, a Flick Knife.' There had already been quite a lot of stabbings in the area and the young Tony was keen to acquire one. He never intended to stab anybody – his attraction to it was based on it being a gadget and he loved those – he just liked to flick it. As he couldn't afford the 12s/6d, he went half with his friend, Christopher Webb (his father was in the navy with Tony's father). In fact, Tony was as far removed from the 'hard case' image he was trying to portray; as one of the smallest boys in the class, he was just trying to redress the balance.

In those days, most of Tony's friends had a nickname and Tony's was 'Mac'. Said Webb: 'One day, a teacher revealed that 'Mac' meant 'son of'. I shrank below my desk as I could feel all the kids' eyes boring into the back of my neck. 'Son of Phee!' somebody blurted out. The mathematics teacher didn't like Tony very much, and from that point, every time we were in a maths class and the teacher mentioned the word 'fee', he couldn't understand why the whole class went into paroxysms of laughter.' In spite of this incident, his nickname remained the 'tough' sounding 'Mac'.

Tony's academic prowess was taking a hammering by the time he got to Class 3A (Arts stream). He came 30th out of a class of 31 pupils. One of his friends, Johnny Bryant, had the dubious honour of being last. In fact, Bryant also made a mark on the entertainment industry by winning the very first edition of the TV talent show *New Faces*. As Tony noted: 'Isn't it strange how the only two people in our year to go on to be professional musicians were the most useless academically!'

It was no surprise that the subject that interested Tony the most was science, but he ended up in the arts stream and was unable to shake off the accursed Latin lessons. By this time, one of his best friends was Dave Wetton and they enjoyed the same types of music. It was 1957 and it greeted the arrival of another big figure on the horizon. To Tony, he was different from the others: 'He was one of the most influential white singer/guitarist/songwriters of all time.' The man in question was Buddy Holly. Holly was the first consistent songwriter/performer to emerge to date. The number of artists that Tony admired was building up and the time was fast approaching when he would no longer be content with just listening to music! There wasn't really a history of musicians in the family aside from Tony's grandfather, who played the banjo.

Dave Wetton acquired an acoustic guitar and was the first of his close friends to have one. It had been a present from his uncle, who had bought it while on shore leave in the Far East and brought it back with him when World War Two ended. It had a painted Hawaiian scene on it (scratched to buggery by plectrums) and Tony knew he had to have one. After much badgering of his mom, it was agreed that he could have one for Christmas. It was 1958 and his mother took him down to Taborn's music shop in Tooting to select his first guitar – he was 14 years old. He chose a Telesforo Julwe. It was a Spanish guitar and a good choice. His early and only guitar teacher even preferred to play it over his own.

His mother insisted on him embarking on some musical education, so she booked guitar lessons for him. The teacher's name was Sam Weller, who was based in Clapham South, and Tony soon started his lessons in earnest. However, it didn't turn out to be as straightforward as he hoped: he couldn't get his head around the dots; he just couldn't work it out at all. This wasn't a total surprise to him as music lessons at school had also been a mystery. Furthermore, he had small hands and he couldn't cover the fretboard properly. There was no other thing for it; after barely ten lessons, he stopped. The next stage was to adopt a style he was comfortable with. It wasn't long before Tony and Dave Wetton got together to practice and dissect the latest sounds. They were listening to a lot of instrumental records. The Shadows, The Fireballs and The Hunters were the ones that garnered most of their attention.

The young McPhee honed his technique by playing along to these instrumental records – he seemed to have a knack for playing by ear. He was forging ahead rapidly and a regular three hours of practice a day was an indication of his dedication. He was very shy of girls and felt more comfortable staying in with his guitar.

Tony McPhee's first public performance in 1959 was an unlikely affair. He was just 15 years old. Every year, the Bec held a Christmas concert.[1] It was quite informal and the pupils were invited to perform; it wasn't compulsory. The performances took many guises, ranging from poetry to piano recitals or even snippets from the great plays. As the event was so casual, it was decided to have a novel format, as Dave Wetton revealed: 'There were nine of us on stage, including John Wild on banjo and Cakey playing a snare drum! We decided to do 'Worried Man Blues'. We called ourselves The Worried Nine. As it turned out, it was quite apt as John Wild was so nervous that he played the same chord for the whole song. It was quite a simple 12-bar song that could have lasted the whole afternoon if you wanted it to. I made a mistake as I started singing before Tony was ready! I had my dressing gown cord tied around my guitar but he didn't have any support for his guitar. We had to wait while he shuffled a chair forward to rest his leg on. But we got through it after that on our mass strum-in.'

They even used face makeup and painted sideburns to make them look older. It backfired a little bit as it took them ages to get it off in the toilet afterwards. Tony doesn't remember much of that day, apart from the garish orange jumper he was wearing, but he remembers what the Latin teacher, Mr Philpot, said to him – it's a classic line – 'Don't you know you are wasting your time with that guitar?' After that performance, they trimmed back to a four-piece.

While they were rehearsing, the problem of amplification cropped up many times. How could they make their acoustic guitars sound louder? They couldn't afford electric guitars or proper amplifiers. It was here that Tony displayed his electrical ingenuity. He started to think deeply about how amplifiers actually worked and set about trying to solve their problem in some way. He owned some throat mics that were War Department surplus (similar to the one used by WW2 fighter pilots) and he worked on the idea of vibration and amplifying that vibration. He combined the throat mics with a Ford ignition coil. The throat mics were then strapped to the bridge of the guitar by their snake belts, which had a cable going into the ignition coil and then out into the back of an old valve radio – and 'hey presto'. However, it didn't always work; he had to mess around with it and they only had five feet of cable each, so they were never going to move around like The Shadows. They stored the radio in the school janitor's room. Then, one day, Tony couldn't get the set-up to work before he realised that somebody had pinched the valves! They never actually played a gig with that primitive set-up. The friends decided that it was time to form a proper group. By this time, Johnny Bryant, who had also got his own guitar, joined them occasionally.

The boys were now fired up to go a stage further. It was decided that they should enrol in the guitar night class at the nearby Ensham Girls School, which was situated on Franciscan Road, Tooting. The teacher was a man called Frank. He was a big, fat man and seemed to have no trouble finding his way around the fretboard, giving the boys hope they could do it also. There were no difficulties in making the class numbers up as lots of boys were all trying to emulate their heroes. Dave Wetton remembers those times very well: 'Frank used to play things like 'Sweet Georgia Brown'. It was all old tunes, but there were loads of subtle chord changes and we all benefited. It gave us a good insight into how music fits together. We all used to sit on the desk and strum along with chords he'd put on the blackboard.' Later on, they hired a separate room at the Ensham Girls School for their own use. They used it extensively. (In May 1961, they rehearsed there eight times alone.)

Such was their love of the guitar, they all enrolled in the same evening class in woodwork, the rationale being that they intended to make their own guitars. They were made in the classic double cutaway shape (hollow but narrow, composed of ply back and front separated by wooden blocks, with thin ply laminate curved around the edges). But when Dave Wetton assembled his bass job, the problems started, as he recalls: 'When I tightened the strings, the whole thing fell apart and I had to rethink ways of making a more robust design.'

For now, though, the time of play was over and it was time to engage in the real world. Tony McPhee left school in the summer of 1960. His only qualification was a GCE in French, but he did have a near squeak in physics and art. At first, it was thought Tony had done well, but his mother opened the results letter upside down. What she thought was a 'P' for 'pass' was, in fact, a grade '9'! He decided, without telling his father, to have the full school holiday. However, as the holiday period ebbed away, his father found out he had left school and told Tony in no uncertain terms to get a job!

He saw an advert in the *Evening Standard* for a soldering job at Great Chapel Street and decided to go for it (the fact that there were lots of guitar shops nearby had nothing to do with it). The name of the company was Jason Kits. He had learnt to solder at home and decided to apply. But when he got there, the foreman looked at him rather strangely and said he was expecting a young lady. The interview went well and he got the job. It was only when he started that he recalled the reaction of the foreman at the interview. The soldering team was made up of women and he was going to be stuck in the middle of them! He had many embarrassing moments, and he confessed with a laugh: 'The women at the factory were really dirty!' He only stayed for a few months before he got a job at the Post Office.

All this time, Tony and Dave were still practising, but the fledgling band had a major obstruction that had to be overcome. Inspired by

The Shadows, they decided they needed a more practical division of instruments. They had to decide who would drop the six-string guitar. As Dave Wetton recalls, there was one decision that was easy: 'It was obvious that Tony was going to be the lead guitarist as he was so much better than the rest of us. We decided the rest by the toss of a coin; I lost and became the bass player and John Wild went to rhythm guitar. 'Cakey' Weeks already had a snare drum, so he became the drummer.' (Cakey didn't get his first drum kit until 23 May 1961.) At that stage, they didn't have a name for the band. 'Cakey' remembers he suggested they call themselves The Four Horsemen of the Apocalypse, but they preferred to remain nameless. At that point in time, all the boys were members of The Shadows Fan Club. In fact, Tony's name on the fan club register was Elmer P Turner. They all gave themselves American-sounding names in the way that Hank B Marvin (Brian Rankin) had done.

One of the first things Tony did when he started to receive wages was to make plans to buy an electric guitar. The guitar he wanted was a Futurama. It looked like a Stratocaster, but, in fact, it was made in Czechoslovakia. However, at the price of 55 guineas, he couldn't afford to pay cash so he had to buy it on hire purchase, and as he was so young, he had to get his father to be the guarantor in case he defaulted on the payments. He didn't have an amp at that stage, but he was over the moon with his new purchase. But as he remarked: 'From that point, I was hardly out of debt.' Soon after this, the rest of the band started to acquire electric guitars and amplifiers and started to think about playing gigs.

It was around this time that they decided a name for the band would be ideal. Dave Wetton suggested The Talismans of Set; this was a reference to black magic and made the band sound very mystical. But it was rejected. In the end, they settled on The Seneschals. The way they acquired this name was quite bizarre. Tony was thumbing through a dictionary, looking for inspiration. He saw the word Seneschals and he immediately liked the sound – it actually means a butler in a castle. Everybody else thought it was a good name, too. At this stage, their repertoire consisted entirely of instrumental numbers. In fact, one of the numbers they used to do was Duane Eddy's '3:30 blues' – the first real blues tune that Tony played.

The band were still going strong, but they hadn't actually played a gig. That was about to change in the most fortuitous of circumstances. Dave Wetton was travelling on the bus with his Burns Weill bass guitar when a man approached him and asked if he was in a band and if he could ask the band to play at his daughter's wedding. They duly played the wedding; it went quite well and they were paid the princely sum of £2, which was a lot of money in those days. However, the money they received was all used to pay for a stand-in drummer – the usual one wasn't available on that day – and the train and taxi fares that had got them there in the first place!

Back in the day job, Tony McPhee enjoyed working for the General Post Office as a telephone engineer (this was before British Telecom was created). His old friend, John Wild, had recommended the job to him. He had even coached him on how to pass the entry exam. He told Tony all about the quadratic equations that made up the test. So he learnt the formula by heart. He didn't really understand it but he was determined to bluff his way through. Tony recalls his issues started early on: 'The next question started, 'Now use this formula…' – I was stumped. The interviewer asked me why I hadn't answered the question and I just shrugged my shoulders. He then took me along to a panel of engineers and they started asking me questions about history, which I could not answer; then one asked me the formula for Ohm's law and I rattled it off. He asked me to apply it, I did and I was in.'

It was a very good job and he enjoyed the many perks. In the morning, he seemed to spend most of his time in the café, then he'd do a couple of hours of work. After an extended lunch break, during which he would saunter to the guitar shops in Charring Cross Road, he'd be back to do another hour of work and then go home. Tony liked his work, but there was no doubt where his priorities lay: 'The only thing I could think about was doing more music.'

As Christmas 1960 approached, there was something that had been on Tony's mind for quite a while. It concerned the subject of eating animal flesh. It all came to a head when he was working in the Smithfield meat market. The carcasses had often repulsed him, but on this day, he was working by a stall. He heard the stallholder say to a couple who had come to collect their Christmas turkey, 'Do you want the legs on?' The next thing he knew, two legs landed right at his feet. This was the moment when he decided to become a vegetarian.[2] At the time, it was so rare that his family and friends were astounded. It certainly showed that he had the courage of his convictions. It was this trait that was to prove so important to him in his later musical career.

The year 1961 was a busy time for the boys if Dave Wetton's diary is anything to go by. It certainly gives a strong flavour of the 1960s. He went to CND sit-downs, demos in Trafalgar Square against the bomb and the still-active fascist Oswald Moseley's demos in Grosvenor Square. He also managed to fit in The Shadows and Chris Barber gigs. In October, they played their first gig at the Ensham Girls School, and on 10 December, they played the prestigious Castle in Tooting, but Dave Wetton noted in his diary that it was 'not so hot'. They had performed badly and missed the chance to get off to a morale boosting start. The one good thing was that they were investing in gear all the time. Tony had acquired his Truvoice amp and Cakey acquired his second set of Premier drums in early 1962. In the same year, Tony bought a Cherry Red Gibson SG, paying 173 guineas for it. This was the guitar that was to become his trademark to fans all over the world.[3]

On 28 April 1962, they played the St Thomas Church Hall at Nunhead, South London – it was the first of many times there. Dave Wetton recalls that the taxi fare was a whopping £5! However, in June, they played a Wimbledon Park gig that highlighted something missing in the band, as summed up by Dave Wetton in his diary: 'Not so bad as we thought – we need a singer'. The first they auditioned was a local lad called Graham Woollard. He was very good at singing Cliff Richard songs, but he didn't seem right for the job overall. The next candidate was someone called 'Greek' John. He tagged along with the band for a while, but he was a 'pain in the arse' and was very brash – he didn't fit at all. The quest for a singer was undertaken in earnest now. Barry Bethel, Reg Foreman and a guy called Dave were tried out in rehearsal. Dave was the only one who actually got to perform with them in public.

Things looked up even further when they acquired their own transport. 'Cakey' Week's girlfriend's Dad, Pat, offered his van and his chauffeur services as a runaround.[4] This meant the days of carting gear on buses and trains were well and truly over. This was just as well because the ingenious Tony and Sam built Dave Wetton a massive bass cabinet. There was even talk about going professional. However, there was a major problem on the horizon for the band as 'Cakey' was getting engaged to Molly and he couldn't guarantee making all the gigs. His days in the band were numbered.

They were getting a lot of bookings at the Conservative Club Youth Movement, but on 25 August 1962, they played a gig at Kemsing, near Sevenoaks (the first gig in the van). By this time, they had even acquired stage clothes. This consisted of Chef's trousers, white shirts and black bow ties. They supported a band called The Dollarbills, the mainstays of the band being the talented Cruickshank brothers. In fact, Tony and John Wild worked with John Cruickshank as Post Office engineers. In early September, they managed to get an audition at the Castle, but they failed it because the promoter didn't think Dave came up to scratch the new singer left shortly after.

They put an advert in *Melody Maker* and a young man called Ray Orchard applied for the job. However, because there was already a famous man of the same name working as a Radio Luxemburg DJ, he became Rocking Ray Wade. At the point of joining the band, Wade became the most experienced member, as Dave Wetton revealed: 'He was older than us, he was very charismatic and he had a good voice.' Now they had a singer, they could expand their material. They started playing Buddy Holly, Roy Orbison and Everley Brothers songs.

By early November, their gigs were going down very well and they decided to have another try at bigger venues. With their new singer in place, it was time to secure another audition at the Castle; this time, they got 'the thumbs up'. Now they were on the circuit, they played plenty of the bigger venues, but it was the Castle (they played on 22 and 29 November) in Tooting Broadway that meant the most to Tony: 'When we played that gig, I thought we'd made it. I always used to wonder why there were always guys standing outside the pub. It was only years later that I found out it was also a brothel!' It also served as a makeshift boxing ring, especially on a Friday night.

The Seneschals had another break when they were rehearsing at the Ensham Girls School on 11 February 1963. A man came down from the nearby Bedford Hotel in Balham and said he had been told there was a band at the club and that he urgently needed one to stand in for The Checkmates, who'd cancelled next week's gig. This was a daunting prospect as, a few years before, they had had a number-one hit with 'What Do You Want To Make Those Eyes At Me For' (with Emile Ford). The gig was a great success. Strangely, The Checkmates turned up very late but, after some agro at the door, were refused entry. It was obvious that The Seneschals were beginning to be in great demand elsewhere. Immediately after the Bedford Hotel gig, they played three consecutive gigs. On 30 March, they played the St Thomas Hall, Nunhead, again. For the cost of 2 shillings (£1.67 allowing for inflation), you could spend the night 'Dancing to the Fabulous Seneschals'.

As they got more gigs, the band grew in stature, playing to bigger audiences. But how did a young, shy and innocent Tony McPhee overcome his reticence? Dave Wetton gave a clue: 'Tony was retiring {meaning reserved] but when you play in a band, you're playing good music and you are together as one, you acquire huge amounts of self-confidence. We were lucky because we played a lot together before we really started gigging.' Tony McPhee had developed his own mindset for performing in public: 'I was shy, but I wanted to do it badly enough. I remember playing my first solo. I was very apprehensive. However, when I played the first gig at the school Xmas concert, I looked out at the audience and thought, 'I can do something you can't, you useless bastards!''

Tony was always trying to advance the band in any way he could. John Wild recalled: 'Tony was always the first at rehearsals; he would set everything up. He had this Swiss Echo tape machine and was always taping things off the radio for us to listen to. He knew what he wanted, but he could never be described as a dictator. He was very persuasive and he convinced us of his vision with the strength of his argument.' They would all learn how to play the latest hits of the day using this method.

Around this time, Tony was starting to venture out to the Marquee Club in London on Thursdays with his brother Sam. The influence of Sam's records was luring him to seek out the blues in the flesh. He later took Dave Wetton and John Wild to witness the delights of the fledgling blues movement. The spearhead of this movement was Cyril Davies and the All Stars, who, by all accounts, were a scintillating act.

One of the blues artists that Tony liked the most was Robert Johnson. He particularly liked his slide guitar playing. At the time, a slide couldn't be purchased from any shop; he had to improvise and make one. He tried various bits of pipefitting, but he was severely inconvenienced when he got it stuck on his finger – it took him a while to get it off. He carried on in this haphazard way until a friend of his, who worked at the Ford Motor Company, made him a custom-made brass model. After that, he never had any problems.

After playing with The Seneschals for a couple of years, there came a twist of fate that was to bring Tony McPhee to his next career move. Tony had gotten to know John Cruickshank at work quite well; he was the singer in The Dollarbills. Luckily for Tony, their guitarist had just left because he didn't want to turn professional. Cruikshank asked Tony to audition for the vacancy, as he knew he was a useful guitarist. He duly passed the audition, although he wasn't overly impressed by their name or by the fact they had a saxophone player; he didn't think the instrument was right for the band.

In April 1963, shortly before Tony officially joined The Dollarbills, he wrote Dave Wetton a resignation letter, part of which reads: 'I'm leaving the group and turning professional with J.C (John Cruickshank) and will be going to Germany soon. Roy Fisher, their manager, phoned me on Saturday saying that their lead guitarist finally decided not to turn pro.' The Seneschals played their final gig at the Bruce Hall, just up the road from where it all began, at the Ensham Girls School. They'd done several previous gigs there and had always gone down well, so it was a good note to finish on. On Saturday 6 April 1963, the end of this era was played out.

Roy Fisher had been associated with the Cruickshanks for a long time; he recalls how it all started:

> In 1958, I was 18 and working as a photographic assistant, travelling to work in West London from South London. Every day, I would travel on the train with an Anglo-Indian guy called Phillip Holmes, and he invited me to his wedding reception – that's where I first met John Cruickshank (then 16) and his brother Pete (then 14). John got drunk at the reception and I helped his brother carry him home. Arriving at their house too late to get my bus home, I was invited by their mother to stay the night, which was the start of my 45-year-old friendship with John and Pete.
>
> A couple of years later, John got engaged, and his future wife's brother, John Lockyear, was learning to play the guitar. John Cruickshank had a good voice and Pete learnt to play bass guitar. They found a drummer called Dave Boorman and 'Eddy Troude' (John) – The Dollarbills were born. I could not sing and played no instruments but was good on the phone, so I started to manage them. The few gigs that came along were laughable. We played a couple of songs before a movie at the Lewisham Odeon Cinema – that was a complete disaster as the rising platform didn't rise.

There were no hard feelings towards Tony because, shortly after he left, the remainder of The Seneschals went to see their old mate. Tony's debut was probably at the Cafe des Artistes, Chelsea, on Friday 10 May 1963. As a footnote to history, the sax player, Jack, didn't know it, but his days were numbered.

However, the truth of it was that The Seneschals had been going in different directions for some time. Dave Wetton sums up the situation prior to the split: 'When we went to the London clubs, Mac was no longer coming with us and we weren't popping round to each other's houses as we had been, so we were beginning to lose the cohesiveness of those previous years. If I was pushed on the matter, I'd say it was the visits to the clubs that got us all hooked on the blues to the point where we all started buying albums individually rather than buying the records first and then going to the clubs. It was a short, sharp intro before The Seneschals broke up.'

However, they all remained friends, and even though they did have a few rehearsals after Tony left, they folded soon after. John Wild teamed up with some local blues men and 'Cakey' Weeks went back to drumming later on to form a band with Dave Wetton and Johnny Bryant called The Shifters. They appeared with such luminaries as The Barron Knights, The Small Faces and Billy J. Kramer & The Dakotas and appeared on ITV's *Ready, Steady, Win* competition. But as 'Cakey' remarked, life in the music business can be cruel: 'The odd thing is that The Seneschals were miles better, but The Shifters got a lot more work!'

Chapter 2 – The House Of Blues

He had a dramatic impact on the band.
Pete Cruickshank's verdict on Tony joining The Dollarbills

It is rock history's duty to attempt to make amends for all these lives of injustice and misery; while white rock musicians strutted in the hallways of five-star hotels earning money from music that was not really of their own making, the true composers were neither recognised nor recompensed.
Chambers Rock Music Guide

Apart from John Cruickshank on vocals, later on harmonica, there was also his brother, Pete, on bass guitar. John Lockyear made up the rest of The Dollarbills – he played lead guitar. It was no exaggeration to say that John Cruikshank was the acknowledged leader of the band. In joining the band, Tony teamed up for the first time with John's younger brother. It was the beginning of a lifelong association. Pete Cruickshank was born in India on 2 July 1945. His grandfather had gone to India to take over a mill. His father was born on the steamship on the way over. Things didn't go well and his father ended up in an orphanage at the age of four. When he was older, his father joined the RAF, where he met Pete's mother, who was a teacher. They got married in India. In 1955, the family left India and came to England in order to give their children a better education.

Pete's mother was a classically trained musician who was trained at the Royal Academy in London. There was always some sort of music going on in the household. He remembers hearing classical music, and although he didn't like it, he believed it subconsciously made an impression on him. As was expected, his elder brother, John, was very interested in becoming a musician and he acquired a drum kit. All his other friends had acquired guitars and the young Pete also got one. However, being the youngest in the group had distinct disadvantages: 'All the others were a lot more advanced than me. I was always making up ground. We needed a bass player, so I decided that it would be something that would give me a unique identity. I paid £20 for a Tuxedo bass guitar.'

The young Pete Cruickshank liked Gene Vincent, Elvis Presley and The Everley Brothers; one of his favourite tracks was 'Cathy's Clown'

(April 1960). The brothers rehearsed in their front room in Wallbutton Road, Brockley, South London. But even this produced problems, as Pete revealed: 'My parents were incredibly tolerant. They did have people knocking on the door about the noise. They told us to turn it down, but we would carry on playing. In fact, we had a 'nasty' put through the letterbox.' It was clear that the parents were giving the children as much artistic encouragement as they could.

The brothers didn't have a name for their band. However, one thing was for certain: John Cruickshank was a useless drummer, so he decided to concentrate on singing. They drafted in Dave Boorman on drums. They decided to call themselves The Dollarbills in deference to the concept of 'all things American had to be good'. It seemed logical as all the artists they liked were from there. They played their first gig at the famous 2I's coffee bar in London. They journeyed there on the train and taxi. As Pete Cruickshank remembered with a big grin on his face: 'We thought we were going to be stars. We carried our gear around London without any covers! We didn't even have covers for the drums.' By this time, John Lockyear was struggling as lead guitarist.

Pete Cruickshank, meanwhile, had his own personal problems. In 1961, Pete started work as an apprentice fitter. He didn't really have his heart in it: 'My dad forced me to sign the papers. He said, 'We are not going to leave this room until you do.' However, when I'd served two years and I was 18, I packed it in. I was old enough to make my own decisions.' It was obvious that, by then, when push came to shove, music was going to win the day.

The Dollarbills played the pop songs of the day by the likes of The Coasters, Elvis and The Shadows. They were having some success just as Tony McPhee came in. It was ironic that Tony had just been offered the promotion at the Post Office, which he had already turned down previously. It may seem obvious now that he would choose music, but he loved his day job. He loved working in electrics and problem-solving, but in the end, there was no serious debate about it. The chance to be a full-time musician was too great. He left the Post Office and turned professional.

The new addition immediately made an impression on his new bandmates. Pete Cruickshank takes up the story: 'We were doing The Shadows stuff quite badly. Tony was an accomplished musician. He was unusual in that he never copied songs note for note like everybody else. Even without an echo unit and Fender, he still emulated the sound. He had a dramatic impact on the band.' Despite Pete's reservations about the band making it before John Lockyear's departure, Tony's arrival opened up new horizons.

Whereas The Seneschals had played only local gigs, The Dollarbills travelled around a lot more. They played places like The Top Hat in Worthing and the famous Sophia Gardens in Cardiff. Tony knew there was a lot of competition: 'Sophia Gardens was huge and there would be many bands playing their 30-minute slot. In a way, it was like a conveyor belt.' They appeared with Vince Hill on Saturday 31 August 1963. On another occasion, they appeared with Chris Andrews; he had a big hit with 'Yesterday Man'. They also played the RAF Air Force Base at Brize Norton, where they were asked if they could play a waltz – they could! They were getting around the country courtesy of John Lockyear's Dad's Thames Van. He was convinced they were going to make it and even started to arrange gigs for them. They approached the Cana Variety agency to get them more gigs. They were told confidently, 'If we can't get you gigs in England, we can get them in Germany.' They had more than enough work at home, so there was no need to go abroad.

Tony McPhee didn't just bring his guitar to The Dollarbills, but he also brought every blues album he had ever heard. From this point, the rest of the band would hear a lot about the blues movement that Tony loved so much. As Pete Cruickshank revealed: 'We only knew of pop; we didn't know where pop actually came from. Tony knew the background and, as it turned out, we soon came to love it, too.' In the early months after Tony joined, their repertoire started to change. One of the early additions was 'My Babe', which was influenced by Little Walter's version. Jimmy Reed's 'Big Boss Man' was another. And, of course, John Lee Hooker and Muddy Waters songs were well represented in the set. There was a short period of inactivity as they honed their act to suit the new direction. Even though John Cruickshank was acknowledged as the leader of the band, Tony had other plans: 'I led from the back. I was happy to manipulate things from there.' It must be said that everyone, apart from Tony, looked at John as the leader.

In an interview with *Record Collector* in 1993, Tony McPhee outlined that he wasn't attracted to all of the blues, only certain aspects of it: 'I loved the primitiveness of the blues. I've never been into B.B. King that much; it's too sickly, too sweet. I prefer the rough, primitive stuff; country players from the '20s and '30s like Leadbelly and Robert Johnson – he's just a total genius. In the '60s, you mistrusted white artists playing the blues … I only wanted to listen to black artists. There wasn't anybody white who was any good back then.' These black artists generally came from the Mississippi Delta, but they gravitated north to Chicago to play the clubs. Leonard and Phil Chess initially owned only one of the clubs before snapping most of them up. In 1947, they founded Chess Records – the vehicle that would bring these artists to the attention of the world.

It wasn't long before a name change was on the cards in order to reflect the way the band had evolved and their future direction. Tony suggested they change their name to the Groundhogs. This was in homage to 'Groundhog Blues' from the 1960 John Lee Hooker album *House Of The Blues*. Tony had perused all his Hooker albums to find the right name. But the decision process wasn't as straightforward as it seemed, as Pete elucidated: 'Yes, it was Tony's idea for the name, but my brother would have been involved in all of this as he was the leader of the band. John is a very forceful character. By that time, we were all blues fans anyway, so that obviously helped.' Tony wasn't the only one who disliked The Dollarbills as a name; it was also hated by Pete, who found it a tad embarrassing. At the same time, John decided to call himself John Lee and this was added on to the Groundhogs, making the full name of the band John Lee Groundhogs. This happened because John was fascinated by the name Lee. The Dollarbills had also sometimes been known as Lee Grant (a mixture of the US Civil War generals) and The Dollarbills. But contrary to what many people believed, the name of John Lee Hooker did not influence his new stage name.

By late 1963, they decided that they needed a piano player. Not knowing any, they put an advert in *Melody Maker*. Only two people applied for the job and only one turned up for the audition. That man was Bob Hall. As he outlined: 'I had applied for lots of jobs because I was desperate to get into a band, but I never had any replies. I had the audition above a pub in New Cross. As I was the only one who turned up, I got the job.' Bob Hall was able to open up the blues even more to the band, as he recalled: 'I had a friend (Dave Carey, ex-Humphrey Lyttleton drummer) who owned the Swing jazz record shop, which was located at 1b Mitcham Lane, Streatham. The Swing Shop was dark and small, with albums downstairs and 78s up on the next level via the spiral staircase. Even though Carey hated the blues, he used to get a lot of rare Crown blues albums in the shop. This was because he had an import deal for jazz records but could only have a certain amount per deal. This meant he had to make up the numbers with other types of music and the cheapest records he could get were blues ones'. Bob Hall spread the word and took the band to the shop to check out the bargain blues section. To Tony McPhee, it was manna from heaven.

In those days, there were not many white people who liked the blues and the records didn't get to the UK via the usual distribution. Blues records got into the country in other ways. Ports like Liverpool were a good place to go, as people would bring them back on boats from various parts of the world. Consequently, the shortage of blues records made The Swing Shop a magnet for blues fans eager to pick up rare albums. But it wasn't just fans that frequented the shop, as ex-employee Len Tempan remembered: 'Many musicians came to the shop. They included Keith Relf, Paul Samwell-Smith and Eric Clapton of The Yardbirds. Later on, Clapton brought John Mayall along and Jeff Beck also came in, as well as a member of The Rolling Stones, but I can't remember which one. One of these musicians asked about a guy he had heard about playing great blues slide guitar. I told him that man was Tony McPhee.' It's clear that Tony was starting to make a name for himself.

The Swing Shop took on extra significance for Tony, as this was where he met Jo Ann Kelly sometime in early 1964.[5] She made a big impression on him, as he outlines: 'I went into the shop and walked up to the counter where I noticed a girl bending down to get her purse out of her bag. I noticed her backside was sticking out. Then she asked Len if he had a particular Howlin' Wolf album. I thought, 'Wow', but then I noticed she had a guitar slung over her shoulder. I knew I had to speak to this girl.' He did exactly that and struck up an immediate rapport. It wasn't long before Tony was appearing with Jo Ann at Bunjies Folk Cellar, as well as The Hole in the Ground at Swiss Cottage.

Jo Ann Kelly had a younger brother, Dave, and he was also into the blues scene, later finding fame as a blues musician himself: 'We were all into acoustic country blues at the time and generally had the impression that we were the only people in the country with that interest. We slowly found other pockets of country blues pickers in Bristol, Reading, Tyneside, Leeds, etc. Jo, Mac, Bob Hall, Steve Rye and I all used to hang around the Swing Shop in Streatham, waiting for whatever blues releases came in. Jo worked a lot at the time with Mac and Bob Hall. I was still at school and the 'kid brother'.'

Shortly after, Tony taped an EP for Jo Ann in his Tooting home. He used his Ampex tape recorder with the wires snaked all over the house.

She sang and played guitar. The songs recorded for side one were 'Long Black Curly Hair' and 'Boyfriend Blues'. The flip side contained 'New Milk Cow Blues' and 'I Looked Down The Road'. The first song was penned by Jo Ann, with the last three credited as Traditional, arranged by Jo Ann Kelly. Tony took the finished tape to a place in the Old Kent Road where it was cut on a lathe, the swarf being sucked up by a domestic vacuum cleaner! In spite of the primitive technology, the sound turned out very well. He completed the job by buying a John Bull stamping kit for sleeve information; only 99 were pressed and they are very rare items indeed. The EP was called *Blues & Gospel*.

Things were going very well as John Lees Groundhogs, especially when they soon realised, to their delight, that Bob Hall was a very good piano player.[6] But his arrival brought to a head a major problem they had to resolve: what to do with Jack, the sax player, who was now superfluous to their requirements. They decided to get rid of him in true music business style. They sacked him the day that Bob joined. They didn't even bother to tell him; they took his equipment and dumped it on his doorstep on their way to the next gig. These boys were learning fast!

At the time Bob Hall joined, John Cruickshank was picking up the harmonica and was proving to be a fast learner, but he was lacking in one area, as Bob Hall noticed: 'John was a good singer, but he didn't have the charisma that the girls went for.' One of the things that inhibited John in this area was the fact he was married at the time. However, the band centred around the Cruickshanks and John was the leader of the band. Bob continues: 'We always left the van outside their house and their mother fed us on many occasions.' Around this time, Tony struck up a relationship with the Cruickshank's younger sister, Jean. At the time, she was only 15, but they were both smitten with one another. The relationship continued for two years.

Playing the blues was having a liberating effect on Pete Cruickshank. One of the main attractions of the blues to him was its artistic freedom: 'I could put my own bass lines with the blues, as you couldn't really hear it on the records. Furthermore, in those days, there weren't many bands playing it and it made you feel like you belonged to something special. It was like a cult. You would chat to most musicians and they'd never heard of the blues.' The first blues record that Pete really got excited about was Cyril Davis and the All Stars' 'Country Line Special'. He was totally won over by that one. In fact, one of his greatest regrets is that he never got to see the great man on stage (he died of leukemia in 1964).

A later visit to the Marquee provided him with his greatest inspiration, as he related: 'We went to see Long John Baldry and that's when I first saw his bass player. His name was Cliff Barton and he played slap bass, but on the electric bass guitar. His playing was obviously improvised and I realised that's how I wanted to play.' As soon as he could, he went out to purchase the same bass as Barton's. So, he traded his Fender for an Epiphone EB2 – it was a semi-acoustic. One of its disadvantages was the very one-dimensional sound it produced.

The early part of 1964 was spent trying to build up support as a blues band. Their change of direction necessitated a change of venues, too. They started getting gigs at places like Studio 51 and the 100 Club in Oxford Street, both hot r&b venues. Dave Wetton noted in his diary that he saw John Lees Groundhogs support The Animals on 28 January at the 100 Club. On other occasions, they supported Jimmy Powell, Five Dimensions and Alex Harvey. But they also ventured out of the capital on many occasions. They played the famous Newcastle A Go Go and they supported Long John Baldry at the Reading Town Hall. That gig showed that certain parts of the country were not quite ready for the blues revolution, as Bob Hall remembers that, out of the four people in the audience, two were bouncers!

They quickly got a foothold on the south coast circuit, which covered towns like Brighton and Worthing. Their material was not all the usual 'standards' because Tony was always interested in playing lesser-known material. One of these was 'Stagger Lee', a hit for Lloyd Price in 1959. Another venue they played was the Star Club in Croydon and it was here that Tony McPhee first met the rising star in the six-string stakes. As he recalled: 'We all went down there to see Eric Clapton and The Yardbirds. I was a fan of theirs. The first thing I noticed was that they were all playing cheap guitars – I thought that was odd. We were invited by their manager, Giorgio Gomelsky, to play a few numbers in the interval.' The band went down very well in this impromptu gig. Tony's next meeting with Clapton would be a lot more significant!

They played regularly at the 100 Club (including on 10 and 31 March, supporting The Animals again). They got to know the manager of the club quite well and it wasn't long before they started to press him about having their own slot. He wasn't keen on this, but he offered them something else to keep them quiet. And as Bob Hall recalls, it was quite a consolation: 'He offered us the chance to back Champion Jack Dupree. The fact he was a piano player helped me because I played, and he was free to concentrate on his act. This included dancing and telling his bad and very dirty jokes. He was a great performer and a very nice man, but he was a bit of a bullshitter.' (The date of this was 7 May, as Dupree made his debut at the Marquee on 3 May, so he was in town at that time.) In fact, Dupree was later quoted in *Record Mirror* saying that John Lee's Groundhogs are the 'Best band I've played with'.

On the back of this work, they got the chance to back two more blues giants. Roy Fisher had prudently contacted their agents. They backed Little Walter on a one-off at a dance hall. Up until then, most of his backing bands had not been up to scratch because he paid so little. The band were looking for a memorable occasion. But things didn't turn out as they had planned or hoped. As Bob Hall outlined: 'When we met Little Walter, he demanded a bottle of whisky as it was the tradition of the backing band. We refused. He didn't like us after that and he wasn't a nice man anyway. He had no stage charisma and he had the cheek to blame us when he didn't go down too well. We were probably the best band he had at that time because we knew his material.' One thing he did have was the ability to clear congested places in seconds when they were on stage setting the gear up. He farted and it was so bad that the band sought out the sanctuary of the floor; soon, it was too bad even to stand there!

Tony didn't endear himself to Walter either, as he recalled:

> I liked his 'Just A Feeling' and asked him if he still played it. He replied, 'How do you know that?' We knew it because we liked the blues. When it came to that number in the show and we started playing it, I suddenly realised I couldn't remember the riff. I thought, 'Oh, shit!' He wasn't happy about 'My Babe' either. I was playing it the way we usually played it, but he was not like Hooker, who could ride over any hitch. He spent the whole song turning round and growling to me, 'E natural'. Another reason why I didn't like him was that he took the piss out of Hooker. I thought, 'You cheeky bastard!' He wasn't a nice man at all; he walked with a limp because someone had shot him. I think someone finished the job when he got back home!

Soon after this, they played two gigs with Memphis Slim, one of them at a converted cinema in London that the band hated. The Club Norek gig was always at two in the morning and hardly anybody would be there. Slim was unlike most of the black artists of the day and was able to protect his interests a lot more. He got into an argument with the promoter, who was trying to rip him off. Bob Hall overheard the back end of the conversation. Slim told him: 'I am not one of those blacks who can't read or write.'

Like a lot of bands, they were out there hoping to make it. However, the reality is that success is often a matter of catching a lucky break; for those bands that get that break, the trick is to make it a momentous one. In late spring, John Lee's Groundhogs got theirs. In May 1964, the great blues man John Lee Hooker flew into the UK for a five-week tour. It coincided with his single 'Dimples' reaching number 23 in the singles chart, his first hit in the UK. As was common in those days, no backing musicians accompanied him, as the cost was prohibitive. John Lee's Groundhogs manager, Roy Fisher, was keeping his eyes open for opportunities. As soon as he heard Hooker was coming over, he made enquiries as to the promoter. When he found out it was Don Arden, he went round to his office to make a pitch for the tour. He was too late as John Mayall had beat them to it, but Arden clearly made a mental note of John Lee's Groundhogs because when the tour was extended and Mayall couldn't make the last week, he knew who could step in.[7]

Chapter 3 – Hooker & The Hogs

> John Lee's Groundhogs are definitely my favourites. They're tremendously nice fellows and very good to work with.
> John Lee Hooker

On 1 June 1964, John Lee Hooker opened his British tour with John Mayall at the Flamengo Club in London. John Lee's Groundhogs were in attendance in the capacity of fans. As the tour progressed, Hooker got a lot of flak from the so-called blues snobs regarding his 'selling out' of his original roots. An infuriated Tony McPhee fired off a letter of defence to *Melody Maker*. It was published on 27 June. It's worth quoting in full: 'John Lee Hooker and Howlin' Wolf are just as much blues men in their own right as Big Joe Williams and Sleepy John Estes. It's true that Hooker's later records are intended for r&b audiences, but his earlier discs contain some of the most forceful and primitive blues of all time. Wolf has always turned out good discs. His latest are exceptional.' He was not frightened to nail his colours to the mast!

Apart from the band grabbing a lot of interest, Tony himself was receiving more than his fair share. In June, he received an offer to join Chris Barber's Jazz band. It was the first offer to join a name band he'd ever had; it wouldn't be the last. Barber was looking for his first electric guitarist (Barber had initially asked the guitarist from 'Them'), but he was obviously impressed by what Tony was doing. Tony never really considered joining, as he was keen to eventually have his own band. Barber's next choice of John Slaughter was more fruitful; John remained with Barber until his passing in 2010. It was to be a decision that Tony called the biggest mistake of my life: 'I would have had more money and been around the world several times by now.'

John Lee's Groundhogs' first gig with Hooker was later in the year on the 6 July when the band journeyed up to the Twisted Wheel Club in Manchester to meet their hero. They were aware of most of the material Hooker wanted to play, but being major fans of the great man honed the tension to greater heights, as Tony recalled: 'We were all very nervous. When I first met him, I thought he looked mean, but it was only later that I found out he was still annoyed with John Mayall. It appears that Mayall's musical arrangements were not to Hooker's liking; he didn't like the wash of Mayall's keyboards, as he preferred it simpler.' This was compounded by guitarist Roger Dean's inability to follow Hooker's idiosyncratic changes.

With the band being fans of the great man, it created an edge that wouldn't normally be there for a backing band. This gig was more than a paycheque. Pete Cruickshank outlined this philosophy: 'We felt we could do it justice as it meant so much to us and I think we did. We saw him playing with Mayall and we wanted to integrate more and be part of Hooker and not just a backing band. We became very much a part of him on the stage.' It wasn't long before they realised those feelings were mutual.

Prior to the gig, they had no rehearsal. However, they knew the songs would all be played in the key of E, as he only played in two keys: when he played solo, it was A, and with a band, it was E. That was all they had in terms of preparation. The band went on and did a few numbers as a warm-up. The opening number with Hooker was James Brown's 'I'll Go Crazy'. The band played it very much in a Hooker style. Hooker must have been impressed with Tony, as he knew all his licks and more. The gig went well, but afterwards, Tony was disappointed as he felt they didn't do him justice. However, he really perked up when Hooker told the band: 'You boys really know my shit!' John Cruickshank explained how they hit it off with him: 'He never did a song the same way twice. But we were ready, as we knew his work. We knew he would go into a 12-bar, but it might end in a 10-bar. I have to admit it was unnerving at first.' Flexibility was the secret of success in backing Hooker. You had to think on your feet. Some bands could, some couldn't.

Hooker was driven up to Manchester in an Austin Westminster. The driver was Pat Meehan, one of Don Arden's odd job men and a very dour character indeed. How Hooker got on with him, one can only speculate. (In fact, Meehan became the manager of the Groundhogs in 1972 for a short time.) This was Hooker's designated transport for the duration of the tour. Meanwhile, the band were merrily travelling in their Comma van, sampling the sights, the sounds and the smells of the English countryside, not to mention the inside of the van! But the two entities were going to turn into one very soon, as Roy Fisher outlined in Charles Shaar Murray's excellent book *Boogie Man*: 'John said that McPhee knew some of his old blues songs better than he remembered them. Therefore, it wasn't a problem and it just went from there. Because he liked the guys and respected the way they played, he decided the very next day that he didn't want to tour with the chauffeur.' Hooker finished the tour travelling in the back of the van.

The social integration was completed hot on the heels of the musical integration! From that moment, John Lee's Groundhogs ceased being a backing band. Now, they were one homogenous entity!

The tour gained momentum very quickly and Graham Ackers captured the excitement that was generated by the band in his review of the Savoy Ballroom gig, Cleveleys, near Blackpool (8 July), for *Blues Unlimited* magazine: 'Hooker came on to a very enthusiastic reception ... he rolled into 'Shake It Baby' with great power ... Every number was received with enthusiasm to such a degree that five encores were performed in all. A special mention is required for the Groundhogs, who played admirably throughout. All in direct contrast to the 'let's see who can play the loudest' approach of John Mayall. In fact, everything was just right – atmosphere, backing, amplification and temperature – and everybody, including Hooker and the 'Hogs', had a ball.' Other material they played included 'Night Time Is The Right Time', 'Hi Heel Sneakers', 'Boom Boom' and 'Dimples'. The latter was his current hit, although it was recorded in 1959.

It is surprising to note that Hooker had a lot to contend with on the tour and it all stemmed from his unfamiliarity with stardom. Back home in the States, he never received acclaim and this is what all blues artists who came over to Europe had to get used to. The extent of this ignorance in the States was witnessed by Mick Jagger when The Rolling Stones were on their first tour there: 'The funny thing was, the kids had never heard of Muddy Waters. They've got the greatest blues singer living among them and they don't even know.' Hooker was a quiet and unassuming guy offstage, but suddenly he had the spotlight on him. This was summed up by their manager at the time, Roy Fisher: 'There were a lot of people, which he wasn't used to and he'd get nervous when he had to go on stage if he had to push through a crowd.' Another problem was his confusion when people asked for his autograph. The cultural shock was compounded by the fact he was illiterate. Hooker's knee-jerk reaction to this was to refuse to sign, but this was obviously causing problems with the PR. It was left to Tony and Roy to teach Hooker how to sign his name. Roy Fisher witnessed Hooker's progress: 'At first, he was painfully slow. But because he wanted to get back to the hotel as soon as possible (usually with a girl), he started to sign JLH, which got the queue down fast.' Hooker was getting lots of attention from the girls and it would increase dramatically on the next tour. It would also cause a few problems, too!

Hooker was very cute and had many ways of disguising his handicap. In the service stations, he would pick up the menu, usually upside down, and say, 'Dave (Boorman), what are you having?' Hooker hated English food; all he wanted was a burger and chicken, but they were in short supply in those days. He hated the humble sandwich and warm beer. On the subject of food, he was fascinated by Tony being a vegetarian. He had never come across one before and he fired endless questions to him about it. The truth is that Hooker couldn't live properly without his beloved chicken. The culture shock worked the other way around, too. Tony recalls that Hooker had a briefcase full of vitamin pills. He'd never seen that before. Tony speculated that he was keen, in some way at least, to promote his health.

As the end of the tour approached, Tony changed his guitar style as the influence of Hooker intensified. This was the point when he slung the guitar strap over his right shoulder and abandoned his plectrum, just like Hooker. It was very strange at first, but he managed to get through the last few gigs. It wasn't long before he felt totally at ease with it. It was yet another indication of how he was looking for something most other musicians didn't have. It is a style he still employs today and was a big contributing factor to developing his own guitar sound that was to pay real dividends in the 1970s. The tour climaxed at London's Beat City on 12 July. They then parted with Hooker, but it wouldn't be long before they met again.

The Hooker tour made John Lee's Groundhogs famous, and in August, they signed with Anglo-American Artists. They were booked for another tour with John Lee Hooker (on 22 September) at the great man's request. Commencing on 1 October, they were contracted for 56 shows at £130 per week. In fact, it was only 28 venues, as the contract stated they had to deliver two 30-minute performances at each venue. By this time, their workload was very heavy to the extent that Pete Cruickshank remembers his fingers were blistering up at that point.

Around this time, they went into IBC Studios to record a couple of demos for Mickie Most. They decided to do Howlin' Wolf's 'Wang Dang Doodle' and 'Rock Me Baby'. Most had heard about the band, but on the day of the session, he clearly had other things on his mind. Bob Hall recalled this session: 'Most was going out with Marianne Faithfull at the time and she turned up in a mini-skirt with laddered fishnet tights. As the control booth was above the stage, I spent most of the session looking up her skirt. Perhaps that's why the track didn't turn out so good.' Mickie Most hated what they had done and he offered the acetate to Roy Fisher for £40. For some reason, the master tape disappeared! Years later, Roy has no idea what happened to the master, but he still has the acetate. By this time, Tony was garnering some impressive notices. In an autumn edition of *R'N B Scene,* an editorial waxed lyrical about two rising stars on the scene. Tony is described as 'a really great guitarist whose work with a bottle-neck has to be heard to be believed.' The second artist they mentioned was Steve Winwood, so Tony was in good company indeed.

As October approached, the band started to prepare for the much bigger scale Hooker tour. A complication was on the horizon that necessitated a change in personnel. With the tour being a month in duration, it was clear that Bob Hall would have to turn professional. Hitherto, he had always held his day job down, even though the rest of the band had pro status. But he was unwilling to give up his career as a Patent Attorney. This was a major blow as Hall was good. Keith Scott (ex-Cyril Davies) played a few gigs and was mooted for the tour, but in the end, they recruited Tom Parker. Nevertheless, as Hall told Charles Shaar Murray: 'The guy (Parker) they got to play was a pub pianist … I had to teach him to play blues, which I did because I wanted to help, but he couldn't feel the way Hooker played.' There was another way to look at it: Parker couldn't have had many better teachers.

Hooker summed up the here and now to *Melody Maker*, where his laid-back style and politeness shine through: 'That John Mayall group and John Lee's Groundhogs are definitely my favourites. They're tremendously nice fellows and very good to work with. They try hard to do everything I want. I really was pleased to see those fellows when I arrived back in England.' The bond between Hooker and The Hogs was going to get even stronger on the tour.

The opening night was at the legendary Newcastle Club A Go Go, and as it turned out, there were plenty of incidents. They had an afternoon session for the teens, but the fun started later. The size of the crowd dramatically increased Hooker's nerves. Roy Fisher related the course of events in Charles Murray's book: 'Most places were jam-packed. In Newcastle, it was big and there were about 800 people packed into this place. The dressing room wasn't at the side of the stage but in the back of the managerial offices.' It was clear Hooker would have to push his way through. But as the band kicked into his intro music, he couldn't be found. Fisher was beside himself. All he could hear was the band playing the intro repeatedly. It turned out that Hooker had pissed his pants; he was eventually found by a policeman in the toilet. But as Tony McPhee recalls, Hooker was always drinking: 'He used to drink a lot of whisky but diluted with a lot of water. Consequently, he pissed a lot. But he was never drunk.' With the place so packed, it was common for the band not to be able to get to the toilet.

They played the Flamengo club on 23 October, which was witnessed by Tony's old friend, Dave Wetton. Another of the dates on the tour was the famous Cavern Club in Liverpool. This gig was attended by a couple of dedicated fans of the band. Bob Glass never forgot the magic of those gigs: 'I was going out with Jo Ann Kelly then; we had seen them in Manchester and were hitching a ride to Liverpool. But by coincidence, the band's van turned up and we piled into the back. There wasn't a lot of room but we fitted in. I remember the fluidity of those gigs. Hooker would get requests to play on his own and he did. Also, Tony and Pete made a great rhythm team.'[8] It seems odd today that the audience's main reason for being there was to dance.

Hooker was 47 and was far older than most of the fans, but that didn't prove to be a barrier to him connecting with them – they loved him. He was very interested in the many females that turned up and was always looking for a chance to chat them up. Apart from the fact he was a star who had a hit single, he also had a stage presence that was utterly mesmerising and this helped in his quest to impress the girls. It wasn't long before he was having success with some of them. But at the Dungeon Club in Nottingham, he realised just how close he was sailing to the wind, even in the far more liberal UK. Roy Fisher revealed how it came to a head: 'I came back into the dressing room and he was in a very, very upset state. He was stuttering away and it was obvious that he was upset. I was trying to work out what had upset him and it was because he had found out that one young lady who had been particularly forceful and had got through to him … he had found out about ten minutes later that she was only 15.' He was a lot more careful after that episode.

Tony McPhee reveals his memories of that gig: 'The place was small and it had two dressing rooms upstairs. I'd left my travel bag and change of clothing in one, but for some reason, we decided to change to the other dressing room. But they were not interconnecting, so I had to go downstairs to go up to the other one. I walked in and John was groping a girl in there. I shut the door and made my way back to the other dressing room. I suddenly realised John was close behind me and he excitedly said with a stutter 'she's fifttteen years old'![9] Tony got a lot of grief as a result of this liaison. Hooker asked Tony to write the girl a letter, which he did, but as he recalls, he didn't write 'I lllllllove you!''

After the gig, the owner of a restaurant invited Hooker back for a meal. He agreed but he insisted the band be included in the offer, too, such was the camaraderie between them. Reluctantly, the owner agreed, but it was to cause problems later on. It turned out that the owner was a big music fan and collected artists' autographs on his wall (at that stage, there was only Ben E King). He asked Hooker to sign, but he still had difficulty signing his name. Hooker kept crossing out his not-so-nifty crayon work because he was not happy with it. This continued until he had covered half the wall. They then sat down to their meal and discovered that Hooker wasn't going to take any shit off anybody. They naturally thought the invitation meant the meal was gratis. However, halfway through the meal, Tony leant over to Hooker and said, 'The waiter is writing things down.' With that, Hooker called over the waiter and said, 'I want you to get a pen and paper and to write down the club, the manager of the club and your name, and how nice you were to me and the band and how nice it was to give us the meal.' There was a moment of tension as the waiter gave the paper to the manager. The manager came over and said, 'Did you enjoy the meal?' And the band had their free meal.

Shortly after the tour started, they appeared on BBC television on a program called *Beat Room*. Also on the bill were The Kinks and Tom Jones. Pete Cruickshank remembered that the Welshman had an astounding voice. But it was The Kinks that made an impression on Tony, as he recalled: 'Dave Davies had a small Italian Elpico amplifier which he plugged his guitar into, then he connected the speaker outlets of the Elpico into his Vox. I thought, 'wow'. It gave the guitar a very distorted sound, which, of course, was his intention, but when they started the sound check ('You Really Got Me'), the soundman came down and said, 'This guitar sounds awfully distorted'. The control booth was situated above the stage and Hooker seemed to be mesmerised by it, as he kept looking up throughout their performance.

They played 'Boom Boom' and 'I'm Leaving', and looking at the footage now, you barely get a glimpse of the band. You see a lot of their hands, but it's all in very short shots. Their segment was recorded very quickly, which was just as well as they went off to a gig afterwards.

They even managed to record a session for Saturday Club at Maida Vale. The program was broadcast on 14 November and included The Isley Brothers and Freddie & The Dreamers. Although, none of them were present when the Hogs did their set.

The tour continued with Hooker in the van and he certainly made a big impression on all concerned, as Pete Cruickshank recalled: 'He used to get his semi-acoustic guitar out in the van. We'd be dozing, but we'd soon wake up. Just hearing the travelling noises of the road and Hooker playing a slow blues like 'Waterfront' in his moving and meaningful way. It was the very essence of John and it would send shivers down your spine. If only I'd had a tape recorder.'

John Cruickshank also has his memories of this time: 'There was a magic event on the road in the van. The whole band were sound asleep (save Dave Boorman, who was driving) after a gig when we were woken by JLH. He couldn't have been very tired as he was singing and playing his guitar. He could compose songs at the drop of a hat. We recalled later how we all gradually woke up to his singing, not wanting to interrupt him in any way, as the moment was truly magical. We were audience to something that was truly unique and to which tickets for his performance couldn't be bought.'

It must be said that Hooker had some annoying habits. He tended to spit a lot in order to clear his throat. The Comma van had a sliding window on the passenger side. Spitting was perfectly normal where John came from. John would be sitting in the single seat next to the window and they would feel a rush of cold air as he turned round, opened the window and spat out. But sometimes, he'd not time it right, so all around the door would be encrusted spit. One time, Pete drew the short straw and had to clean the offending area. On another occasion, they were invited back to Tom Parker's house, where he proceeded to spit on the fireplace, only realising afterwards it was an artificial one. Even though Tom's wife was shocked, she didn't say anything, like a real trooper.

The toilet problems continued at the Bure Country Club, Bournemouth. Hooker urinated in the corner of the dressing room as he couldn't get to the facilities, but Pete Cruickshank had foolishly left his new stage shirt in the vicinity. When he picked the shirt up, he complained the shirt was wet. Tony vividly remembers thinking, 'I know what's happened here'. Another problem was the autumn weather. Hooker didn't like the cold very much. In fact, he couldn't tolerate it at all. As Roy Fisher recalled in Murray's book: 'He'd be up in the usual seat with a coat, a scarf and hat, a blanket over his knees, the heater on and still complaining about the cold. We'd all be there in T-shirts saying, 'Oh my god', with sweat pouring off us.'

The tour's conclusion didn't end the association with Hooker, as the Hogs were booked to make an album with the great man. But before that, they had a single to record with a top American producer.

It now appears Hooker had been hustling for his erstwhile backing band. In an interview with Max Jones of *Melody Maker*, he gave a hint of what happened to the recent *IBC* Groundhogs recordings: 'I was so impressed with the Groundhogs on this tour, I contacted Calvin Carter of Vee Jay Records right away with a view to recording them over here. And I sent a demo disc of two songs by the group for him to hear (Roy Fisher gave the demo of 'Wang Dang Doodle' to Hooker). He phoned me back and then sent a cable saying he was coming over to London and would offer them a contract and record them here.' Carter was showing a special interest in talented white artists as The Beatles had really taken off by then. This was the band's chance to make a name.

Carter duly came over and the band picked him up in their van from the Hilton Hotel. By all accounts, Carter was hoping to find a new Beatles playing blues. This gave the whole enterprise an edge. But things didn't get off to a good start, as John Cruickshank outlined: 'It was nighttime and Carter was in the back; I was sitting in the passenger seat, turning round and talking to him. But I could see he was nervous and he clearly didn't want to speak to me. I thought it was odd, but I only found out later that he thought I was driving as I was sitting on the left-hand side.' After the initial awkward introduction, Carter turned out to be very nice. They chose Phillips Studios in London. The date of the recording was on 19 November.

The recording session finally got underway and they chose 'Shake It', which was really Hooker's 'Shake 'Em On Down' and 'Rock Me Baby', delivered in the B.B. King style; they had covered this in the Mickie Most session. The outstanding thing about these recordings is that John Cruickshank was obviously a great singer. He had a voice with oodles of charisma. In fact, as Pete Cruickshank recalls, Jo Anne Kelly was a great fan of John; she thought he was a tremendous singer. The band's ex-piano player, Bob Hall, played a part in proceedings: 'Tom Parker used my arrangement for piano because it's exactly the same one I used later on Savoy Brown's debut album.' The session was considered by all to be a success. But John Cruickshank had a shock when he finally received a copy of the single because he had a songwriting credit with Carter. Carter was a canny operator and was well used to the techniques of getting around publishing credits. He knew that changing just a single word could facilitate such a transfer of rights. It was all rather shady stuff as it meant that, somewhere down the line, someone missed out on their due reward. Calvin Carter was pictured in the 28 November edition of *Melody Maker* outside the studio shaking hands with John Cruickshank (the paper wrongly stated it was Jimmy Reed). The confusion was probably caused by the fact that, at the time, the picture was taken when they were on tour with the blues giant. They got the tour through Don Arden, who was clearly impressed with how they handled Hooker.

They commenced the tour with Reed on 1 November at the Flamengo, London. But Tony McPhee remembers the doubleheader in Birmingham (at the Ritz and Plaza) and a gig in Guildford the most: 'As we were packing our gear away to get over the other side of Birmingham, I noticed Jimmy went over to the support band to congratulate the way they'd backed him!' But there was a much more pressing problem on the music front, as Tony revealed: 'Reed had a habit of not tuning his guitar and we were coping well with that problem. However, when the *Blues Unlimited* review of the Guildford gig came out later, they blamed us! I thought that was out of order because it was obvious where the problem was. They always hated us anyway. The only good review we ever got from them was on the first Hooker tour.'

Around this time, Tony had a meeting with one of his heroes, but if it hadn't been for the timely intervention of Pete Cruickshank, it wouldn't have happened. They had played a gig earlier in the evening but managed to get back to catch a couple of numbers at a Blues Festival. Howlin' Wolf came off stage and Tony and Pete were standing at the bottom of the theatre's fire escape. Steam was rising from Wolf's head but Tony was apprehensive about speaking to him because he had read in *Blues Unlimited* magazine that he didn't like white people. However, Pete was not so shy in coming forward, as Tony relates: 'Pete didn't believe it at all and introduced himself as 'Mr Burnett' (Wolf's real name): 'I am the bass player in a band called the Groundhogs, who play a lot of your songs.' At that, Wolf turned slightly to look way down at me and asked in his massive voice, 'Is this another lil Groundhogs?' Wolf invited us back to the hotel, and as we walked into the foyer, we couldn't believe it – they were all there in the shape of Wolf, Sleepy John Estes and Hubert Sumlin. It was 1964/65 and all the waiters were white; you could tell they weren't keen on serving drinks to these black guys. Wolf had an acoustic guitar and he started playing 'Down In The Bottom' – it was amazing. I still can't work out how he managed to put so much attack into his bottle-neck playing – we just stood there stunned.' So, Tony spent the most memorable night of his life in the presence of those three blues giants. It meant that, by the end of the decade, Tony had played with or met the majority of his blues heroes!

The band later went to see Howlin' Wolf at Cooks Ferry Inn, London. Tony was just as interested to see his guitarist, Hubert Sumlin. The show was split into two sets and Tony remembers that Hubert was a genius in the first set and only brilliant in the second.

By the end of the year, there were the inevitable comparisons between the blues artists they'd backed. Roy Fisher summarised each character that the Hogs backed and how difficult it could be, starting with Hooker: 'He was a gentleman, always polite, and in that way, totally unique, unlike Little Walter and Jimmy Reed, who were totally uncouth … Walter was obnoxious and bad-tempered and got upset very, very quickly. Jimmy Reed was okay on stage when he was playing, but in between times, he drank too much and complained about absolutely everything.' Bob Hall was in no doubt who was number one, as he recalled: 'I was later in The John Dummer Blues Band that backed Howlin' Wolf, but I think Hooker was the greatest of all the blues artists I was involved with.'[10]

Contrary to many reports, they did not record the album with John Lee Hooker at this time. It was mooted, but the reason why it didn't happen appears to have been lost in the mists of time. Before he left for home, Hooker gave a ringing endorsement to the band: 'I'm bound to say that John Lee's Groundhogs are one of the best groups you have over here, and it fits in with my type of music perfectly … I'm proud of them. I am sure they'll become a great favourite of British blues fans and they'll be known in America in a few months from now.' For all of Hooker's hopes, it didn't quite pan out that way. The single appeared on Interphon across the pond and it bombed, ensuring a no-profile situation in America. However, the failure to consolidate the success of 1964 into 1965 is more inexplicable.

Chapter 4 - The Cold Wind Of Change

The blues can be boring but I play things in different keys.
John Mayall's pitch to Tony McPhee to persuade him to join the Bluesbreakers

The blues clubs were disappearing, so I accepted the situation.
Tony McPhee on the switch to soul

John Lee Hooker came back to England in spring 1965 and John Lee's Groundhogs were mooted to cover the tour. But in the end, they didn't get the job as John Mayall and the unknown Cops & Robbers did the honours. In and around Hooker's tour, John Lee's Groundhogs recorded an album with him. In an interview with *Melody Maker*, Hooker revealed he was not short of material: 'I know one I'm going to do is 'Seven Days & Seven Nights', a new one of mine. I've got some more, too, but right now, I'm undecided as to which to do.' Hooker went into IBC Studios with ten other songs. However, Tony McPhee related a problem they had to Bob Brunning in his excellent book *Blues: The British Connection*: 'Tom Parker wasn't able to vary the bar counts, so what we had to do was let Hooker play his blues sequence, which was about 10 ½ bars and then he had to mark time until Parker had finished and then start off again.' Another problem was that Mickie Most insisted they record at low volume and this didn't help to create a live atmosphere. Tony thought that his guitar sounded more like a banjo at the low level, so he used a lot of slide to give it more sustain.

The album sleeve indicates the sessions were held in May/June 1965. But Tony remembers only one session (he is correct). Pete Cruickshank gives an insight into how the sessions went: 'Hooker would tell us the song we were going to do. He would sing the song, I'd sort out the bass line there and then we'd run it off. Most of the tracks were one-takes; it was very impromptu. I listened to it recently and thought I could have done better with more time.' It has been said by Hooker aficionados that the album was not a major addition to the Hooker catalogue, but it is a solid piece of work. However, as Charles Murray writes in *Boogie Man*, there are certain things we have to bear in mind: 'Though the album may not have been the artistic triumph for Hooker, it was a considerable achievement for the fledgling Groundhogs, winning their spurs by keeping musical pace with an acknowledged master.' It was also an achievement given the relative lack of experience in recording that John Lee's Groundhogs had at that time.

One of the standout tracks is 'Little Girl Go Back To School', which is not a million miles away from Sonny Boy Williamson's 'Good Morning Little Schoolgirl'. Perhaps Hooker was still smarting from his experiences on the 1964 tour of the UK. 'Don't Be Messin' With My Bread' could also allude to his shenanigans with wayward promoters, but a cursory glance at the lyrics reveals the subject is a lot closer to home. The slow blues of 'Waterfront' invoke all of Pete Cruickshank's memories of Hooker strumming away in the back of the van. It is a beautiful slow blues, with the Hog's tastefully restrained backing working to great effect. The listener is transfixed as Hooker laments his 'five years of torture'. Strangely, the cut that was originally mooted as the title track, 'Seven Days & Seven Nights', doesn't stand out that much.

The album was released in the States under the title *And Seven Nights* on the Verve-Folkways label – it was quickly deleted. It finally got a UK release in 1971 and this was probably because of the Groundhogs' success in the album charts. Sadly, the album was thrown from 'pillar to post' as all sorts of underhand tactics manifested themselves. It was billed on one release as John Lee Hooker with John Mayall & The Groundhogs (Mayall had nothing to do with the album). Tony McPhee's sleeve notes reveal that even the music was changed to some degree: 'Although we did have a brass section later on in the original Hogs lineup, any versions you may have heard of songs from this album with brass were added later by persons unknown.' Another attempt to promote the album also failed as ex-'Who' producer Shel Talmy managed to acquire 'Mai Lee' and 'Don't Be Messin' With My Bread' for his Planet label, but the single flopped.

Listening to the album today and taking into account how fast it was recorded, it is an achievement. But Tony McPhee is rather matter-of-fact about it: 'I look at that album as conveyor belt stuff, really.' It's a major contrast with the way albums are made today. It seems that a lot of bands seem to get bogged down in the studio.

John Lee's Groundhogs were now playing gigs at the famous Marquee Club, where they met prolific producer Mike Vernon.[11] He had ventured to the Marquee to see a band he'd had a tip on, but John Lee's Groundhogs' luck was in as they were also on the bill. Vernon had heard of John Lee's Groundhogs, but for some reason, he didn't like the name, so he thought they must be bad. But it turned out that, when he heard them, he was impressed by their authentic blues. It wasn't long before he suggested they put a few tracks down at Decca Studios in West Hampstead Heath, London. They recorded 'Big Train Blues', 'Can't Sit Down' and Earl Hooker's 'Blue Guitar'. Although nothing came of these tracks, the latter ended up on a blues compilation in the 1970s.

It's important to note that, in between Hooker's 1964/65 tours, the music scene in the UK changed and it spelt disaster for the blues. There was one major reason for the demise of the pure blues bands: another type of music, called soul, had invaded the shores and it initiated big changes. It wasn't long before some artists started to 'put the boot in' to the trailblazers. Pete Townshend provided Charles Shaar Murray with the evidence: 'The irony was that they (US blues artists) all seemed too pathetic, John Lee Hooker in his checkered jacket, doing his cabaret … somehow, they weren't able to attend to the quantum jump that we'd made.[12] But another big name saw Hooker in 1969 and testified to the contrary: 'I took pictures from the side. He was an amazing performer, just him and his guitar. He stood there with his chin pushed out, stamping his foot in rhythm – he looked like a god.' The witness was Bill Wyman of The Rolling Stones.

One of the major attractions of soul was its dynamism and its pure sex appeal, epitomised by the godfather of soul, James Brown. It wasn't long before John Lee's Groundhogs embraced this new genre! However, the winds of change were blowing in different directions, too. A radical game-changing example of this was emanating from Liverpool. The Beatles were showing to all and sundry that it was possible to write original material, and once you did, you could go off in a myriad of directions. It is one reason why the fixation with soul didn't last much longer than the blues. But for the time being, soul was having its day in the sun.

The popularity of soul had the effect of gradually drying up gigs as the blues clubs either closed down or jumped ship. This was especially acute outside London. As Pete Cruickshank sums up, the band had no choice but to go along with it: 'We liked a track called 'Further On Up The Road' by Bobby Bland, but we needed some brass to do it justice, so we acquired some. The soul period was my brother's influence as he liked James Brown a lot. It did put us on a more commercial path, but we had to keep the work coming in.' They saw that the visiting US soul bands were picking up regular work throughout the country. These included Jimmy James & The Vagabonds and Geno Washington. But this conversion worked better for John Cruickshank because his powerful voice projected the new material to the hilt.

The shift to soul brought some problems to the surface in the band. It was clear that Tom Parker struggled to play soul very well, so he left in early September to join The Mark Leeman Five (which included Brian Davison, later to find fame in The Nice). Short of a keyboard player, John Cruickshank took the initiative. He phoned up Terry Goldberg, the previous Mark Leeman Five keyboard player, and offered him the job. As Goldberg was looking for a gig, he accepted Cruickshank's offer and the informal transfer was complete. Goldberg's first job was to negotiate a week's tour of Scotland. However, he never really settled down and only stayed a month. This ushered in a period of time when the band was without a regular keyboard player.

Around the same time that Parker left, Dave Boorman vacated the drum stool. In fact, he was sacked. John Cruickshank reveals the reason why he had to go: 'Dave was a pain in the arse, and by this time, he was becoming very unprofessional.' It fell to John, as leader of the band (it must be said that nobody actually looked at John as being the leader at the time; it was only in retrospect that it was more obvious), to tell him he was out, but at least they didn't dump his drums on his doorstep! They even put a hilarious cover story out that Boorman had left to try his luck as a professional footballer. They delved into *Melody Maker* for a replacement. They chose Terry Slade, who, by all accounts, was a great drummer.

The shift to soul, although necessary, was not to everyone's liking. But what did Tony McPhee think of the change? He was quite philosophical about it: 'The blues clubs were disappearing, so I accepted the situation. It meant I had a lot less to do as I tended to play more rhythm guitar. I remember very well when John came round to my house and excitedly told me he'd heard James Brown's 'Papa's Got A Brand New Bag' and it had a great guitar part. But when I heard it, there was hardly anything in there.' However, the truth was that they never really did become an out-and-out soul band as they merged it with the blues. So, in a way, not only did they create their own sound but they retained their integrity. In an interview with James Johnson of *NME* in 1972, Tony admitted that he was never totally won over by soul and he was always looking over his shoulder at other bands who were still on the original path: 'The point was that The Yardbirds went on to become better while we got stuck into this soul thing. I was watching how well The Yardbirds were doing while I was plugging along with 'In The Midnight Hour'. It was a bit sick.' In fact, The Yardbirds had bailed out from blues and were treading a path towards pop.

Shortly after their switch to soul, they went into Regent Sound in Denmark Street, London, to record a couple of demos. They recorded 'Someone To Love' and 'Hallelujah'. The former is a rollicking adventure with the brass to the fore and with John Cruickshank's expressive vocals – it's quite catchy, too! Bob Hall returned to play some piano for them. The latter is a lot more downbeat. Years later, someone suggested to Tony that he had written 'Hallelujah'. His reply was emphatic: 'I would never write a song with such a title.' In fact, The Sensational Nightingales recorded the song, which was originally called 'The Storm Is Passing Over'. It's an obscure track and it was Bob Hall's suggestion to do it as he had bought it when he was a student. Nobody else had heard it before. It was, however, around this time that Tony started to think about writing his own songs.

Roy Fisher tried to get Shel Talmy interested in the band's new direction. Talmy was still trying to get his fledgling Planet label off the ground. Glyn Johns, who engineered the session, recommended they do 'I'll Never Fall In Love Again'. It's a shame the single didn't make an impact because, right from Terry Slade's crack of his snare drum, it's a tour de force. Again, the brass is prominent. This consisted of David Ware on trumpet and Fred (they never did find out his surname) on sax – they sound a great combination. But it is perfectly obvious that Tony is less enthusiastic. The reviews were very good. The 28 January 1966 edition of *New Musical Express* filed it under 'Recommended' and trumpeted: 'One of our most underrated R&B groups … Bouncy, full of the joys of living. Features the throaty, infectious tones of the band's leader.' *Record Mirror* weighed in heavily: 'There is no doubt it's one of the great examples of selling the blues by the lead voice, with smartly laid down backing. Nice tempo; workmanlike all the way. Could catch on.'

Perhaps one of the reasons why it didn't catch on was because of the saucy references to a 16-year-old girl. Talmy was uncomfortable with the subject matter, but it didn't stop the record from being released. The significance of the flip side is that it's the first song written by Tony McPhee committed to vinyl. The title, 'Over You Baby', is a play on words and its meaning can be interpreted in different ways. Tony's acute sense of humour is to the fore; he liked his humour slapstick and surreal, just like his heroes, The Goons. This was something that would crop up regularly in Tony's work in the future. It's not a major work, but the main aim was to get his first work out on vinyl.

In early 1966, Terry Slade left the band. He'd had a better offer from a band called Sunshine who had got a deal with Warners. After a short search, Colin Huntley became the last drummer for John Lee's Groundhogs. It was decided that they would finally fill the vacant keyboard slot, too. Mick Humbey duly took Goldberg's place in the band; he was the band's last keyboard player. He got the job because Terry Goldberg was always going on about the virtues of the Hammond organ, which was then in vogue. Georgie Fame and Graham Bond were making the instrument famous. They were really keen to get Humbey, even though he would turn out to be band's least proficient keyboard player. It's obvious they were desperate to secure the instrument as a possible route to success. They told Humbey a big fib that he could earn £8 a week, and on the strength of this, Humbey went out and bought the expensive Hammond on Hire Purchase.

In early February 1966, Tony was invited to record with Champion Jack Dupree on the album *From New Orleans To Chicago*. It was another Mike Vernon-produced session. Initially, he was due to play electric lead on all the cuts, but the session was given an extra edge when Eric Clapton turned up. Obviously, room had to be found for him and it resulted in Tony playing less lead. Coincidentally, in August of the previous year, Clapton had left Mayall's Bluesbreakers to 'go around the world' with some of his musician friends (they got as far as Greece). As Tony recalls, it all started at a gig: 'Mayall was playing at the Ricky Tick, Windsor. I met Eric there and he told me he had made enough money and wanted to go on a world trip. He mentioned that John was a megalomaniac. I wasn't interested, but Mayall came to my Tooting home and offered me £40 a week. He even said, 'The blues can be boring but I play things in different keys.' He then tried to get my mom to get me to join when I went to the toilet!' Mayall has been around the block a few times, but he recalled humorously: 'It's true that Tony was my first choice for Eric's replacement and Tony did turn me down.' It turned out to be a wise move in the end, as Peter Green took the job but was kicked out as soon as Clapton returned.

The Dupree recordings took place at Central Sound Studios in Denmark Street, London. Tony plays slide guitar on two tracks: 'Third Degree' and 'Shim, Sham, Shimmy'. Clapton plays lead on both cuts, with Keef Hartley on drums. Tony plays acoustic guitar on the rest of the tracks, with Dupree on piano. Tony remembers 'Going Down To Big Leg Emma's' very well as he outlines the impromptu nature of the sessions: 'Jack had written the song, but before we recorded it, he wanted to improvise the lyrics. He started off with the first line and asked me to come up with something that would fit, but I couldn't do it. He was a very nice man and Clapton was very easy to work with.' The late Gus Dudgeon, who went on to fame with Elton John in the 1970s, engineered the session. The album was released in April 1966. Oddly enough, John Mayall is supposed to be playing harmonica on the two electric guitar tracks, but Tony doesn't remember him being there.

The extent to which John Lee's Groundhogs altered their sound can be summed up by an incident at the Cromwellian Club in London. Tony painfully relates it: 'I thought the gig was dire, and during the set, the manager came up to me and said, 'What band's this?' I told him and he said, 'It isn't; I saw John Lees Groundhogs play with Hooker and it isn't the same band."' To Tony, it was a blunt reminder of just how far he had moved from his blues roots. However, John Cruickshank had this to say about this period: 'Tony was the only one in the band who was against the shift to soul. We were playing great and going down a storm in most places we played.' To complete the misery for Tony, as they were packing away the gear, a cocky young man told them to get off the stage. He had a Hofner pianette under his arm. That man was Reg Dwight, later to become Elton John. Tony never did like him after that and when they were both on the same bill a few years later, he deliberately ran over time (the only time he ever did) just to annoy the headlining be-sequined 'superstar'.

It was the spring of 1966 and the band were going nowhere fast. They were even introduced by Rod Stewart at the Marquee as the Groundhogs Big Band! It was the final humiliation for Tony. It was difficult to believe that, less than a year before, they were backing the great John Lee Hooker on a major tour of the UK. The final straw was when John Cruickshank decided he'd had enough of touring. He was a married man and a father and didn't want that tough lifestyle anymore. The last gig was an all-nighter at the Battersea Town Hall. Tony knew it was all slipping away long before all of this. He'd had enough anyway, but he hadn't a clue exactly what he was going to do next.

Chapter 5 - Have Guitar, Will Travel

> Jo Ann Kelly was remarkable as a vocalist and guitarist and gained immense respect for her authentic grasp of a musical genre dominated by men.
> Tony McPhee writing about his dear friend.

Just after the Hogs disbanded, Tony went into the studio with Mike Vernon to record a couple of singles. Vernon had just launched his own Purdah label and was keen to increase the catalogue. But it was no ordinary label; it was more of a cottage label. Only 99 copies were pressed of any single in order to avoid tax and that's why these singles are so rare today. Some big names succumbed to Vernon's charms. They included Eric Clapton, John Mayall and Savoy Brown. The facilities were made available by dint of a wheeze. The Decca studio was only at Vernon's disposal to audition new bands. It was something he sidestepped nimbly in order to launch his own concern!

These cuts represent Tony McPhee's first solo venture. He recruited his old mate Pete Cruickshank on bass and another old mate, Bob Hall (piano), plus Vaughan Rees (drums). Tony didn't know Rees as he was brought in by Vernon. What gave the session an extra edge was that Tony was singing for the first time. Considering the short duration of the session, these are assured performances. They recorded 'Ain't Gonna Cry No More', 'Someone To Love Me', 'You Don't Love Me' and 'When You Gotta A Good Friend' (Bob Hall is not on the last one). The recordings were released as two singles in July 1966 (probably recorded in June). The standout track is 'Someone To Love Me', which includes a great rhythm backing and some spirited lead from Tony. He purloined the riff off Charly Patton. Tony is the first one to admit that contemporary blues songs were rarely totally original.

The session with Vernon is also notable because this is where Tony acquired his TS moniker. It was Vernon's idea as he liked using initials for stage names, such as 'JB' Lenoir. He asked Tony what his middle name was (it's Charles), but Tony didn't like that idea because TC was also the name of a famous cartoon character, Top Cat, who, though lovable, was a bit of a scallywag. Tony thought no more of it until the initials appeared on a US album sleeve. After that, the name stuck. But when Tony later phoned Vernon about royalties, he was only able to speak to his secretary. She had a brief consultation with Vernon, who told her to tell Tony that the 'TS' stands for tough shit! However, there is a postscript to the story. In 1968, the four tracks appeared on a best-selling blues compilation album called *Blues Anytime Vol 1 & 2.*[13] It appears that Vernon sold the tracks to Immediate Records and made a lot of money from those cuts.

Around this time, Alexis Korner asked Tony to go on the road with him. Korner was still doing his *Five O'Clock Club* on television. This was an amazing show and indicates what a smooth operator Korner was to persuade the BBC to have a blues segment in a children's television show. So he asked Tony to meet him at the Giaconda Cafe in Denmark Street in a 'couple of weeks' to discuss things. The problem was that Tony forgot to make the appointment and it turned out that Korner didn't forgive people who missed appointments. He heard later from other musicians that Korner had told them not to trust Tony McPhee. It didn't diminish the respect he had for the great, old blues man, however.

By July, Tony was struggling to maintain his professional status. In the nick of time, he received a call from Dave Nicholson, who was the manager of a band called Truth. He was looking for a guitarist. They had recently had a hit with a version of The Beatles song 'Girl' and their current single was a version of The Kinks' 'I Go To Sleep'. Tony was impressed with the single but only joined the band for the money. Desperate times called for desperate measures! The nucleus of Truth was composed of two singers: Frank Aiellou and Steve Jameson (the former ended up in Cozy Powell's Bedlam). Tony was part of a backing trio that was made up of Ray Stock on drums and Dennis Taylor on bass. Tony was in the band for a couple of months; he played a lot of gigs but never made any recordings with them.

Tony McPhee's career was clearly lacking direction, and his next job, though very interesting, illustrated the point. He got a call from the elegantly named Basil Charles-Dean. He was the manager of Boz & the Boz People, who had just secured the support slot for a Dusty Springfield tour in early September. Boz later ended up in King Crimson and later became Bad Company's singer/bassist, but in those days, he didn't play an instrument. Tony got on well with him and things were soon looking up; he even got paid for rehearsing. This gig was turning into luxury as he initially travelled in Basil's sleek Vanden Plas Princess. The tour kicked off on 12 September at the Astoria, London. Unfortunately, the car got 'used' (Basil was not pleased) by Boz and they found themselves relegated to finishing the tour in a mini. At the tour's conclusion, it was obvious to him that he couldn't maintain his professional status. He was forced to go back to full employment in September 1966.

Tony got a job with Pullmans, who specialised in the maintenance of dictating machines. The company was situated on Old Street, London. It wasn't long before he launched his own band, albeit part-time. The name Herbal Mixture was inspired by his vegetarian status and his interest in alternative medicines. He didn't think long about who was going to play bass. Tony had retained Roy Fisher as the manager. Consequently, Fisher fired off a call to Pete Cruickshank. As it turned out, Cruickshank was still playing pro but in the most bizarre of circumstances, as he recalls: 'After John Lee's Groundhogs split up, I got a job in a seven-piece Jamaican band called Ossie Lane & The Red Hot Band. I can't remember how I got the job, but I think it was because I had a certain pedigree. I was the only white guy and my nickname was 'spooky'. We played Jamaican clubs and I had a great time.' The call from Tony put an end to that gig. Even though Pete had to go back to working nine to five, he'd had enough of Ossie's band anyway.

They recruited 17-year-old Mike Meekham on drums from the *Melody Maker* classified ads section. He had a Keith Moon 'I'm here' style, according to Pete Cruickshank. This was essential because playing in a three-piece meant they could not carry any passengers and Pete remembers Meekham as a fine drummer. They started off doing soul, a lot of Sam & Dave numbers, which Tony liked. They also did 'I'll Keep On Holding On' by the Marvelletes. The songs were all executed in an outrageous beat/rock style. However, the psychedelic era of rock was kicking in and other influences would soon make their mark, too. They were quickly signed by Columbia and it wasn't long before they went into the studio. This was partly due to Bruce Higham, whom Roy Fisher had asked to be the co-manager of the band. The recordings highlighted a few problems, as Tony wasn't sure whether to handle the vocals. At one stage, Roy Fisher suggested they try out a singer he knew. Rab Monroe did indeed record a couple of demos, but they got rid of him because Tony thought he wasn't a very good singer.

They went into IBC Studios, Portland Street, to record the McPhee-penned tracks 'A Love That's Died' and 'Tailor Made'. Both of these cuts are what could be called 'rockers' and the band are very together. The former has a great intro that sounds rather like Pink Floyd, except that this was months before Floyd ever went into a studio. The cut might have improved if the haunting intro had been reprised more. Still, it's a solid debut, but it's clearly a band at the learning stage. The flipside is a really catchy tune, making it a value-for-money coupling. Norman Jopling reviewed 'A Love That's Died' in the 15 October edition of *Record Mirror*: 'Quaintly named, starts most promisingly, but it deteriorates into a rather routine performance and song.'

The next single they recorded was a much more significant piece of work. 'Machines' is the first social comment that Tony ever wrote. It's a statement that there is more to life than working a machine in a factory. He was clearly feeding off his own experiences and frustrations. It also underlines his determination not to succumb to that life. But as he remembers, there was another aspect to this song that the 1980s brought to fruition: 'In those days, there was the idea of having a job for life. I didn't believe in lifelong security and I was shown to be right later.' 'Machines' is also memorable for its excellent guitar solo.

When listening to this band's work, the most satisfying aspect is Tony's distinctive voice. Strangely, he was inspired later on by an unlikely source in his determination to be a singer, as he reveals: 'Hendrix had always said he couldn't sing, so I thought I'll do it, too.' 'Machines' was released in December and *Record Mirror* was enthusiastic: 'Good bluesy sound on this jerky, somewhat unbalanced slice of earthiness. May get lost, but plugging could help it through.' Furthermore, the *New Musical Express* picked it as their record of the week! The review ends by urging people to listen to the record when it's aired on *Juke Box Jury*, which was the legendary television pop show hosted by David Jacobs, although it never got an airing as far as is known.

Glyn Johns was engineering the sessions; he also worked with The Who. He regaled the band with stories of Pete Townshend and Keith Moon ripping the towel dispensing machine off the wall. Tony was baffled and recalls these conversations: 'I enjoyed the stories but my initial reaction was 'Why?' I have never done anything like that on the road or anywhere else.' Tony was there solely for the music and had a healthy, economical attitude to the whole process. Although he enjoys the practical jokes, he was not into damage and demolition.

Apart from the influence of John Lee Hooker, Jimi Hendrix and Hubert Sumlin, Tony's technique for writing entailed playing random chords until he came across something that sounded unusual. This is what interested him and ensured he had a better chance of creating something that was different. Well, that was the theory. It didn't always work early on, but this technique paid supreme dividends a little later. However, the lyrics didn't come easy. He usually left this to the last minute, but it was a bad move on the 'Machines' session. Johns was getting paid a stupendous £4 per hour for the session. At one stage, Tony wanted to sing the line, 'Vegetable matter', over and over but Johns persuaded him he needed proper words. Tony needed lyrics and fast. He went to the toilet and sat down on the seat in the foetal position and had a brainstorming session. This ended up being a favourite future technique for writing lyrics. In this fledgling writing period, Tony was never able to create a unique sound in Herbal Mixture, although he made a brave attempt and came close.

As well as the material they recorded, Tony had other self-penned songs they played live. 'Mr McGhee' was important because it was the first song that he wrote with chord changes that were out of the ordinary. The song's subject matter was the world of advertising. There was no Mr McGhee; it was a name that Tony plucked out of the air. Another song was 'Eleven Year Old Man', which was about a rather simple-minded man. 'Spontaneity' was another song they played live, but it was never finished to Tony's satisfaction and it always had different lyrics. As a result of the limited opportunities the band had to record, these songs went unheralded in the studio.

It was clear that they hadn't got an original sound that would put them ahead of the pack, so Roy Fisher set about giving the band an edge. Tony remembers his embarrassment when he recalls how it came about: 'I had a call from Roy, who said we had a gig at Middle Earth. I said, 'Great', but then he told me he'd told them that we were different. He said we had to dress up like we did that time at Jo Ann Kelly's flat.' They then raided her wardrobe and put on some of her clothes for a laugh. Now they had to appear in public like that. They got behind the idea and went to junk shops and bought pith helmets, beads, old ladies' hats and anything else they could wear. Tony even made himself a pair of Bermuda shorts from a cushion cover. However, as Pete Cruickshank remembers, it got worse than that: 'I had a green sparkly face and I dyed my hair copper coloured. My sister helped me on that one. Strangely, I met my wife when I had that face on. Looking back, it was all a bit embarrassing.'

Tony was still at the day job, but he found solace in the workplace with a strategically placed radio – this was to unexpectedly play a part in shaping the band's repertoire. Something came on the radio that hit him like a ton of bricks, so he turned it up full blast. It didn't last long at this level, as his co-workers soon turned it down, but he thought the song was awesome. The record was 'Hey Joe' by Jimi Hendrix and it was soon incorporated into the act, along with Tim Rose's 'Morning Dew'. This was during the time when they were starting to move away from soul, as a lot of bands were doing. It has been suggested by some journalists that one of the reasons why soul's appeal was limited in the UK was because it became related more to US performers. Of course another reason was the emergence of the Mersey beat type sounds, where guitar bands had really taken off with their more catchy material. Things are rarely mono-causal.

By early 1967, they were still raiding junk shops for unusual clothes. Now and again, they would get the dreaded call from Roy Fisher, who was also a photographer. He would tell them that he needed more pictures. They'd drive to Hyde Park and change into their gear, emerging from the back of the van like butterflies. They would then spend the next hour prancing around, having their photos taken not only by Fisher but also by bemused Japanese tourists.

Tony was still keeping busy on the session front. The Mike Vernon connection paid dividends as he was drafted in to play on an Eddie Boyd album. On 21 March 1967, he played slide guitar on 'Dust My Broom' and 'Save Her Doctor'. The album was packed with luminaries such as Peter Green and John McVie. A lot of the recordings that big-name blues artists were making at that time simply came about very informally. The way it worked was that a producer like Vernon would offer a couple of hundred pounds to make an album, so it was done in rapid time. In April 1967, Tony teamed up with Champion Jack Dupree again – Mike Vernon was producing. They went into a studio near Islington, London, where they recorded 13 original cuts. These tracks were never released and they have since been gathering dust. The tracks were credited to Jack Dupree and Tony McPhee, except that is not quite accurate, as Tony didn't have any part in the writing, but Dupree was generous enough to cede half the credit. The tapes have recently been discovered by Vernon, and in 2004, Tony McPhee signed a contract with Dupree's daughter to allow for their release.[14]

Gigs were always in short supply, although they did play the Marquee Club four times. On 27 September 1967, they supported the legendary Jeff Beck Group, who were making a dry run for Led Zeppelin in the blues-rock stakes. The truth is that they would both follow Cream's lead. Luckily, by this time, the crazy clothes had been abandoned for Regency clothes, which were the height of fashion. They took their inspiration from early 19th-century clothing, reinterpreted for the modern day, initially for Mods, by iconoclastic designers such as Mary Quant. One of the major outlets for this clothing was the iconic Granny Takes A Trip in London, which started in 1966 and counted George Harrison and Jimi Hendrix as part of their clientele. There was to be no Granny Takes A Trip visits for Tony as he was so broke that he had to ask Jeff Beck if he had a spare first guitar string, as he had snapped his. The band were drifting along now and seemed to be going nowhere. Worse was to come when Mike Meekham allowed his girlfriend, whom he was infatuated with, to dissuade him from playing the drums. It came to a head when he was late for a gig at the Marquee on 16 December. The manager of the club, John Gee, went berserk and that was more or less it.

The band limped until the early summer of 1968, when Tony had an interesting offer. He joined The John Dummer Band. Dave Kelly played guitar in the band and he recalls how it came about: 'I asked Mac if he fancied joining the Dummer Band. I'd joined about a year earlier as a singer & slide guitarist. Then the lead guitarist was Roger Pearce, but he left quite soon as I don't think he liked the less 'modern' direction the band were going in. I thought Mac had nothing planned at that time; we (Dummer Band) had a record deal and I thought we needed a lead guitarist – and a bloody good one. Also, we were friends. Furthermore, Mac shared the vocals with me in the band.' For a short while, Tony was in two bands. But he was still loyal to Pete Cruikshank and Mike Meekham, as he stipulated to Kelly that if Herbal Mixture took off, he would leave to go full-time with them. But shortly after this, Herbal Mixture folded.

As well as John Dummer on drums, there was also Thumper Thompson on bass (they went on to form the rock and roll revivalists Darts in the 70s). Dave Kelly was still quite young and inexperienced then and his exuberance got them into trouble at a gig in London, as Tony recalls: 'We played a gig with Sam Apple Pie at their own club. At the end of their set, they played an Elmore Jones number that we played in our set. Dave Kelly heard this and said, 'Let's show them how it's really done'. My heart sank, as I don't like that sort of thing. I knew it would end in disaster and it did! We were total shit; we even started off in the wrong key.' Dave Kelly also recalls these events: 'Yes, sure do, they were getting on my nerves, I thought they were pretty basic. I don't know why they bothered booking other bands as all their mates (90% of the audience) wanted to hear only them. However, I think the longevity of my career has proved my point. Were the Dummer Band shit? It was probably not one of our better gigs; we had the ability to be absolutely brilliant or absolute crap, and at the time, I didn't know enough to be able to put my finger on what happened to make the difference.'

In spite of the odd disaster, the band were building up quite a name in the blues world, and on 2 July 1968, they appeared on a *Top Gear* radio session. Just after that, they recorded the album *Cabal*. Tony was pleased as Jo Ann Kelly was also involved and he always liked working with her. The original John Lee's Groundhogs pianist, Bob Hall, also joined the sessions. The songs are a curious mix of the old and the new. There are songs by John Lee Hooker, Little Walter and Willie Dixon, as well as new material by Dave Kelly. Even Tony's early solo Mike Vernon period is reprised with 'When You Gotta Good Friend', but at a faster tempo. Dave Kelly explains how he got a songwriting credit: 'This 'old song by Tony' was, in fact, a much older song by Robert Johnson. At that time, Johnson's songs were up for grabs as the copyright laws weren't as protective as they are now. Presumably, Mac had 'trad arranged' his version. The version by the John Dummer Band was my arrangement.'

There's even space for some solid social comment in the 1930s song 'Welfare Blues', which features a great vocal from Tony. The lead guitar duties were shared; Dave Kelly was an accomplished guitarist in his own right. He recalls how they divided out the guitar playing: 'We had some songs prepared and busked some in the studio, some with Jo on vocals. I don't remember how we worked out who would play lead; it just worked out organically – horses for courses, etc. I remember more the recording of our first single 'Travellin Man', which was a John Lee Hooker song, with me taking the Hooker lead vocal part and Mac taking the middle vocal part a la Eddie Kirkland.' The highlight of Tony's contribution is 'After Hours'. It might not be the best track but it features a gutsy vocal and a storming guitar solo. Tony was into new territory on this album and he thought some of it was false. He remembers how they did three versions of one track and then spliced the best bits of each one to make a hybrid number. He wasn't keen on those tactics.

Cabal was originally scheduled for a September release, but it was delayed for a few months until January 1969. *New Musical Express* was gushing about it: '(The group) really gets an exciting, pulsating rhythm going, and the vocalist, Dave Kelly, really gets out his message. Great party maker.' *Melody Maker* added the good and the bad: 'The band achieve just the right balance and swing, even handling the difficult slow-medium tempo well. Though they have mastered the (blues) idiom, their influences are too obvious and they lack vocal flexibility.' The album still stands up today and can be filed under a 'great blues album'. There are some top-class performances. Apart from the lead guitars, the music is superbly supplemented by Bob Hall's piano and John O'Leary's harmonica, creating a dense sound. Tony McPhee left as soon as the album was recorded because he had an offer to go to United Artists. His departure was so swift that he doesn't even appear on the album cover (his place was taken by Adrian 'Putty' Pietryga). When Tony departed the band, he left with a new partner. Christine Payne had previously gone out with John Dummer and Dave Kelly. Tony wasn't even looking for someone permanent, but they hit it off well. They were to be married a few years later.

The way Tony McPhee got involved with United Artists is the epitome of serendipity. Roy Fisher recalls how this came about and it was all to do with his desire to rent a studio in Ebury Street, London, to shoot music videos:

> At that time, music videos were starting to be the big thing, but there were not a lot of video recording studios and I thought this place would be good for that purpose. I contacted the man who owned the building, and on meeting him and explaining my plan for a video in the studio, he let me sign a six-month lease on the understanding that I would need time to raise the capital to develop the idea. It was on contacting companies in the entertainment business to see if they would be interested in investing in my plan that I met with Andrew Lauder, then head of A&R at Liberty. In conversation, I mentioned managing the Groundhogs during the time they backed John Lee Hooker, and he said he had seen a couple of the shows and asked what the band were doing now, as he would be interested in offering them a record deal.

The rest, as they say, is history.

Roy Fisher immediately phoned Tony up at work and asked for a meeting at a café near Green Park tube station: the conversation centred on re-forming the Groundhogs. Seconds after Tony heard the offer, he effectively turned pro and didn't even go back to work in the afternoon. He also handed his notice in with The John Dummer Band. He then rescued Pete Cruickshank from a building site. They got Steve Rye, who was a friend of Jo Ann Kelly, on harmonica. The only slot left to fill was the drummer. But that would remain a problem until quite late in the day. This offer was especially fortuitous because blues was back in vogue again, or a hybrid version of it. Fleetwood Mac had formed the year before and they were playing what was called blues-rock with great success and it wasn't very long before Jimmy Page formed Led Zeppelin from the ashes of The Yardbirds. It hadn't been long before that there was only John Mayall and one or two others on the original blues path.

Dave Kelly stayed in The John Dummer Band for a while longer. He went on to have a successful career culminating in the legendary Blues Band. He performed in that band until the day it broke up in 2022. He outlines his feelings on what working with Tony McPhee gave him: 'Mac was the greatest influence on me in my early days of learning to play blues. He showed me how to tune the guitar to open tuning, gave me my first slide and sold me my first decent acoustic guitar. I loved and still do love his quirky style of playing lead – totally unlike all of his contemporaries. He didn't do the usual B.B./Freddie King style but was rather influenced by Hubert 'sublime' Sumlin. You ask me about Mac as a guitarist and my first feeling is the same when people constantly refer to me as a guitarist – what about the vocals?'

At the same time as the reformation of the Groundhogs, Roy Fisher put into action some more projects: 'I originated the idea of the 'Groundhog Series' of albums and put the idea to Andrew Lauder. I also devised the concept of each album and got the artists together who recorded on them. They were mostly artists we already knew from the London blues/folk clubs that Jo Ann Kelly was playing. Tony did the production work. We gave them the opportunity to record for a major label then got accused of ripping them off because they didn't get any royalties. They did not realise that the albums did not sell enough to even cover the recording costs! They were only meant to help them get more gigs.'

The first of these projects was a compilation album called *Me And The Devil* and it was scheduled before the Groundhogs went into the studio. The album was produced by Mike Batt and was recorded at Marquee Studios in September 1968.[15] There was quite a talented roster of artists assembled, including Jo Ann Kelly, Dave Kelly, Andy Fernbach and, of course, Tony McPhee. Tony's original idea was to get a small audience into the studio to give it more of a live feel. However, Batt didn't think much of that idea; although the technicians tried a few claps, it was quickly dropped. Tony appears playing acoustic and slide guitar on the title cut, 'No More Doggin'', 'Death Letter' and 'Rollin & Tumblin'' – the latter was with Jo Ann Kelly, who provides a riveting vocal performance. In 1998, Tony had this to say about Jo Ann in the sleeve notes of the re-issue of the album: '(She) was remarkable as a vocalist and guitarist and gained immense respect for her authentic grasp of a musical genre dominated by men. She was almost certainly the only white British female playing acoustic slide guitar.'

The sleeve notes for the album were written by Mike Raven and he asked the million-dollar question, 'How can a well-fed, well-educated, young white musician ever do justice to a music originated by starving, illiterate, middle-aged Negroes from the Deep South?' The question was mainly pointed at the vocals. How do you put across human suffering with conviction? At the end of the year, Tony got his chance to answer the question in an interview with *Melody Maker*: 'I think you can compare it with the instrumental side of the blues. It's like copying Hubert Sumlin's sound on guitar. I don't put anything on for the blues. I try not to copy anybody in particular when I'm singing, but I like the way Son House uses words and that influences me. It's a way of using words; you bend them like you do a note on a guitar. Really, it's no effort for me. I couldn't sing any other way, not on blues, without having to think hard about it.'

Me And The Devil is a solid collection of songs, but, much to Tony's disappointment, it didn't chart – he didn't have time to dwell on that. In the next few weeks, he would have to fill the drum stool as the Groundhogs' first foray into the studio was imminent. How he eventually got his man came about in strange circumstances.

Ken Pustelnik was born on Friday 13 March 1946, near Blairgarry, on a farm in the highlands of Scotland. His family were well-steeped in the art of drumming. His grandfather had been a regimental sergeant major in the legendary Black Watch. He ended up as a pipe major in the even more famous Scot's Grey's. He later played jazz drums, and even his uncle was also a drummer. He only recently found out that his father was an American GI and he had been a guitar player. Couple this with his Scottish mother, who gave him a Polish upbringing, and mix this with his American father's German background and you have a rather eclectic family situation. Suffice it to say that Ken Pustelnik's musical legacy was vibrant.

The family moved to Bristol in 1951 and that's where he was brought up. When he was about ten, he started listening to the great jazz Hammond organ players Jimmy Smith and Jimmy McGriff. At the time, he enjoyed the sound. He also liked country blues and the mountain music of the Appalachian variety. The famous Carter family were a shining beacon to him then. But it wasn't long before percussion influences imposed themselves on the young boy. He heard a record on Radio Luxembourg called 'El Watusi' by Ray Barretto and that knocked him out. Barretto's bongos are heavily featured and two men arguing complement these furious sounds, as he remembers: 'That was a great track, and looking back, it was an early version of rap.' He later found that Barretto was famous in his own right and recorded many film soundtracks – he was inducted into the International Latin Music Hall of Fame in 1999.

Later on, he got into Miles Davis, Charlie Mingus and the usual suspects. Classical music also got the once over. He clearly had a voracious appetite for music that was drawn from the four corners of the world. By the time he was 18, he was thinking deeply about why music happens. He even formulated a theory that music happens geographically and that rhythms happen due to temperatures. Vietnamese and Indian music was especially at the top of his list then. In fact, one of his most influential albums was *The Drums Of India*. It could be said that what Ken was listening to was world music – and it is – but more important than that, it is simply the concept of anything goes.

At this time, Ken Pustelnik sported long hair before it was fashionable. He was sitting in Bristol city centre when a guy came up to him and said, 'I love your image; I want you to be my drummer'. He describes what happened next: 'I went back to his house, where he opened his garage door. It was full of equipment. I told him I don't play the drums, but he convinced me. His name was Alan Clarke and he was a dead ringer for the lead singer of The Hollies; he even had the same name.' After that, he scraped £50 and bought his first drum kit. The Premier kit lasted right until the first Groundhogs album. The Pustelnik family legacy of drums was heavily imbued into him because he is completely self-taught. From the first time he put the kit together, he sat down and just played them instinctively. It wasn't long before Ken was playing drums in the band and he started to bring in his friends, such as Rob Freeman. Over the passage of time, Clarke was squeezed out, leaving them with a lot of equipment. This band developed into The Deep Blues Band.

It was 1962 and they were still playing exclusively in the garage. They were into country blues and skiffle. Robert Johnson and Lonnie Donnegan were the ones they most revered. The frustration of not having any gigs led them to a masterstroke. They decided to form their own blues club. It wasn't long before they had clubs in Bristol and Gloucester. They didn't even have a name beyond The Blues Club. It was very egalitarian and they would have free and easy slots where members of the audience would be invited to perform. It wasn't all low-key; the clubs were also booking name bands like Fleetwood Mac and The John Dummer Band – its possible Tony performed there later. There were always big crowds for these gigs as the area was so starved of name bands. But that was part of the problem; they had no contact with London and that was where it all happened. But that was to change soon.

The Deep Blues Band were avid readers of the music press, and in late 1967, there were plenty of exciting things to read. It was here that they found out about the plight of Memphis Minnie. The story reported she was unable to pay for the medical treatment she desperately required. The article mentioned that there was going to be a benefit for her at Club 51, London. Being not very versed in the correct etiquette of such things, they piled into their van on the appointed day and drove to London in true hippy fashion. There was nobody there when they arrived. Perhaps just as well because they were weirdly attired. As it was still early, they decided to set up their gear. Nobody challenged them initially, but eventually, somebody did ask if they were the house band, to which they replied in the affirmative. As is no great surprise, the big-name players that did turn up came late after the gear was set up.

Ken Pustelnik recalls these events: 'As it got dark, the stars came out. John Mayall came in and introduced his hot new bassist, Andy Fraser. So they both played with us. Then Bob Hall played with us; Andy Fernbach and Dave Kelly were also there. For some reason, Tony wasn't there.' The evening was a great success and raised a good deal of funds. However, it was also important because the capital had a taste of a good one-off band they had never heard before.

The Deep Blues Band played the blues in a totally off-the-cuff fashion. They were out of the mainstream London circuit; they made their blues statement without any due reference to anybody else who was around. Ken proffers the extent of this: 'The Deep were playing blues in a rockabilly style. Ours was more like a hoedown in Mississippi. We were like skiffle, but we had electric instruments. The London-based bands played Chicago blues with loads of technique. It was a culture clash.' However, in the wake of the benefit, The Deep's personnel were being raided by a furious onslaught from the capital on a weekly basis. With Ken Pustelnik's patience wearing thin after every phone call, he received one from Tony McPhee. What transpired was quite odd, as he recalls: 'He said, 'I want you to join my band.' So I said, 'You've never seen me play.' He was quite willing to go on the recommendation of Dave and Jo Ann Kelly. I didn't want to join without an audition.'

The audition was duly arranged at Club 51. As well as Tony and Pete, Roy Fisher was in attendance at the back of the hall. Ken didn't like him; he didn't like 'accountant'-like people in suits. However, Roy Fisher never wore suits then or after, so it was obviously the other record executives. Ken remembers the magic of that evening and also what he brought to the band: 'When we started playing, it was like 'bang'. Pete and Tony were die-hard musicians; I was more into avant-garde like Andy Warhol and Stockhausen. I am a sophisticated music person but a primitive drummer. So when I played, it didn't come out like that because I stripped it down to its elements. That's why I hated drum solos.' It was this 'only use what's required' philosophy that impressed Tony. This is the magic ingredient that Ken brought to the Groundhogs. He was the oil and Tony and Pete were the water. In theory, it couldn't work, but this 'imbalanced mix' was to give them something that no other band had. However, the selection process irked Ken. He was asked to come back the following day to the club, and after much procrastination, he was invited to the Marquee Studios. There was just one problem – he had never been in a studio before! However, the second audition went well for Ken.

He was now a member of the Groundhogs, and in 1971, at the height of the band's fame, he gave an interview to *Record Mirror* about what playing in the band meant to him: 'It's about the only magical thing left. I'm not terribly romantic anymore – I've been through it. And I haven't any more illusions about pop. I value it for what it's worth … I still go out to see groups. Playing is an attitude, I guess. I never really grew up and never will. At school, when I first saw the old Groundhogs playing, I wrote their name on my haversack and I'm still basically a fan.'

Chapter 6 - Light Was The Night

> I do think, and did then, that Tony is, and was, a superb talent – very original and yet classic in his approach.
> Mike Batt

> Tony is, without doubt, a genius and the best (bar none) bottleneck guitarist in Europe, as well as a quite amazingly fast and accurate conventional guitarist.
> Journalist John Tobler writing about Tony in 1970

When Ken Pustelnik entered Marquee Studios on 5 October 1968, it wasn't the only new experience for him that day, as he hadn't met all the band members. He was introduced to harmonica player Steve Rye just before they hit the first note. Unfamiliarity wasn't the only problem for the band, as studio time was severely limited and, of course, they hadn't played any gigs together. Furthermore, the studio was only four-track (like most others at the time); it was hardly the kind of scenario that would conjure up a good album. As it happened, it didn't turn out so bad. Mike Batt was their Liberty producer.

Tony McPhee was still in the early stages as a writer and only had three songs for the album. But this set-up gave him the chance to develop fast. The first of his songs is 'Rocking Chair' and it's a solid opener, with Tony's voice in fine form. In fact, apart from two tracks, he took all the lead vocals. Steve Rye takes the lead vocals on 'Early In The Morning', which is Tony's second original song. Listening to Rye's more conventional voice on that cut highlights what an interesting voice Tony possessed. The other McPhee-penned cut is 'Married Men'. It's odd because he can't recall why he chose that subject matter; he certainly wasn't married at that stage. The track is showcased by Rye's harmonica and Tony's restrained licks. Tony decided to reprise 'No More Doggin' from the *Me And The Devil* album. On that album, Tony tackled it with his acoustic guitar, but here, the band inject some electric punch into it. It was played until the disbanding of the Groundhogs and remained a firm favourite with the fans.

The opener of side two is 'Man Trouble'. The rhythm section, perfectly in time, nail everything down and make this a most interesting proposition. Tony is content to take a back seat on this one. Rye takes lead vocals again on 'You Don't Love Me'; it is catchy, but it's a million miles away from the album's closing gambit. 'Still A Fool' is a great blues song and showcases Tony singing about the downs of a relationship. The album was released on Liberty in November 1968. Many years later, it was reviewed by Dave Thompson of *Allmusic*: 'Again, if you arrive at *Scratching The Surface* in search of a fresh 'Cherry Red' or 'Status People', you'll probably be disappointed. But if you want to hear the blues sluicing straight out of the Southern England Delta, there are precious few better introductions … *Scratching The Surface* ranks among the finest albums to emerge out of that entire period, a moody shuffle that includes an epic recounting of the Chicago classic 'Still A Fool'.' The band have expressed disappointment with the finished result. It's true that it isn't a polished album, but what else could have been done under the constraints of time? Tony acknowledges that there are a lot of mistakes on the album and describes it as 'conveyor belt stuff' – but it does have its moments.

Mike Batt recalls the session didn't always go well: 'During the recording of the album at Marquee Studios, just behind the Marquee Club in Wardour Street, one of the songs was so long and I was so tired that I fell asleep over the recording desk during the take – (so did the engineer) – and we were woken by the band, who had finished the song and wanted to hear it back! Not the best way to show a band how much you care!' This was the impression he created as all the members of the band recalled that Batt didn't like the album. Batt was also involved in the shooting of the album sleeve. Roy Fisher decided that it would be good to show the band in a pool of water. With that in mind, they journeyed to Hamstead Pond with photographer Michael Hasted and found a pool.[16] It was freezing cold but the band waded in and proceeded to patiently pose for half an hour while the shots were taken. In the cover shot, Pete Cruickshank looks like he's had enough and is taking steps to the bank – he really was on his way out!

However, Mike Batt was so impressed with Tony that he decided to use him on his next project. Hapshash and the Coloured Coat was made up of Nigel Weymouth and Michael English. They had a fairly successful debut album, and to some, it was described as a psychedelic classic. Interestingly, Batt pinpoints how good Tony was at interpreting what he wanted:

> *Western Flyer* was recorded at Marquee Studios just after the first Groundhogs album. It was a bit experimental. I think I probably had

> *Music From The Big Pink* (The Band) in my mind when I put that project together, as well as half a dozen other psychedelic albums. I played piano, Tony played guitar and it was really exhilarating working on it, playing and producing. We would run through the songs probably once only, using chord sheets I'd prepared, and then we'd do a take, probably THE take. Tony played some great stuff, very freaky, just right for what I wanted. Then I took the finished four-track tapes, containing our rhythm section performances, over the road to Trident Studios, which had the only eight-track machine in town – and where The Beatles had just recorded 'Hey Jude' – and we transferred the tapes to eight-track, leaving four open tracks, which I used for weird acid rocky effects like the girls singing and waving tinkly things.

The album was released in late 1968, but it didn't do very well.

Even though Tony was doing what he wanted, the value of regular sessions cannot be underestimated in his development as a musician: 'You have to think on your feet as you haven't got much time. When they start playing, you have to follow. It certainly gives you confidence in your ability.' As Batt testified, Tony McPhee was a very experienced hand in the studio and most effective at doing exactly that. The regular work continued when Andrew Lauder got Tony more work with another blues giant in the studio. But this time, he was in a coordinator role.

Big Joe Williams was in the middle of touring the UK and had some free time between gigs. A deal was struck to record an album for Liberty. That it all happened so quickly can be judged by the fact that Tony had to borrow a Vox AC30 amp for Big Joe from Ken Pustelnik's flatmate Putty (real name: Adrian Pietryga). He had been the guitarist in Ken's old band, The Deep. Roy Fisher recalls the casual nature of the session: 'We sat him in the studio, got the engineer to just set the equipment and let the tape run. He had half a bottle of scotch and played non-stop till the bottle was empty and that was the album.'

As Big Joe was performing on his own, with no overdubs, Tony admits that there was not much work for him to do, and contrary to popular myth, he didn't perform on the album, although he wrote the sleeve notes. Tony describes the run-down nature of Big Joe's guitar in the notes: 'It is an incredibly dirty old Harmony Sovereign, which is the blues guitar next to the national, held together in parts with various forms of sticky tape. The three extra pegs required to make up the complement of nine strings are screwed to the top of the head. He uses a de-armoured pickup with volume control and a connecting lead patched up with insulating tape.' At the end of the session, he told Tony it was the best recording he'd ever made.

Big Joe Williams was a former cotton picker from the south of the US. He'd had a hard life and, clearly, had been treated badly for much of the time. His trademark was his walking stick, which displayed badges, each one being a place he'd been to. He was quite a character and a nice guy, but he obviously overestimated Tony's standing when he asked him: 'Have you got a model T Ford?' This lack of transport taught Tony that you don't mess with Big Joe Williams, especially if you're a taxi driver. At the session's conclusion, they had to get the amp and everybody else back home. However, after they called a black cab, they soon realised they needed another one. Somebody suggested they call a mini-cab, and on hearing that word, the black cab driver indicated he wouldn't take them (this was the time of the fierce rivalry between the two types of hire car). The driver got very vocal and an argument ensued. Tony recalls what happened next: 'Big Joe came up to the driver with his walking stick in hand and said, 'Get out of here!'' The driver legged it out of there!

After all of these sessions, it was time to get back to Groundhogs business. And what better way could there be than to re-acquaint themselves with the man himself, John Lee Hooker. Hooker had written a letter prior to the tour asking for his old backing band. It was Hooker's first visit to the UK since 1965. Only Tony and Pete remained from the band that had toured with him previously. However, Ken Pustelnik and Steve Rye were to get on well with the great man. The tour kicked off in late October 1968 and it was almost like the old days. Hooker had heard *Scratching The Surface* (Tony took him into the studio and played him the whole album) and he recommended they release 'You Don't Love Me' as the single. They followed his advice!

Just after the tour started, they played a doubleheader on 9 November. The early gig was at the Boston Glyderdome. At the gig's conclusion, they had to pack up the gear and drive back to London for a gig at The Roundhouse, where they were supporting Led Zeppelin as John Lee Hooker's backing band. This was a gig that would go down in music history, as this was Led Zeppelin's first appearance in London (previously, Jimmy Page's band had been known as The New Yardbirds). Even though London was obviously the centre for all things, thanks to Ken Pustelnik's connections, they were also getting gigs in the

West Country. These were mainly in Bristol and Gloucester, and with it being starved of music, they hired bigger venues. It was interesting to note that some of these drew bigger crowds than the London gigs.

For Steve Rye, the experience of working with Hooker for the first time was a revelation. No one could ever accuse Hooker of not giving enough 'air' for his band to breathe, but that didn't interfere with him connecting to his audience, as Rye once commented to Bob Brunning: 'I never saw him give a bad performance; there was good and extra good. He was very easy going and very generous with solo time; he certainly didn't hog (pardon the pun) the stage in any way. But he had a lot of trouble with his tuning. In fact, Tony used to tune his guitar for him. Still, he was exciting and he always managed to win over young audiences.' Hooker was proving to Rye that he was a big character. However, Rye was a bit of a character himself. Ken recalls him very well: 'He was a fiery bloke, but he was a hypochondriac. He'd carry a thermometer around with him and he was always taking his temperature. We'd be in the back of the van coming back from a gig at four in the morning and he'd be shaking his thermometer on the side of the van. One time, he accidentally smashed it on the side of the van; he was distraught!'

All the travelling soon brought back memories as Hooker was up to his old tricks again, wearing layer after layer of clothing in the van, even though the heater was turned up full. Everyone else was frying! It was especially hard for the band on this tour as they had a lot of bad weather, but they all gelled as before. However, as Tony comments, there was an issue: 'Hooker didn't take to Ken's drumming. On stage, he would sometimes turn around and say, 'Backbeat, backbeat'. This was because Ken would sometimes play on the on-beat and Hooker didn't like that.' It was clear that this would happen as Ken's style was so off the wall, there was no way that he could have fitted in with Hooker's [more] basic requirements. Ken's unique style of drumming would pay dividends when they got back to Groundhogs business, which was the main thing, but such musical differences didn't get in the way of the friendship between the two men. Ken Pustelnik remembers that you got on the wrong side of him at your peril: 'I went with him to buy a suit in the King's Road, Chelsea. You can imagine what they thought when this bloke came into their shop with a pork pie hat on. I whispered to the assistant, 'He's a famous American musician. You could see the £ signs on the assistant's face.' Hooker picked a suit he liked and asked how much it was in dollars. The assistant said it was about $25. They wrapped it up and it came to a little bit more. Hooker leant over the counter and said, 'When you tell me a price, that is what I pay!' We came out the shop and I understood why he was one of the first black artists to make sure he got his money back in the States.'

However, Hooker, as well as being a tough negotiator, was also very warm and caring. Pete Cruickshank recalls an incident during that last tour: 'Just after our first child was born, Hooker came to our house in Catford. We showed him the baby and he said, 'Oh no, it's a boy!' The next thing we knew, he gave us a bracelet for our son. It was engraved, 'To Paul from John Lee Hooker'. He still has the bracelet.'

The tour continued in early February 1969 when they were booked for a short six-gig Harold Davidson-promoted tour with Champion Jack Dupree, Aynsley Dunbar's Retaliation and Jo Ann Kelly. The most prestigious of these gigs was the opener, held at the Royal Festival Hall on Saturday 8 February. Sound issues abounded, which made the job of the opening act a little more difficult. It just so happened that it was the Groundhogs – minus Hooker. Their set included a version of Sleepy John Estes 'Express Man' and Freddie King's 'Welfare Blues'. However, the band were later augmented by some welcome additions. Bob Hall made a joyous return for the tour and Jo Ann Kelly delivered powerful versions of 'Let Me Love You' and the old barnstormer 'Rock Me Baby'. After that, Hooker came out and played solo for a spell. Tony Wilson of *Melody Maker* describes the scene: 'Seated on a piano stool, John's mellow, haunting voice, backed by his distinctive amplified, semi-acoustic guitar filled the Festival Hall with 'Serve You Right To Suffer' and 'One Room Country Shack'.

The Groundhogs returned to finish the set with him and it generally went down well, in spite of the gremlins. They even recalled Jo Ann Kelly to help them out with 'Boom, Boom'. There was another aspect to the tour that went unheralded. There was a matinee tour with a gig late afternoon and that included the likes of Roland Kirk, Tubby Hayes and Philly Joe Jones. It was the latter that made an impression on Ken. He sat through a lot of these shows and was mesmerised by Jones's drumming. He'd never heard a jazz drummer bash his kit so much. But even though they were at the bottom of the bill, Ken considered these giants to be the real thing.

The tour was a success and Hooker fired off a parting shot to *Melody Maker* that had a familiar ring to it: 'I wouldn't work with any other band. Before I came, I sent a letter to Britain asking for them to work with me.' It's an amazing ringing endorsement for the Groundhogs, considering all the bands he had worked with in the UK and elsewhere. As the band said their farewells to Hooker, Tony McPhee didn't know it, but he would only meet the great man one more time.[17]

By the spring of 1969, it was becoming more and more apparent that the traditional blues was going out of fashion. A lot of the blues adherents were mixing it with something else that later became known as blues rock. John Mayall, Ten Years After and Led Zeppelin – their first two albums in particular – are classic examples. Pete Cruickshank sums up the dilemma that this transitional period presented: 'Tony thought that sticking to the blues was very restrictive. There were many blues purists who didn't like this move. We wanted to say goodbye to being strictly a blues band.' Towards late spring, Steve Rye was becoming more and more unreliable and it was becoming obvious that he had to go. Tony reveals the root of the problem: 'We had to play two sets at one gig. When it came to the second set, we couldn't find him. He was eventually found in a nearby pub really drunk. It was just getting worse. So we asked him not to do any more gigs.'[18] They put out a cover story that suggested his dismissal was illness-related, but he was actually sacked. Later on, Steve Rye went back to work with Jo Ann Kelly, Sonny Terry, Brownie McGhee and Dave Kelly.

Just before the Groundhogs recorded their second album, Tony produced a heavyweight multi-artist blues album called *I Asked For Water, She Gave Me Gasoline*, recorded at Central Sound Studios, Denmark Street.[19] Tony is on four of the cuts. Teaming up with Jo Anne Kelly provides a satisfying opening gambit. 'Oh, Death', a duet between Tony and Jo Anne, perfectly displays Jo Anne's voice. Tony closes side one with 'Gasoline'. So far, Tony's contribution is limited to acoustic guitar, but for the next number, he plugs the amps in as the Groundhogs utilise their talents. 'Rock Me' is a lively, even foot-tapping cut. The band provide a platform for Jo Anne's expressive vocals. The final contribution from Tony is the self-penned 'Don't Pass The Hat Round', which is a great blues song in its own right. Overall, it is a fine blues album; however, the Hogs were about to announce the 'death of the blues'.

One of the artists on the *Gasoline* album was Andy Fernbach. The Groundhog Series – an idea of Roy Fisher and Andrew Lauder to promote some of the blues artists in the Liberty Records stable – wasn't totally mapped out in 1968. In some cases, it just happened, as Tony related to an American magazine in 1972 how he came to produce Fernbach's album: 'The first one was *Me And The Devil* and that was just the initial one of lumping everyone together and seeing what came out. Some people were stroppy about it and some people weren't and Andy wasn't. He was the easiest to get on with … so we decided to do an album with him.' Tony produced the album just after the Hooker tour (it was released in June 1969). *If You Miss Your Connexion* was unfairly slated, as Tony emphatically recalls: 'I thought it was a decent album, but some reviewer called it the worst album ever made. After I read that review, I went back and listened to the album and I couldn't see how that statement could have been made.' It was the first time that Tony received a totally negative review. He didn't know it, but it foreshadowed the shape of things to come. For the record, Pete Cruickshank and Ken Pustelnik played on the album.

The departure of Rye gave the band a new lease of life and they were becoming tighter than ever. But was there a specific time that this move away from blues was mooted? Tony recalled to John Tobler in the re-issued album's sleeve notes: 'Well, it was made for us, really, because John Walters (BBC radio producer) decided that he hated blues. He decided that The Nice was a blues band! We figured it was time to get away from it.' Just after the departure of Steve Rye, it was decided the time was right to acquire a roadie. The workload was increasing, so Roy Fisher employed Mick Hubbert, their first full-time roadie. Up until then, Roy occasionally helped with the shifting of the gear. He would also act as a part-time driver and had driven the Ford Thames van up and down the country. Hubbert liked the job, as it was clear that there was a firm platform to make great music: 'Roy showed me the way things were wired up. We all travelled in the same van; there wasn't much room, but the band got on well together and there wasn't any friction at all.'

In June 1969, the re-vitalised slim-line Groundhogs went back into Marquee Studios to record the follow-up to *Scratching The Surface*. This time, Tony was producing the album and had even created his own publishing company called Groundhog Productions. They were still limited by the four-track desk, but they had a good nine months of gigging behind them (not that many gigs, actually). It paid off as they came up with a minor classic. The album was teasingly entitled *Blues Obituary*. The album's opener is 'BDD', which stands for 'Blind, Deaf & Dumb'. Tony remembered it from an acetate he'd heard of an old blues song; he liked the tune and put some words to it. He was clueless as to who wrote the original tune. It's a catchy number and was even chosen as a single, but the most interesting aspect of the cut is Tony's playing. His finger picking style gave his playing a distinctive sound. Strangely it made number one in Lebanon! Tony was miffed when Chicken Shack coincidentally released the rather similarly themed 'I'd Rather Go Blind' just before the Hogs album was released.

The second track is 'Daze Of The Week' and is another example of Tony's play on words. Its slow blues beginning belies how it develops towards a ferocious climax. As Ken Pustelnik explains: 'I'm the psychedelic freak-out merchant. I'm very good at anticipating the right groove. We never played a track at the same speed twice. That's why we would sound like a different band by the end of a tour. Tony responded to it and we played off one another.' Tony remembers it differently, as he reveals: 'The first time I saw a freak out – it can be described as a discordant meandering – on stage was by The Yardbirds and I thought it was great. In fact, all three of us were into it.' This was the first totally unique song Tony wrote for the Groundhogs. It wouldn't be the last.

'Times' is a number that Tony wrote based on a Blind Willie Johnson track and 'Mistreated' is an old Tommy Johnson song. They didn't know it, but the latter was to remain a firm favourite for 40 years. 'Mistreated' is a good example of how Tony was developing his own guitar sound. It's a classic riff from him, coupled with his convincing vocals. You really believe him when he sings, 'Baby, what have I done that's wrong?' 'Natchez Burning' is a Howlin' Wolf song from the 1950s and tells the story of how the Ku Klux Klan burned down the church in Natchez, Mississippi. However, if anyone needed evidence of how far the band had travelled since the first album, then the last cut would provide it.

'Light Was The Day' was another of those McPhee wordplay games. It was lifted from a Blind Willie Johnson song called 'Dark Is The Night'. This featured a world music intervention of epic proportions from Ken Pustelnik, as he outlines: 'I got a lot of Indian records off Andrew Lauder: the records were from the basement of UA. I listened to them over the weekend prior to going into the studio. I tuned the drums to highlight the Indian rhythms I was going to play. Tony had a song called 'Dark Is The Night' where he played a wailing spiritual, which had an African feel. In other words, I came up with my version of Indian drumming to a gospel.' 'Light Was The Day' is a track, more than any other on the album, that showed they were developing their own unique sound. As recently summarised by Dave Henderson of *Mojo*: 'This track was the jumping off point, a re-evaluation of the blues that opened the door.' It is an atmospheric delight. Tony used a nine-string guitar on this track and it really highlights his excellent slide work. It was yet another example of his outstanding contribution in this field. He got the guitar from a junk shop for just £15.

John Tobler witnessed some of the recording sessions. Tobler admitted he had heard a flood of bad reports about the band. He was there on Andrew Lauder's invitation. It was the first time he had ever been in a studio. He recalled his experiences for *What's On Where* in 1970: 'The recording studio was really exciting. Efficient, perhaps, but the music was knockout, literally. It was such a surprise. I raved about the Hogs to all I met and gave them all the publicity I was able to at the time … then I saw the Groundhogs on stage for the first time and yet another facet of their excitement hit me. It was just too much. That was at the Marquee, and they were probably playing second to somebody like The Taste and producing an incredible night for electric blues freaks.' But it wasn't just the band that Tobler liked: 'Tony is, without doubt, a genius and the best (bar none) bottleneck guitarist in Europe, as well as a quite amazingly fast and accurate conventional guitarist.'

This second album was a real step up from the debut as the band continued to move away from the blues, which Tony believed to be 'too restrictive.' But what kind of band were they? What kind of music did they play? Ken sums it up: 'We'd got swing rhythm, it's a jazz thing, trad-jazz, folk-blues, electric blues and even free jazz is in there, but it's in such small measures. 'Daze Of The Week' was the shape of things to come. We didn't like to be defined. The press liked to control everything and they were always trying to shape musical trends.' But this was one band that they would fail, and in the end, they took their retribution. But that was a few years away yet.

Like a lot of bands, they were paying a lot of attention to the album sleeve design. In acknowledgement of the musical shift, Roy Fisher came up with the idea of calling the album *Blues Obituary* and the cover featured that concept. Said Pete: 'It was us saying goodbye to the blues.' Roy Fisher arranged the photo shoot to take place at Highgate Cemetery, North London. They paid 15 guineas for the privilege of a three-hour shoot. He also hired the clothes from Moss Brothers and a classy 1919 hearse. Tony was transformed into a vicar with Ken and Pete as coffin bearers. They even managed to persuade their friend, Hoss, from the band Screw, to play dead as the 'body' in the coffin. Tony is seen as giving the last rites to the blues. The book that the Reverend McPhee is holding (this was his idea) is the bible of the blues: Paul Oliver's *Blues Fell This Morning* (he still has the book).

Roy Fisher recalls an amusing incident from the shoot: 'The funny thing about the end result that is not widely known is that the pious look on vicar Tony's face was not so much from his acting skills but because the guy who volunteered to be the corpse was too tall to fit the coffin with his shoes on, and with them off, he had the most evil smelling feet that were wafting up under Tony's nose.' When they finished the shoot, something rather strange happened; Tony takes up the story: 'I, in my vicar's garb, walked off in front, and after a while, I realised that the hubbub of voices had gone, and I was in this cemetery, which was all overgrown, walking past these crypts with these little busted headstones, and there was this clap of thunder. I thought, 'Oh, I'm in the shit!' and I sort of dashed, hoping I was heading the right way. I did a big circle and I found myself at the gates again, quickly donned my civilian clothes and buggered off.'

The album was released on 5 September 1969, and to coincide with this, they decided to make a publicity stunt around the shooting of the album cover. Roy Fisher knew a freelance publicist who got his secretary to phone up the *News Of The World* Sunday newspaper. The secretary, who went under the name of Angela Wilson, complained to the paper that she recognised a gravestone in the picture as her grandmother's and that this caused her a lot of distress! The paper fell for it hook, line and sinker and the story appeared with the lurid headline, 'A Pop Group On Grannie's Grave', with a picture of the entourage standing by a number of graves. However, it didn't have a significant impact on sales.

The *Ipswich Evening Star* said that the album was 'strictly for the pure blues fan (and I say that with a guilty feeling). Good slide lead work and a wonderful wailing bass.' *Allmusic* recently paid special attention to one track in particular: 'The traditional 'Natchez Burning', arranged by McPhee, fits in nicely with his originals, while the longest track, the six-minute-and-50-second 'Light Is The Day', features the most innovation – a Ginger Baker-style tribal rant by drummer Ken Pustelnik, allowing McPhee to lay down some muted slide work while Pete Cruickshank's bass drives along with the mayhem … Blistering guitar on the opening track, 'B.D.D', sets the pace for this deep excursion into the musical depths further down than Canned Heat ever dared go.' Gushing praise indeed! *Blues Obituary* was the last of the Groundhog Series albums.[20]

It can be considered nothing less than a triumph. In just under a year, Tony proved that he could juggle several projects simultaneously, work with different artists and come up with high-quality work.

In 1969, they re-acquainted themselves with the Marquee Club in London. They played their return on 7 February and played another 12 times that year. It had been just over three years since the last time. It did help that the manager of the club, John Gee, was a great fan of the band, calling Tony 'a fine player in the bottleneck tradition.' Around this time, Tony got to perform with Howlin' Wolf, but alas, his hero Hubert Sumlin wasn't in the band. Wolf was backed by Tony's old mates The John Dummer Band, and during the gig, he was invited on stage to play a number. That was a great moment for him.

Just after they recorded the second album, Tony played an impromptu gig. Dave Wetton got married on 21 June 1969 and invited all his old friends. He hired a band called Tangerine. In between sets, Dave & friends borrowed their instruments. The band included Tony on lead, plus future *New Faces* winner Johnny Bryant. They then proceeded to play about half a dozen numbers, which went down a storm. As Dave adds: 'Poor old Tangerine didn't want to come back on again after that, especially the lead guitarist.' You couldn't blame him either!

On Saturday 8 August, they appeared at the ninth National Jazz and Blues Festival at Plumpton Racecourse. As usual, there was a prestigious bill for the three-day event, with Pink Floyd, The Who and The Nice headlining. The Groundhogs played in a big marquee off the main arena in what was called the Village. Ken recalls he watched the astonishing King Crimson, as they weren't too far from the main stage. The band played a short set featuring a bass solo by Pete. The show was witnessed by Paul Chitty, who was seeing the Groundhogs for the first time, and, suffice to say, he was impressed: 'We came across a three-piece playing some really good blues. The guitarist was getting some incredible sounds out of a Gibson SG … We missed the beginning of the set, but the music was so good it seemed to go on for ages … When a song required the use of a bottleneck, the immaculate-looking SG was put down and a Fender Stratocaster that had seen better times was used.' By all accounts, the small crowd was impressed. The problem at this stage was effectively getting the message across that this band were going places.

Shortly after, the band went on their first trip to Germany. They were booked for two weeks at the famous Star Club in Hamburg, where they shared the bill with Samson. It was no holiday, as each band played alternate half-hour sets for the whole night. The crowds weren't that great, either. Pete Cruickshank recalls that, even though they had well over a hundred people come in, there were only about ten watching the gig at any time. The problem was that people were coming into the club only because the admission fee included a certain number of drinks. As soon as they consumed them, they were off. The highlight of the residency was when Vanilla Fudge played the club. The place was packed to the rafters and there wasn't enough room to swing a cat. The greatest rhythm section he ever saw transfixed Pete. Not only were Tim Bogert (bass) and Carmine Appice (drums) great players, but they had oodles of charisma and they gelled impressively. At the end of the Groundhogs' set, Tony was accosted by a journalist, who asked him a lot of questions: 'He eventually mentioned the VF album *The Beat Goes On* and I realised he thought I was with Vanilla Fudge; the conversation faltered and we both walked off bemused.'

Back in England, they continued playing sporadic gigs. Mike Hubbert remembers one of them in particular: 'Ken lived in Earls Court with a guy who synthesised Mescaline (it's a hallucinogenic drug derived from the Mescal cactus). Ken had taken a lot of Mescaline and I had to carry him to the van to get to a gig we had somewhere in the Midlands. He played the gig, but the following day, he apologised to Mac for not playing the gig. He just couldn't remember it at all. He experimented like that.'

In late 1969, they found themselves supported by heavy rockers Earth at a gig in Birmingham. In fact, Earth were not far off from changing their name to Black Sabbath. Mick Hubbert remembers seeing their guitarist, Tony Iommi, inspecting the amplifier that Tony had built for himself. Iommi was intrigued, as it was quite large and looked like a 1930s radio. Hubbert invited him to pick it up; Iommi obliged, but his reaction was of surprise: 'Fucking hell, it's so heavy'. Initially, Tony built his gear because of necessity, but now he had faith that he could build something that the off-the-shelf models couldn't give him. But as he told *Melody Maker* in 1970, there was a method in this: 'I make my own equipment, too. It's the way I like it, being totally involved, but it has a terrible effect on your time.'

Chapter 7 - Thank Christ For The Groundhogs

> Without him, it would have been just another album among many. The album wouldn't have made it, no doubt about it.
> Tony McPhee summing up John Peel's contribution to the sales of *Thank Christ For The Bomb*

> I hate the glorification of war. I hate how people were duped into fighting. Not much changed between WW1 & WW2 for the soldier.
> Tony McPhee

Tony McPhee spent the early part of 1970 writing the band's third album. *Blues Obituary* had left them hanging onto the blues by their fingertips, but this new album would ring in the changes on three fronts. The first was a complete divorce from the blues. Secondly, all of the material would spring from Tony's pen, and finally, it was the only time he went into the studio with all the material written beforehand. He reveals a cogent reason for this: 'I wanted to prove I could do something away from the blues.' For someone who was known totally as a blues man, it was a big challenge. However, there were a number of steps that he took to facilitate success.

It was Roy Fisher who came up with a suggestion for the title of the album, wanting something controversial, as he recalls: 'I was sitting in Andrew's office and we were trying to think of a concept that Tony could write. That's when I thought of *Thank Christ For The Bomb* off the top of my head.' The world was potentially teetering on the brink as the US faced the USSR, both armed to the teeth with nuclear weapons. However, the contradictory thing was that Tony McPhee, known for having progressive views, took a different stand on nuclear disarmament on the album. It was a view that was based on the impossibility of both sides disarming simultaneously: 'I looked at the deterrent side of things. Some people came up to me and said, 'Did you mean that?' On this occasion, they were my views.'[21] Tony outlined his full view on this in a Liberty press release:

> All material things can be wiped out, erased, destroyed – including stockpiles of atomic bombs. They can be dismantled and the nuclear materials used for much better purposes. This is in the minds of many people. Destroy the bomb and you destroy the threat of annihilation.

> But you cannot destroy knowledge. It is implanted in the human brain and it cannot be erased until the death of that individual. Before that time, knowledge can be passed to thousands of other minds and can never be destroyed short of the confinement of those people who have it, which is an impossible task. Therefore, the atomic bomb must be an accepted evil of the 20th Century and, in effect, all that is stopping East and West from tearing themselves apart is the destructive force of their own weapons. So, for peace, we can thank the bomb.

Pete Cruikshank outlines his views on the title of the album: 'It was a statement against all the ban the bomb marches. We would have had another war if we hadn't had them. We didn't welcome the weapons, but while they were there, it stopped others from starting WW3.' Ken Pustelnik was succinct: 'It just might be possible that this was why there had been no major war since WW2.'

At first, Tony wasn't too enamoured with the title, but it didn't take long after that for the thing to take off, as he recalls: 'The more I thought about it, the more I thought, why not? It gave me something to really get my teeth into. Also, it appealed to my atheist tendencies and the old argument of how a benevolent God could let these catastrophes happen.' But Tony didn't see the 'bomb' as a creative starting point. He later said his initial thoughts concentrated on the WW1 soldier's plight. Furthermore, only the title track deals with WW2 whereas the first three deal with WW1.

Even before Tony finished writing all the music, he had decided to instigate a new lyrical approach, as he explains: 'I told the band I wanted to make it something like The Who's *Tommy*. They thought I meant a rock opera. I quickly told them that I meant a concept album and they breathed a sigh of relief!' The band felt much more comfortable with that adjustment. He had previously touched on social comment and the drudgery of the 40-hour week with Herbal Mixture's 'Machines', but now he decided to slant some of the lyrics in that direction. The new album would boast not one but two concept pieces that were both connected somewhere in the middle! Family's debut album, *Music In A Doll's House*, had influenced him greatly, as he told *NME*: 'It really knocked me out. It gave me an inkling of numbers that could produce a feel or mood apart from the actual playing involved.' Sometimes, these things are difficult to extrapolate. As Keith Emerson noted with *Sgt. Pepper* and its influence on The Nice: 'It wasn't the music, but more what you could put on a record.'

As the title hinted, Tony kept coming back to the theme of war, but he had an image of a World War One soldier copping a 'blighty' one. In other words, he imagined an injury, such as losing a foot, which would mean that his fighting days were over. When he actually started to write the lyrics, they seemed to all have a common thread running through. As he related it on the liner notes of the 2003 digitally re-mastered CD: 'I realised that every song was about the way that, in a world crammed with people, there are levels of alienation, from individuals living isolated in one room through to communities that cannot accept individual differences and countries that are unable to communicate with each other.' But alienation didn't cover everything that he wanted to express. The more he thought, the more he came to the word alienness. This sounded better because it invoked a total state of something. It was obvious to him that the subject of war couldn't cover the massive brief he'd set himself and so other areas were developed on side two.

Just before recording commenced for the album (they had already recorded some demos in late January), they went along to their first BBC radio session at Maida Vale in London. On 7 February, they premiered two new songs – 'Garden' and 'Eccentric Man' – both destined for the new album. The other track they recorded was the outstanding 'Mistreated' from *Blues Obituary*. The sessions were usually recorded in the evening and Tony always enjoyed them.

They only had two track recorders at the BBC in those days. So, if you wanted overdubs, it was necessary to play an original recording onto a second machine and record the overdub at the same time. It was a painstaking process, but after a few sessions, they got used to it. A BBC session was considered to be an opportunity to get some good exposure. Tony considered the corporation to have excellent recording facilities. Before recording began, they would sneak into a large orchestral studio and play around with the instruments. There were pianos set up to sound like jangly pub pianos, spinets and large, expensive Neumann microphones on booms. One night, Pete tripped over one of the mics and the whole thing came crashing down, so in the manner of the great and good, they snuck back out and didn't tell anyone!

For the new album, Tony wanted a different studio, one with all the latest technology. The first two albums had been recorded in the primitive Marquee Studios. At the time, this had met their needs, but there was no way that he was going to endure a studio with only four tracks on this occasion. Tony had a lot of ideas about the sound, too. One of his favourite songs at the time was Fleetwood Mac's 'Oh, Well'. He considered it to have 'an amazing sound' and he decided the band would record where that was made. He asked Roy Fisher to find out where it had been recorded; he found out that it was at De Lane Lea Studios, London. It takes more than studio equipment to make a great sound. It just so happened that the in-house engineer was the talented Martin Birch, who had engineered Fleetwood Mac's album and went on to engineer/produce Deep Purple.

Tony needed to hone his production technique as he set about creating a unique sound for the band. The material he had written was interesting and it was because of this that he hit it off with Martin Birch. He really liked what they were doing. Tony had resurrected an old technique in the process of writing the new stuff: 'I sort of remembered how I used to write stuff for Herbal Mixture and I used that formula of just hammering chords that shouldn't fit – notes that shouldn't fit.' However, as Tony reveals, these changes had the potential to create schisms in the band: 'I wanted to use the three-piece band fully. So, I wrote the bass parts as well. I didn't want the usual root notes. I was writing these different chord sequences and I wanted everything whirling about. I wanted bass parts that would coincide with everything else. Pete is a fine player and I did give him the opportunity of writing them, but he later admitted he couldn't do what I wanted.' He had to leave Ken Pustelnik to his own devices, however, as he didn't know anything about drumming.

Recording began on 18 February 1970 at De Lane Lea Studios and carried on into March (the last session was on 3 March). Tony had written four cuts that made up the main concept. As with most albums, the opener is always an important choice and this is why 'Strange Town' succeeds more than most. The start is unusual; Tony reveals how he achieved it: 'Most riffs start with the root note. I decided to start the riff below the root note.' That's why it feels like you've missed the first few seconds of the intro! It's a perfect example of hitting your audience like a ton of bricks. But the opener is effective in other ways. Tony's distinctive licks continually soar and descend and things are never on an even keel for long as Tony has a strong improvisational streak in his playing, creating a huge dose of excitement. Tony's lyrics of alienness refer to the larger community and there's more than a nod to Herbal Mixture's 'Machines':

I don't believe these people
Spend all their time
Walkin' round, lookin' so glum.
They think that life is for workin'
To secure their pension
When retirement come.
Ah, but they don't realise
It's right before their eyes
Life is for livin'
Right now before you die.

The second track, 'Darkness Is No Friend', is a perfect example of the unusual bass sound that Tony was after. It's important to reiterate that Pete always interpreted what Tony wanted and really hit the button on this one. There's more of a hint of the inspiration for the band's next album in there, with its references to daylight and darkness bringing their own horrors in equal measure. The chorus illustrates that Tony was prepared to take a back seat as Pete's bass dominates proceedings. However, it's the unusual ending that steals the show on this cut. Tony had always liked Little Richard's abrupt endings, so much so that he decided to put several of them together in a loop and that is how he got that swinging jazzy 3/4 feeling to create a jarring effect.

The last two tracks reveal alienness through war: 'You are told by your country to go to war and nobody wants to', says Tony. Set in the First World War, 'Soldier's lyrics empathise with those unfortunate men who fought against their will, but it's told through the eyes of someone like their sergeant major. The lyrics tell a horrible story and are worth quoting in full:

Soldier, fix your bayonet before the enemy come,
'Cos you won't have time, when they start to climb the hill, y'know.

Soldier, when you see 8,000 climbin' up on you,
Don't see them as men, just see them as enemies of the King, y'know.

Soldier, Don't think of runnin', your death is just as sure.
If you don't face it now, you'll face it anyhow in front of the squad, y'know.

> Soldier, stand firm in your trenches, don't let them break the line.
> Because these dirty Hun are all bastard whore's whose son's not fit to live, don't you know.

The music is deliberately laid back because Tony wanted it to contrast with the heavy lyrics. He was making good use of the extra tracks available for overdubs. On this track, he intertwined two guitar solos: 'I loved doing them. They had nothing to do with each other except for being in the same key. One was muted but then came out strong. I was looking for a change of colour as often as possible.' It's Tony's finger-pick style that gives this song an extra dimension: 'I feel I have an advantage with my pick style because if you play with a plectrum, it will always sound staccato. But playing with your fingers, you can use the thumb, the nail or even the fingertip and this gives you more tones. You have a lot more scope.'

Another unusual aspect was provided by the vocal delivery because Tony inserted a lot of 'y'know's at the end of the first three verses. In theory, it sounds absurd, but it worked, creating a kind of rhyming effect. This made an impact on a lot of people and, later on, with a certain radio DJ, who was to play a major part in the album's success. Many consider 'Soldier' to be the band's finest moment.

Pete Cruickshank had a testing time during the recording of 'Strange Town' and 'Soldier' as, the night before they recorded these tracks, his Gibson bass had fallen off the stage at a gig at The Black Prince, Bexley. It was discovered that the neck had been broken at the head. At the last minute, he borrowed a Fender Precision from the studio's reserve of instruments. It was the first time he had used that model for years.

The title track opens with some gentle acoustic guitar. It was the first time that Tony featured the instrument so prominently on a Groundhogs album. Martin Birch accidentally wiped an acoustic intro from the beginning of 'Soldier'; at first, they were gutted, but in retrospect, it wasn't a detrimental move. Or as Tony preferred to call it, 'even the cock ups worked'. *Thank Christ For The Bomb* moves from the muddy trenches of WW1 to the 'two big bangs' that were supposed to signal the end of WW2. All of this is achieved in a few Dr Strangelove-type lines, illustrating an effective less-is-more approach. The acoustic section fades out and gives way to an upbeat march that belies what is to come next. This segment was inspired by seeing John Cruickshank's band performing a song called 'Reflections' (it was a song that Tony had written years before). The procession soon gives way to a freak out as the band career towards the track's riveting climax of the two atomic bombs at the end of WW2. Martin Birch had a friend who was working on an electronic symphony and Tony heard some of it. He had these two big explosions and Tony Martin's friend said they could use them. Pete Cruickshank remembers it a little differently: 'It was Martin's idea as he had seen two galaxies crashing into one another in a sci-fi program.' However, it is clear, surprisingly, that nobody thought about it representing the two atomic bombs, which became and still is the accepted interpretation. The coincidence of two explosions at the end of a song that was about thanking Christ for the bomb led to fans believing they were hearing the US bombing of Hiroshima and Nagasaki in 1945.

The sound quality far outstripped anything they had done before. Tony's idea to record at De Lane Lea had paid off handsomely. Ken Pustelnik outlines another factor that worked for them: 'We never had any arguments in the studio about music and that's floored many a group. I remember for one section, we wanted to move the sound around, so we had several people all lined up along the desk panning from one speaker to another. It was painstaking, but we did it. We all had to turn a volume gain to make it run along the various channels and then we had to sequence it. It would be easy to do that today.' Tony related the intensity of it all to *Disc And Music Echo*: 'I really went to town on everything – double-tracked voice and overdubbed guitar – and the result was far more satisfying. I can't listen to the other Groundhogs albums.'

The second side also presented a concept, but it was subtle and was mostly overlooked with all the publicity surrounding the first side. In fact, Tony had deliberately buried it, as he told *Melody Maker*: 'I haven't made it blatantly obvious, but there's a theme running through the second side: I just didn't want people to compare it with *Tommy* or something.' On the face of it, it's a bunch of disparate cuts, but on closer inspection, it tells the story of a man who becomes disillusioned about his life. The opener is 'Ship On The Ocean' and it features another of those unusual intros. The first two lines give a clue: 'I'm like a ship on the ocean that's rolling from side to side, But I'm not drunk I'm just dissatisfied'. It's clear from later lines that the person is materially well off but lacking any direction in life. In some ways, he is searching for something.

The next track is 'Garden' and is one of the best on the album. Tony readily admits that he pinched the main riff from The Beatles' 'Come

Together', but it's well disguised. Martin Birch had a good idea for the guitar solo. He suggested to Tony that he put the mic at the other end of the studio; the slight delay gives it a fading sound. By now, there is inertia that hangs over our wealthy man and he yearns for a return to the past in order to start again. Tony points out that possessing wealth is not the be-all and end-all of things, as he confirms: 'If you have so much money, what is there to strive for? I do believe in the work ethic. In a way, I foretold what was to happen in the future. You see professional people giving up their high-paying, long hours job and moving to the country to live a simpler life. You didn't see that then.' The lyrics make it crystal clear:

But I'm not going to cut a single blade of grass
My garden will look just like the distant past,
Before the days of agricultural land
Before the time when pebbles turned to sand.
When I leave this house I'm going to stay
I'm forsaking my comforts to live another way
Get my clothes from heaps, my food from bins,
My water from ponds and have tramps for all my friends.

'Status People' starts with a punchy bass intro that has Tony slotting into the groove nicely. This develops into a hard-hitting riff with Ken in great form. Tony explains the mechanics of sounding different: 'The magic number of notes is 12 but I decided to group these notes in twos, threes and fours. On 'Status People', I grouped them in 3 x 4. It was a formula, but I used it to sound different, not the same.' The track explores the searcher's current social standing and Tony is quite clear about where he stands on this: 'You have these people that need to be part of something. Why don't you be yourself? People seem to need status; I think they must be shallow.' 'Rich Man, Poor Man' showcases a rollicking riff and explores the essential differences in society, which, in the song, is a 'cross-section' of humankind.

The final track is 'Eccentric Man', a convenient label for society to put on a man who gives his wealth away. He has found what he was looking for. The journey from a Chelsea mansion to the benches of the Embankment is complete. It's a crunching riff from the outset and it climaxes with one of Tony's longest solos on record. It was no surprise that this was chosen as the single. The band didn't really harbour any hope of it being a hit; it was more of a ploy to get airplay. When the album was being cut, Tony and Ken went along to listen to it. At the end, Ken said: 'I like that, I think!' Tony took an acetate home and put it on while he was eating his dinner. He found himself eating faster and faster. It was a sign of his excitement at what they had created, so much so that he thought, 'If this doesn't make it, nothing will.' It was obvious that the album was a great one. Tony was succinct: 'The album was like a jigsaw puzzle that came together.'

One of the things that occupied everyone's mind was the design of the album cover. Andrew Lauder knew of a design company called Clearwater Conception, as they had provided posters for various bands at gigs that he had seen. Andrew got to know of Alan Tanner, the artist who had drawn them. One of the things that Tony was certain that he wanted was artwork rather than photographs. Tanner came up with a brilliant idea. He took two famous photos from the First World War and reworked them by superimposing the faces of the band. The images, therefore, contradict the title of the album – the images on the cover are from WW1 and the title is more closely related to WW2 – making it all the more interesting. In discussions, it was decided to use poppies in some way, but the way that Tanner used them is breathtaking. On the inside cover is an old photograph of a group of men of the time of 'Soldier'. The photo has the quality of a negative. This emphasises their ghostly faces and invokes an idea of them situated outside a recruitment office en route to the bloody trenches. The double-winged plane above them is bombing them with red poppies because the feeling is that most of these men will be scattered in some field somewhere in Europe. Tanner also provided the emotive poem on the inside cover. It was a candidate for one of the most effective artwork concepts of the year.[22] When Tony took the work for the album cover into Andrew Lauder's office, his secretary told him there is no such word as 'alienness'. Quick as flash Tony's riposte was 'There is now!'

As a result of Tanner's good work, it was decided that he be used again to inject some more personality into the band. In the discussions that ensued, it was suggested that he should do a drum skin for Ken. The design would be a Groundhog, as it was most apt. But it didn't take long for the project to hit a snag. Shortly after doing the sleeve for *TCFTB*, Alan Tanner went to work for Alan Whitehead (who painted sleeve covers for the Genesis albums *Trespass*, *Nursery Cryme* and *Foxtrot*). It seems that Whitehead grabbed the project away from Tanner and it was Whitehead who painted the Groundhog (which looked like a cross between an otter and a prairie dog with a fat tail). Consequently, he sent in a bill for a large amount of guineas! When the band found out that Tanner hadn't done the work, they refused to pay.

With the album safely in the can, they made their second trip to Germany. It was an eventful trip, just like all their visits there. Ken got chatting to some US military personnel on the ferry and they opened a bottle of spirits. But what he didn't know was it was spiked with LSD. Just after he drank some, it had a dramatic effect on him. At one stage, he ran through the lounge with a girl, but he had her head under his arm because he thought he was the front of a camel. He remembers it like it was yesterday: 'I could see Tony walking towards me from a distance from the other end of the boat but he stayed the same size to me, even when he reached me. He was walking like Popeye.'

With the weather about to turn, the band were in for a trip they'd never forget! The boat was flat-bottomed and had no stabilisers. It was a last-minute replacement for the usual boat and was too small to undertake such a long trip, made worse by the storm they ended up in. Roy Fisher recalls the mayhem: 'Everyone on board was sick except for me and Tony. I went to find Pete, who we thought had fallen over the side. I found him in the toilet, which was awash in shit and seawater. He told me to fuck off and leave him alone. I guess he felt a little undignified with his head down the bowl and ankles swimming in shitty water.' One of the crew was tied to a rope for safety and had the dubious honour of bailing out the toilet of all the puke and crap with a bucket. Roadie Mick Hubbert took the drastic step of going down into the hold and spending the trip on the mattress in the van as it alleviated the seasickness somewhat. They wouldn't forget their voyage on the Viking III in a hurry!

In the morning, they (apart from Pete) went to breakfast and Tony could see the vast estuary of the Elbe, but the ship had taken such a hammering over the night's storm that it was sailing at an angle so that, through the starboard windows, he could see the sky, and on the port side, the water. Every now and again, the boat would lurch and all the breakfast rolls and plates would come crashing down and head along the corridor. The stewards would fill the shelves with fresh bread, and the next time the boat lurched, it would all come crashing down again.

After this eventful crossing, they supported the rapidly disintegrating The Nice at the Ernst Merk Halle, Hamburg, on 28 March 1970. There was a riot when the organisers started showing slides advertising Coca-Cola. There was a level of radicalisation within West German students, and as a result, they didn't take to seeing these corporate images of the USA. Germany proved quite different from anywhere else they had played. The rock music industry had not spread to all corners of the world then, as Ken related to *Melody Maker*: 'Managers and agents are illegal out there, so contracts don't mean very much.' The tour went well and they returned home with a less interesting crossing, and to that, they all breathed a sigh of relief.

The band were getting more exposure in the press now and Tony was fielding questions regarding the chemistry of the band. In one interview, Tony revealed that political views within the band were an in-house issue: 'Politics is an issue between me and Ken. It is all down to me being a moderate and Ken being an extremist.' They did have more than a few lively debates, but their political disagreements never became an issue. Where did Pete Cruickshank stand in this? In an interview with *Zig Zag* the following year, Tony gave a hint: 'Pete is basically very lazy – he plays because he likes it and it brings him a bit of bread – and that's it … that's his philosophy as far as I can make out.' Pete was keen to put the record straight regarding his attitude: 'I was stuck between Tony and Ken squabbling pointlessly, and as I was not a political animal, all I wanted to do was play.' It must be stated that there were different levels of sloth in the organisation, as Tony told *Zig Zag*: 'The factor that gets us going has always been Roy. You see, I'm as lazy as Pete, really, and though I've got a lot of ambition to do things, I don't particularly want to start them off. But Roy always manages to get us moving.'

In early May, the band played a gig in Brighton. The Brighton Film Festival was on and they had just shown *Rock Around The Clock* and *Blackboard Jungle*. Consequently, there were a lot of Teddy boys wandering around the town. It appears that a few of them ended up at the Groundhogs gig; the original band had cancelled, so they had been booked at the last minute. It was a decent-sized place with the seating made up of metal tubing chairs with padded arms. As Tony was announcing the next song, he heard a cry from the back of the hall requesting some 'rock 'n' roll'. Tony's retort – 'we don't do rock 'n' roll' – was greeted with a beer glass that sailed over the crowd and landed on Ken's cymbal. Ken relates what happened next: 'A chair was thrown on the stage and it landed right in the middle of my bass drum. A kid from the audience got up and started to extricate it. I noticed from the gloom an arm with a beer glass in it that ended up being broken on the kid's head. All hell broke loose, so I made my way to the front of the stage. Pete was still playing; I don't know why! All I remember is a chair flying towards me. It hit me on the bridge of the nose. I was out cold.' The upshot was that he had to go down to the police station to make a statement. His souvenir was two big black eyes and a permanently damaged nasal tube!

On 9 May, the day after the Brighton gig, they made an appearance on the strangely named progressive music program *Disco 2* on BBC television. This show was the forerunner to the famous *Old Grey Whistle Test* and was fronted by *Melody Maker*'s Richard Williams. The studio format presented them with an issue: they had to mime. Tony related the embarrassment to *Zig Zag*: 'They stick you in this studio, standing on a chalk mark ... Ken and I were between the speaker, connecting with the odd thump; it took all my powers of concentration to pull it off.' They mimed to 'Garden', but the problem was that Ken was looking like an endangered panda with his black eyes. As he recalls: 'It was quite a small room, but they had these big gantry cameras with hydraulic arms. The cameraman was seated on it and they zoomed right close to me. The cameras kept changing lenses. That was all I needed.'

On 14 May, the band were booked to appear on John Peel's *In Concert* radio program. The show was recorded at the Paris Theatre in Lower Regent Street, London. This was Pete Cruickshank's favourite venue for these sessions. He thought it was a fabulous theatre, with its plush seating and intimate atmosphere. Ken remembers this venue very well for two reasons: 'We always played well there; we always seemed to be on the button. I remember John Martyn supported us on one occasion. He was doing his sound check while we were standing on the side of the stage. I thought it sounded good, so I thought I'd play my drums along with it. Soon after, Pete started playing bass; it sounded good. But Martyn's body was getting more and more hunched in his chair. He was retreating into his shell. I thought, 'What a miserable bastard!'' Even though Ken was annoyed at Martyn, it must be said that time is limited in a sound check and he was probably concerned about not getting it right in time. These appearances on BBC radio helped build up more of a following.

In June, *Thank Christ For The Bomb* was released to some critical acclaim. But sometimes, you need more for an album to make it. On occasions, you need a little nudge in your favour at the right time. Just after the album was released, John Peel played 'Soldier' on his Sunday afternoon radio show – the following week, thousands left the racks. Peel waxed lyrical about the track and he loved the 'y'know's'. Tony confirms: 'Without him, it would have been just another album among many. The album wouldn't have made it, no doubt about it.' Writing in a *Melody Maker* column, Peel called 'Soldier' one of his favourite tracks of the year.

The album was released on Liberty, and within a few weeks, it peaked at number nine. This represented a major success after all of Tony's efforts to get into the charts. He summed up his feelings about this time: 'It was exciting, but once Peel picked up on it, I knew it was going to be a success. It was lovely.' However, in an interview given at the time with *Melody Maker,* he was keen to point out that he wasn't going to leave his roots behind and was still in control of his career: 'I still enjoy playing the blues and feature a couple of things on stage: 'Me And The Devil' and 'Groundhog Blues' … I still enjoy the odd acoustic gig which comes along once in a while, but right now, I'm purposely out of touch with the blues.' For the moment, it was only on vinyl that they had deserted the blues.

Melody Maker gave it a top rating and praised Tony to the hilt as a producer and musician: 'McPhee has drawn on his long experiences in all facets of the music industry and he is one of the most original and calculating guitarists in Britain. He really used the bare minimum of three musicians to the best advantage.' An unknown publication picked up on the sound that the producer was looking for: 'Played during a period when little acknowledgement is given to a bass player … who plays a far more rugged and imaginative bass than is accepted, thus succeeding the beautiful plunge down an octave or two to depths where all notes are transformed into a naked, metallic grinding.'

Disc & Music Echo gave the album a four-star rating and emphasised the unique sound of the band: 'The effect of the counterpoint guitar phrases, with bass and drums well in the background, is a change that other groups would do well to follow.' However, the *Jazz & Folk Blues Society* was less praising: 'It should be subtitled 'Thank God For The Off-Switch' … I'm sure that cavemen must have made better records.' It's clear that some people still hadn't forgiven them for deserting the blues.

On 1 July 1970, they returned to Germany for a series of dates. The audience's reaction varied wildly. As Ken reveals: 'In North Germany, they were very aware. It is really down to the students. They want to hear political stuff. We played a University in Hamburg and we had representatives of the Baider-Mienhoff gang coming in and asking us very seriously, 'What is this *Thank Christ For The Bomb* about?' I thought I'd better be careful what I say here!' It was an eventful tour in other ways, too. They encountered the full spectrum of political views. They played a right-wing University in southern Germany, where one promoter sounded them out about touring South Africa (then under apartheid)! On the border with Switzerland, they played at a casino where the gig consisted entirely of instrumentals because Tony had lost his voice. There was never a dull moment with the Groundhogs in Germany.

They also played a festival in Essen with Black Sabbath. It was an indoor venue and also on the bill were It's A Beautiful Day and Flock (the latter included Jerry Goodman, who later joined the famous Mahavishnu Orchestra). There were two stages, one at either end of the arena; as one band played, the other's gear was taken off for the next band to set up. Black Sabbath played their set, but something was wrong with the other stage and Flock were unable to start their set. So, after a while, Tony offered to play first to allow the fans to hear a band, even though it put the running order out. No doubt the fans would have agreed to such an arrangement and the promoter was for the idea, but Flock refused to do this and the fans were kept waiting for ages. The upshot was that the festival overran and the Groundhogs never played, but at least they got paid.

The problems continued when they were stranded at the Atlantic Hotel in Hamburg. They weren't actually in the hotel but in an annexe where all the bands stayed. It was a kind of theatrical Bed and Breakfast. The promoter, Bodo Aldez, was supposed to give them some money halfway through the tour, but he decided to do a bunk. The band were penniless and they were reduced to cooking soup in their hotel room and sneaking around to the supermarket to get cornflakes. Pete Cruickshank recalls the events: 'We used to stand on the balcony and watch people eating in the street. In the end, we had to wait for our agency to send us some money.' The manager of the hotel was losing her temper with roadie Daryl Payne (Tony's brother-in-law to-be). They used to cook the soup in his room and it was a bit of a shit-tip, but when the manager found out, she illustrated to Tony, while pointing at Daryl, that she had an economical but practical grasp of English: 'Your room good, his room shit!'

There was still a few more German gigs left, but it was clear some venues weren't equipped to stage rock shows. At one place, they had to get the gear in through a window! As roadie Mick Hubbert concluded, the Germans couldn't organise a 'piss up in a brewery', but it was more to do with the local scene not being well developed. Hubbert went absent without leave in the middle of the tour and it left the band in the lurch. In fact, Pete Cruickshank had to do the driving! The Germans did get some things right, however. The band were directed to a cattle market, which they then found out was the venue. The stench was vile and they thought there was no way they could play there, but four hours later, the band played the gig and the smell had disappeared (the promoter had the place sprayed).

On the 5 July, they played the Kiel Festival at the Oseenhalle. Also on the bill was Black Sabbath again. It all went well until they got on the ferry coming back. Ken and Ozzy Osbourne got locked up in the ferry's cells because they insisted on seeing an American film that had been dubbed in German. As Ken remembers: 'We thought it was great to hear a German dubbing John Wayne's voice. But they insisted we had to watch the other film being shown in English. That's how we ended up in the cells. To add insult to injury, our Transit van broke down and we were towed off the ferry by Sabbath's Transit.'

Pete Cruickshank remembers an amusing incident: 'We were playing an indoor festival in Hamburg. Steamhammer were on before us and they went down well. The band had gone off and the roadies were dismantling the gear. We were on the side of the stage thinking about going on. Then, one small group of people started stamping their feet. It wasn't long before the whole crowd were going mad, so the roadies had to put the gear together and Steamhammer came back. It was an amazing thing to see. At the same festival, we were told we had to be off by midnight. We timed it so all the encores were finished before our allotted time. But then it happened again, so the promoter was forced to ask us to get back on stage; otherwise, there would have been a riot.'

Summertime brought the festival season into bloom in the UK and the band were booked for three of them. The first one was the tenth National Jazz and Blues Festival. This was promoted by Harold Pendelton and was basically the Marquee's own festival. The band had gone up on the bill since the previous year's appearance on the small stage named the Village. On Friday 7 August, they appeared third on the bill to headliners Family. The program notes acknowledge just how far the band had travelled: 'Tony McPhee must have woken up one morning and suddenly realised where he really was. They are now so different and so much better that they could well be one of the outstanding successes of the whole festival: 'Thank Christ For The Groundhogs'.'

The second festival was a week later at the inaugural Folk, Blues and Jazz Festival at Krumlin, near Halifax. Held over three days, it was a major event, but it still attracted a number of big names like Pink Floyd, Ginger Baker's Airforce, Manfred Mann and Fairport Convention. The Groundhogs were scheduled to play on the opening Friday. It's impossible to quantify how the £2.10 cost of a weekend ticket compares to today, but suffice it to say, it was about the price of an album!

Trouble started on the Saturday when the band turned up mid-morning to be told they should have been performing the day before! The entreaties to Roy Fisher to look at the contract fell apart when he told them he didn't actually have one. Then, Jo Ann Kelly (who was performing that day) came over and told them there had been many forged tickets. It also appeared that the local Yorkshire mafia had put the squeeze on festival traders and it was unlikely anybody was going to be paid anyway. Tony recalls what happened next in his liner notes to *Split*: 'The promoter then decided that he could fit us in and our attitude was that, as we were only getting £100 for the gig and we were there, we wouldn't be losing a lot if we didn't get paid and we were sure the audience, who were sitting in a muddy field (yes, it was raining as well and plenty of it, too) would like to see something happening on stage.'

Their impromptu performance saw them appearing between top folk acts Fairport Convention and Pentangle. Ken recalls the mood of the moment: 'We saw these people under a sea of plastic. When we started playing, they went mental.' This positive attitude paid dividends because their photographer friend, Chris Richardson, took some shots of the performance, which would be used to dramatic effect on the cover of the next album. After the show, they went to the bar where they saw the bands that had refused to play, like Pink Floyd. The festival was a complete disaster and the Sunday bill didn't even take place. The two promoters were in a bad state and they did a bunk; one of them was not seen for three weeks. He was last seen walking the hills, mumbling about how much money he'd lost.

Even though 25 thousand people attended the Krumlin festival, their next outdoor date would completely dwarf that. The 1970 Isle of Wight festival was a watershed in such massive outdoor events. The previous summers of love that had drawn the curtain on the 60s were about to be shattered by a more hard-nosed, insidious and ultimately unworkable attitude shown by a small section of the quarter of a million crowds. This minority were taking the 'hippie' ideal to an unworkable level. The festival scene was turning ugly as the new cry went up of 'music should be free'. Joni Mitchell's set was interrupted as she was heckled with their slogans. Sections of the surrounding fences were torn down. There was no one to stop them and thousands of people piled in for free. The Groundhogs were lucky that they missed the mayhem, as they had performed on Thursday, and this time, they did turn up on the right day!

The Isle of Wight was the biggest gig they ever played in the UK. Tony recalls that they had almost missed the boat to the island. On the ferry, they chatted with the Mick Abraham's band's drummer. Strangely, soon after they got there, promoter Rikki Farr came over to them and asked them to go on early because the Mick Abraham's band didn't have a drummer. Tony didn't say anything about the meeting on the ferry, so they went on stage early. The mystery of the disappearing drummer was never solved. Thursday 27 August was only a warm-up day, but there was still a big crowd that greeted the band. It was a weird experience for Ken, who was there the year before with his girlfriend as a spectator, as he remembers: 'We slept in a field that was by this big hotel and it was where we stayed in 1970. When we walked on stage, the roar of the crowd was like a jet engine. It was so powerful a noise that it was almost primaeval.' One of the music papers reported on the two-day warm-up: 'Groundhogs, featuring some really excellent bass guitar work from Pete Cruikshank and the splendid 'Eccentric Man' from their new album.'

It is often taken for granted, but many artists have to get over the hurdle of performing in public. It has already been noted that Tony conquered his with his inner belief in himself. To him, if that was what was required, then so be it. But how did the rest of the band cope? Pete Cruickshank reveals his approach: 'During the Hooker period, I drank whisky for some Dutch courage. But I started to be sick a lot. You have to remember that everything was geared to the gig in the evening. I later went onto beer.'

Recalling a gig at Mothers, Birmingham, he points out that you have to be careful on gig day regarding substances: 'There was a black DJ there and he came into the dressing room before the gig and offered us a smoke. I didn't want to say no, so I had a couple of drags. I don't know what was in it, but everything was suddenly in slow motion.' There was a lot of face washing and walks outside, but it wasn't enough. He had no idea how he was going to get through the gig. The following day, he asked the roadies what his performance was like; their reply was 'great'. As usual, Ken Pustelnik took a very practical point of view regarding stage fright: 'I never really suffered with nerves. Stage fright is a condition. I like performing and I like to see the audience response to what we do. That's why I never had nerves because I never saw it as a problem to walk on stage to do that function. It never occurred to me.'

Tony McPhee married Christine Payne on 4 September 1970 at the Wandsworth Registry Office, London. Master guitar maker Tony Zemaitis and his wife were witnesses. Tony knew Zemaitis because he was a friend of Jo Ann Kelly. But there wasn't to be a honeymoon. Shortly after the wedding, the band embarked on a short home tour supporting the great American blues band Canned Heat. They got the tour after Andrew Lauder signed them to Liberty/UA Records. Pete Cruickshank recalls the tour: 'Canned Heat were great and they had lots of charisma. I watched them every night and learned a lot.' As the autumn leaves started falling, they began to think about recording their next album. However, the seed for that work had already been planted in Tony's head. The trouble was that he didn't know it!

Chapter 8 - One Way Split

I wrote *Thank Christ For The Bomb* and *Split* on riffs. I knew my melodies were not great.
Tony McPhee

The joke backfired on us when it became our signature song.
Ken Pustelnik on 'Cherry Red'

Half of the Groundhogs' *Split* features the musical tremors of a disturbed mind.
Notts Evening Post

Within just a few months of the release of *Thank Christ For The Bomb*, Tony was already fielding questions about the next album from sections of the music press. He had indicated as early as August that they were trying to find new songs. Burnout from the album, tour, album treadmill, etc., had not kicked in yet, but it was not far away! However, the events surrounding the theme of the next album had its germ well before *Thank Christ For The Bomb* was released. The actual inspiration was even earlier than has first been thought.

The story goes that Tony McPhee's aberration of May 1970 was the inspiration for the lyrical content of *Split*. While there's some truth in that, it really was the effect. The cause had occurred a few weeks earlier. The band usually went round to someone's flat after a gig for a get-together. Tony remembers one such night when they went round to Ken's flat in Earls Court. Tony had tried dope once before, but it never really affected him. Ex-roadie Mike Hubbert confirms it: 'Tony and Pete were never really into drugs that much.' On this occasion, Tony remembers Ken's mate, known as Putty, 'in an oozing lump' on the floor. He was completely blitzed! Putty had been handing out some hash cake and it clearly had some body to it. There was an empty milk bottle being used as a bong but Tony didn't fancy having a smoke of that either. But the next occasion, he wouldn't be so lucky.

The night after a gig in Huddersfield, Tony and Christine were invited back to Mick Hubbert's flat for a curry. Mick had a Canadian lodger who had made up some joints from a pile of cannabis dust left over from the grass that Ken had been given. Tony remembers coming back from the gig the night before and trying it with no effect. He remembered thinking it highly amusing that the seeds had been left in and the joint would occasionally bang like an exploding cigar. However, his complacency was abou to get the better of him. He recalls the events: 'I shared a joint that the Canadian guy had made up. Mick's television (*Star Trek* was on) suddenly divided down the middle. Everybody else seemed to be having a good time, but I was feeling strange. I went to the bathroom as I needed something elemental and turned on the tap, but I started to grow like something from *Alice In Wonderland*. I tried to play the guitar to gain some focus, but I was losing reality and all I could see were spirals. My heart was beating so fast that I thought I was going to explode. Mick asked me to look at the curry, as the last time he looked, it was growing out of the pan. I went into the kitchen and opened a window and the garden looked like a Martian landscape. Mick's wife was there, so I latched on to her because she was sober and I needed someone like that to get me through. I even started to pass out, but after a few hours, it subsided. I'm sure that episode opened the door a bit, which I couldn't close, to *Split*.'

Just a few weeks later, in May, Tony and Christine took their landlady's son, also called Tony, out for a walk in Green Park, London. It was a boiling hot day, and later that night, Tony couldn't get to sleep. It was then that he had a panic attack:

> I started to think and it came to me – how on earth can I possibly exist? I still have trouble explaining it ('Split Part One'). It was a denial of existence, so I tried to run away from the thought; I ran upstairs to the top of the flats, but it was too dark, so I turned on the lights – too bright ('Split Part Two'). I couldn't get away from the thought all night. I tried stroking the cat to get my mind channelled off it. We had this old fridge and I could listen to the sound of the motor when it started up. I eventually fell asleep from sheer exhaustion ('Split Part Three'), but when I woke up, the feeling came back to me straight away. I used to look at the toilet bowls and they were alien. We were surrounded by buildings which overshadowed me; I was completely paranoid. Looking back, there were a few months when I would have believed anything; a door opened in my mind and I couldn't shut it. I don't fear it now. I used to.

The morning after, he put it down to schizophrenia. It was much later that he recalled the get-together after the Huddersfield gig and connected it with this incident.

As time went on, he realised that this was too big a thing to ignore with regard to his work. He started to think about incorporating this experience into the band's repertoire. However, there was a big obstacle in that he had always found personal lyrics boring and self-indulgent. But there was something that swung it in favour of recording these thoughts within the confines of the group. An interview with *Sounds* outlines the clincher: 'I thought I'd put it down because I know a lot of people who are getting the same thing; I was very confused at the time and I thought I was going nuts, so what I wanted to do was put that down to show anyone who's got it that they're not alone.'

The main problem for him was how to write the words in such a way that would come across as universal rather than pompous. This was to provide an interesting challenge for him. They entered De Lane Lea Studios in November 1970 to record their follow-up to *Thank Christ For The Bomb*. In the very early stages, he still wasn't sure about the theme. However, when he found out that Martin Birch had suffered similar aberrations (Ken was also in the same position), it justified his original idea. In order to write successful lyrics, he found himself taking the rough mixes home and working the words out. It's a far cry from the Herbal Mixture days of sitting in the fetal position in the studio toilet!

All the preparations paid off; in just a couple of weeks, the album was completed. The joyous opening gambit of 'Split Part One' belies what's ahead. The double-tracked guitars and the steadiness of the band create an ambience of calm and this is reflected in the first two lines of the verse. However, as the track careers to its conclusion, the ambience changes dramatically, as the band descend into freak out. This is summed up in the last two lines and cuts through to Tony's worst fears:

> In the dying embers of a burnt-out day,
> When morning seems a thousand hours away,
> Dark prevails and the light gives up the fight to stay.
> The blackness thickens and surrounds.

'Split Part Two' starts with some frenzied wah-wah and tremolo work. Tony had acquired the wah-wah just after *Thank Christ For The Bomb*. Also, it must be said that the riff to 'Split Part Two' is one of Tony's catchiest. It had started life as something he played in the sound check. Then, it graduated to being used in one of the improvisation sections at gigs. By the time he started writing the album, it had developed sufficiently. The middle section solo refers briefly to the blues before the band really start to kick in. The impossible situation that Tony found himself in is summed up in the first lines:

I leap from bed in the middle of night,
Run up the stairs for 3 or 4 flights,
Run in a room, turn on the light,
The dark is too dark but the light's too bright.

The ethereal chords on the Hammond to transition between 'Split Part Two' and 'Split Part Three' create a dreamy feeling. 'Split Part Three' is really about the peak of Tony's aberration. Exhaustion is reached and there are no more depths to plummet. There's a nice section where Pete plays a catchy bass line and everything else slots in around. The end is manic, with a raunchy solo from Tony.

'Split Part Four' concludes the concept. It opens with a juicy blues lick and continues in that groove. Tony delivers a great vocal with lots of references to the Almighty and salvation. The lyrics acknowledge that some people do turn to religion in times of crisis, although Tony didn't. Perhaps these lyrics confused some people. Ken plays with a lot of feel on this one and delivers some great snare drum work. However, as he confirmed to *NME*, these noises were not what they seemed: 'All the weird sound effects are accidental really and we didn't even know we'd recorded the closing section of side one.'

Split succeeds on many levels. However, as Tony reveals, he was aware of his limitations as a writer: 'I wrote *Thank Christ For The Bomb* and *Split* on riffs. I knew my melodies were not great' (later, he exclaimed, 'I can't believe I said that'). In fact, the story and the riffs are so great that any melodic deficiencies become irrelevant. The 'Split' side of the album runs for 20 minutes, but it seems to fly by, displaying a more organic sound than *Thank Christ For The Bomb*.

Side two is made up of a number of disparate tracks. 'A Year In The Life' was inspired by The Beatles track 'A Day In The Life'. The song is about the seasons and the passage of time. It features some muscular drumming from Ken. The underrated 'Junkman' is an iconoclastic number, like 'A Year In The Life'. The vocals for 'Junkman' were recorded at 3 am when Tony was coming down with flu. The song is about how modern food production techniques have not only skewed how it is made but also how certain elements of the food are removed and used to make yet more profit. Tony had been into healthy food for quite a while and had educated himself on the lamentable state of the modern diet. The lyrics indicate knowledge of the subject that goes beyond 'Joe Public'. He bemoans the removal of the wheat germ from bread and molasses from sugar; by implication, the best things are taken out, thus leaving junk food. Although not in common parlance at the time, it's interesting to note that Tony was using the term 'Junkman' in a song describing what is now commonly known as 'junk food'.

They had six tracks in the can but were a little shy of a complete album. In desperation, Tony turned to a track that he had written on the Germany tour in the summer. In fact, it was first tried out in a school hall on a day off. The track had since become a regular in the set, but nobody had thought about it for the album. It was a number called 'Cherry Red' (it was named after the colour of Tony's Gibson). It inadvertently became their signature song. As Tony recalls, some things are way beyond the horizon: 'You can't really tell how a track is going to do. I had no idea it was going to be so big. In the end, it was a millstone around my neck, and by the late 70s, I refused to play it.' 'Cherry Red' was recorded in one take and they employed some tricks that they used on *Blues Obituary*.

It's a tour de force, with its wailing guitars, driving bass and crashing percussion, topped by a weird falsetto delivery. Tony liked the idea of doing falsetto. It was another new experience – he was always experimenting. With minimal overdubs, it's still a cornucopia of sound. With the backing track in the can, Tony set about putting the vocals down. When Martin Birch put the music on, Tony was not quite in position, as the mics were 20 yards at the other end of the L-shaped studio. The stunning opening kicked in and Tony let out a clearly audible shriek on the record. Eyeing a cowbell, he picked up a drumstick and whacked it on his dash from desk to mic – that was recorded for posterity, too!

'Cherry Red' was actually a bit of a joke. Ken takes up the story: 'We sort of said, 'Let's do a piss take.' It was the Groundhogs plays Led Zeppelin – an in-house joke. We thought riff songs were good but simple. Originally, 'Cherry Red' was in the act before we recorded it, but it was very bluesy. The joke backfired on us when it became our signature song.' There was another joke that was connected with the track and it concerned BBC radio sessions. Tony was not averse to taking a shortcut or two: 'We'd go in and Malcolm Brown (producer) would say, 'Alright lads, 'Cherry Red' again? We've got a few of those.' We once used an old version of the track. Nobody seemed to notice.'

There's a degree of mischievousness in 'Cherry Red' that belies Tony's serious attitude to his music. In 'Split Part One', the lyrics portray the darkness of his flat. The working title was 'Nocturn in A flat', although the song is in A major – serious-sounding stuff. However, 'Cherry Red' tells the story of a special girl he met who gave him the runaround – a humorous contrast to the weighty 'Split' themes. But who was this girl and where did he meet her? Did he see her again? The answer is simple – the whole story is bogus. He gives a clue as to why some of his lyrics follow this path: 'Some phrases come out of your head. There is no pattern; they just fit. There is no creativity; it just happens.' When viewed in this way, it can be dangerous to take his lyrics too seriously, no matter how solemn the themes may be. This concept was later developed to the hilt on *Hogwash*.

Even with the addition of 'Cherry Red', they still had five minutes to fill. This was the excuse that Tony was looking for – a return to the blues. There were already references to their roots on *Split*, but this was going to be a full-blown affair. 'Groundhog' is another old stage number they fell back on and Tony outlined to *Sounds* how it came about: 'As we were pushed for time, I thought we'd put it down … and I think it works quite nicely with the rest of the numbers.'

In some interviews, Tony stated that 'Groundhog' was done because he couldn't get the vocals right on another track. That was a cover story, as there was no other track. But it was more than that; it was Tony's statement that he still dug the blues. In order to get the sound he wanted, he put the guitar through two amps and then used ten mics to record them. There are no drums on this track, but Tony got a percussion effect by attaching some bottle tops to his shoe and tapping his foot against a wooden board. This certainly fooled a lot of people. 'Groundhog' is John Lee Hooker's song and is Tony's tribute to the great man. It's quite a journey from 'Split Part One' to 'Groundhog', and as such, is a much more eclectic journey than *TCFTB*.

By the time they had finished the final mixing, it was early morning. The whole process took just two weeks. They were so elated that they decided to give Andrew Lauder a preview. With a copy of the tape in hand, they walked up Oxford Street, into Mortimer Street and the UA offices. They went into Lauder's office, where Martin Birch put the mix onto the Revox machine – amazingly, they hadn't made any copies!

There was a moment of horror when the depressed play button brought forth a sound that could only have been described as rubbish. They looked at Martin, whose facial contortions had changed to a sunnier side. He realised that he'd put the tape in the wrong way! All was then revealed and it sounded great. It was a very strong album throughout. However, not quite everybody agreed with that. Tony recalls: 'Around the time of *Split,* I remember Ken saying to me, 'I've noticed that, on every album, you put a weak track on.' I thought, 'What!' I have never put a filler track on any album. Other people may have thought that, but I can honestly say I never put anything on that was substandard to me.'

With the album in the can, they entered 1971 with the belief that things would get even better. In February, *Thank Christ For The Bomb* was released in the States.[23] Around this time, Tony decided that he needed to upgrade his gear. He had shown interest in what Hi-Watt (his existing gear) and Marshall had to offer, but by the end of March, he'd gone over to Laney. The reason for the change in the first place was his old gear was obsolete. One of the problems was that, although he had built his own amplifier, he had never bothered to have it housed properly.

The rigours of touring had taken its toll, but as he told *Zig Zag,* the new gear was not only up to scratch but also gave him more room to manoeuvre: 'There's not really much to choose between makes, but this Laney stuff gave out what it claimed to give out and seemed okay ... though I've made some alterations to improve the tone because I'm as interested in getting a good sound as I am in volume.' There was another factor in choosing Laney. He discovered his octave splitter (this device could repeat a note Tony played an octave higher or lower, thus creating a new interesting sound) worked better when using the wah-wah pedal. It gave him a lot more tones than the others – he was a great fan of Hendrix's 'Machine Gun'. He wanted to explore effects more fully.

Tony was also looking to improve his instrumentation and he turned to an old friend. He commissioned Tony Zemaitis to make an electric guitar for him. Zemaitis had already made a 12-string guitar for Eric Clapton and was gaining a reputation for quality instruments. Zemaitis turned the tables and asked Tony if he could improve on the performance of some Lawrence pickups he was using. Tony's reputation for his technical knowledge was pretty widespread in the business. He had a go, but he was unable to help on that occasion. One day in March, Zemaitis showed Tony a guitar he had made. It was the first one he made with a metal front and he explained that it was only a prototype and he would make another if Tony didn't like it. It was beautiful and Tony was stunned; because it was quite early in Zemaitis's career, he only paid £175 for it – it was a real bargain as well. Tony McPhee still owns his prized guitar. It wouldn't be long before its value would go through the roof. Shortly after Tony received his guitar, Zemaitis started work on a bass for Pete Cruikshank.[24]

In February, Tony and Christine moved to a cottage in Haverhill, Suffolk. This meant that the band lived quite far apart from each other, but he made it clear to the *Suffolk Free Press* that it wasn't an issue: 'Some groups live together, but it doesn't work out.' As far as he was concerned, a hard-working band like the Groundhogs already saw enough of each other and the rest of the band also agreed. Christine was also interviewed. The paper noted that she was also a vegetarian. However, she certainly didn't see her husband as anything other than an ordinary guy: 'Even when I go along to hear him play at gigs, it doesn't seem like Tony up there on stage.'

With the amount of travelling the band were doing in those days, the result was a lot of boredom, so to relieve some of the tension, they devised silly ways of passing the time. They would have mock fights that sometimes got out of hand. Once, they were being driven by Charlie McLeod down the Caring Cross road in London. Tony was sitting in the front and he was turning around, play-thumping Pete. Charlie had gone through a red light and was speeding; it wasn't long before an unmarked police car stopped them. The policeman asked the driver, 'What's your name? Death!' Charlie must have been impressed because he later joined the Police force.

On 6 February 1971, they recorded a *Top Gear* session for John Peel. The most significant gig they had around this time was at The Roundhouse, London, and it was here they got a lucky break. In the audience was a certain Mick Jagger, who was scouting for a support band for an upcoming Rolling Stones tour. After a phone call from Jagger, Roy Fisher went to meet him and Trevor Churchill the following day at the 'Stones' office after he rang to see if the group would be interested in supporting them. The deal was done and it was a good opportunity for the band to get more exposure, but it wasn't all roses. The contract was signed on 1 March for Chrysalis and the deal was £400 plus petrol for nine concerts. The money looked even less, however, when they realised that most of the gigs had a matinee show. The tour started three days later at the Newcastle City Hall on 4 March.

This was a poignant moment for Tony as he had seen the Stones back in the early days at Studio 51. In those days, the crowds were not that large for a blues band. In that period, he also saw them many times at the Richmond Athletic Club. He watched them grow, as he recalls: 'The Stones went from strength to strength, featuring on tours with Bo Diddley, etc., playing the big gigs like the Lewisham Odeon whilst the Groundhogs had made it to Studio 51! So it was quite an honour to actually be asked to support them.' Jagger remarked to the band that he didn't think they would do the tour because they were successful in their own right. Pete Cruickshank, in fact, knew Bill Wyman, who lived close by in Beckenham.

This was the first time the band had played to consistently large audiences and the atmosphere at these gigs was phenomenal. After the Coventry gig on 6 March, there was a day's break, so Tony went home to Haverhill. One of the reasons he went home was because Christine was heavily pregnant (their son, Conan, was born on 16 April 1971). He planned to catch the train to Glasgow from London to arrive in good time for the Playhouse gig. Tony thought there was bound to be a train every hour. In this, he was seriously wrong because there were only two trains per day. By the time he got to the station, he'd missed the first one and the last one was going to get him there after the first show started. He was pleasantly surprised to find Keith Richards on the train and they journeyed up together. Of course, Richards was secure in the knowledge that he would make their first show. Tony missed his and a local band called Merlin stepped in as support for the first performance. It was not their night, as their gear hadn't arrived, so Tony had to use Keith Richards' Fender Amp, which he hated.

The following day, they played Bristol Colston Hall, but Tony had some running repairs on his mind. He was wandering around the backstage catacombs with a soldering iron in his hand looking for a power point to complete some repairs to his amp – he wasn't sure how it was damaged. He came across a slightly opened door and pushed it; Jagger and Bianca had been squatting behind the door like a pair of naughty children and Tony sent them flying. He was met with the sight of Mick and Bianca sprawled on the floor, giggling in a cloud of (coke) dust. It was also the first time Tony had seen an entourage. Keith Richards had a guy that followed him around and it was clear where he was coming from. They called him a 'professional ponce' and all he seemed to do was to be at the beck and call of his mentor. And that, no doubt, included fetching the drugs and taking the rap as the need be.

Tony told *Sounds* that he remembered Bristol quite well and, keeping the 1969 Altamount Festival in mind (security was provided by a group of Hell's Angels; they were not shy in using their muscle, and in the many scuffles, a fan was stabbed by one of them and died), reported the same mistakes: 'The hairy audience gave us a good reception despite the presence of a dozen or so bouncers deployed around the hall. As soon as the Stones came on, they lined up against the curved stage, facing the audience with their arms crossed.'

One of the gigs turned out to be quite un-rock 'n' roll, as Tony related in his diary of the tour in *Sounds*: 'It was at The Big Apple in Brighton, which is above a cinema. We were asked to keep the volume down for our set so it wouldn't disturb the filmgoers below … but with two and a half thousand asses acting as sound absorbers in the floor, there was no real problem.'

It was then onto Leeds University for the Groundhogs' most famous gig. They had already met up with their one-time engineer, Glyn Johns, who was recording the gig for The Stones using their mobile studio. Tony reminded him that they still owed £20 for the Herbal Mixture session. As Johns was rich and famous by then, he'd obviously forgotten about such trifles. He even offered to tape the Groundhogs' set for them. Though he said he couldn't tape the whole set, it turned out that they were using a backup tape as a fail-safe. It was recorded on a combination of the two machines. It was a blistering performance, opening with 'Cherry Red' and finishing with a pulsating performance of 'Eccentric Man'. At the end of the night, Johns got Jagger to present Tony with the tape. It was fitting, as the Stones were very approachable, although they never had much direct contact with the superstars.

Bill Wyman told Tony and Pete that he envied them as he missed playing the smaller venues and being able to choose their own material. Pete was disappointed that he never got to speak to Mick Jagger and Keith Richards. But Ken did: 'At Leeds, the dressing rooms were upstairs above the stage of a sports hall. Their dressing room had tables of food, but there was no one to eat it. Keith Richards couldn't get into the dressing room, so we took the lock off for him. He came back a few minutes later with a bowl of liquorice allsorts as a thank you. It was a touching but pitiful moment.' But as Tony recollected,

'The Stones usually would have eaten before they got to the gig, so the rider was often plundered of far more than liquorice allsorts.'

The band were well received but Tony remembered The Stones were a bit off. They hadn't toured for a while and they were rusty. Tony recalls one of the shows: 'Coventry was bad for them. They did 'Midnight Rambler' and there was a part where Jagger took his belt off and hit it on the floor. At that point, the band were supposed to hit their big note. Unfortunately, they were all out of sync and it ended up as a mess.' The tour ended at The Roundhouse, London. Ken recalls an interesting event: 'At the end of the gig, we walked into their dressing room, which was packed with all sorts of hangers-on. We made our way to the band to thank them and say goodbye. Everybody stopped and stared at us; they probably thought, 'Who the hell are these guys.'

In an interview with James Johnson for *NME* just after the tour, Tony noted what a culture shock the tour was: 'It may sound a little strange, but what I liked about the whole thing was being told what to do. It was nice to have a tour manager telling us what to do, how long to play and to get everything sorted out.' But the two-show format caused a lot of problems for the band, as Tony recorded in his *Sounds* diary: 'It's just that, not too often on this kind of tour, a second band is treated like a pimple being slowly squeezed out of its half-hour set because the house was late getting in or the main band overran.' As he confessed later, he was dubious of the whole thing and expected to get slagged off by the music press for supporting The Stones, given their own success at the time.

It was quite surprising for Tony when he found out that UA was planning to put out 100 copies of the live Leeds recordings as a promo in the United States. These were distributed to DJs and quickly became collector's items. As he admits, he was bemused: 'I didn't know why they needed it as we had two albums out. I thought it was inept because they should have been promoting our last two albums more.' The reason why the album was distributed in the US was because it was in anticipation of a tour which never actually materialised. (However, the album did come in handy in 1979 when Tony found himself broke. He found out from a Canadian fan that copies of the album were going for £100. Tony contacted UA to see if they could find the tape, with the hope of making some more copies. However, at the time, he was told that the master tape was lost.)

Split was released to coincide with The Stones tour and sold over 7,000 copies before the first week was out. Before long, it had sped to number five in the charts. However, this could have been much higher because, as with *Thank Christ*, Liberty had pressing and distribution problems and they didn't get the albums in the shops in enough quantities. This had devastating implications and limited their success.[25] The album was released to enthusiastic reviews in the press. *Sounds*, while stating that it wasn't as good as their previous effort, made it clear that McPhee, the songwriter and producer, had come up trumps: '(He) has proved that he can take a basic theme – in this case, the experience of a metaphysical psychosis – and expand on it cleverly.' The paper also pointed out a trait of great producers – economy of effort: 'He (Tony) succeeds in capturing all his own guitar excitement and the driving rhythmic force of Ken Pustelnik and Pete Cruickshank, which an independent producer might have failed to do.' *Disc & Music Echo* were just as gushing: 'In a way, the Groundhogs are the nearest thing we've got left to the now defunct Taste.' The less mainstream *Music Business Weekly* put the album down succinctly as 'Definitely one to watch.' Their music was reaching far and wide now as *Capital Journal* of Oregon, US – concentrating on Tony's success as a producer – noted: 'The music is a superb example of how a commanding guitarist doesn't have to obscure an all-out drummer or an assertive bass player.' The album attracted many new fans of all ages![26]

They had invested a lot of time in the album sleeve and rightly so. Artwork was already established as an integral part of promotion and sales. However, Denis Knowles, who was in charge of distribution and promotion, remembers that the plans were becoming a little bit too ambitious: 'There was a short delay in forward planning as Roy Fisher wanted a complicated sleeve consisting of several round separate photos, each diminishing in diameter, held together by a paper fastener in the centre.' Roy Fisher confirmed recently that this was briefly discussed and then dropped. Denis elaborates: 'We settled for photographing the diminishing photo discs as flat artwork, hence the final outcome. I can't remember whether this held up the sleeve supply, but sleeve artwork was always a big issue and rightly so, as it was an integral part of the whole product.'

As soon as *Split* hit the shops, it made a positive impact with its distinctive artwork.[27] Chris Richardson's photography sat well with the best work of the day. The sleeve worked out so well that it could be looked on as a lucky break that Alan Tanner couldn't do it. He'd taken the subject matter and made an inspirational cover that brilliantly encapsulated the concept. The starkness of the inside picture reveals the band in their minimal glory and portrays their fierce intensity. The shots were taken on that rainy day at the ill-fated Krumlin festival the previous year – some good had come out of that disastrous day. The fact that Tony was photographed with a white Fender Stratocaster confused a few people. In fact, he had borrowed the instrument from his brother-in-law, Daryl Payne. He needed to change from the Gibson SG for some of the numbers, as it worked better with his wah-wah pedal. Furthermore, the live shots of the festival reinforced the idea that, even though it was a studio album, you should come and see this band performing because they are great on stage!

It was inevitable that Tony would field questions comparing their last two albums, especially as it was already marked as a success. *Zig Zag* magazine duly obliged, starting with *Split*: 'It's different … it creates a different mood to me. *Thank Christ* always left me feeling very satisfied; this one leaves me satisfied but also irritated because it's so much more vicious and intense. All the numbers poke you somehow, whereas the last one relied on melody more and was comparatively relaxing.' It's clear that the vibe that surrounded the concept of *Split* had pervaded the music. There is a lot more tension on *Split* for that reason. But another factor that distinguishes the two albums is that *Split* has a lot less overdubs. The arrangements are less complex than on *TCFTB,* and consequently, it does have a 'live' feel to it. There are compelling reasons to believe that *Thank Christ* is actually a consistently stronger album, but it was this on-the-edge feeling of the latter album that tipped the fans' vote.

In April, United Artists' publicity agent, Ronnie Bell, got them onto the long-running BBC chart show *Top Of The Pops*. He had been around in the business for many years and had a lot of connections at the BBC. When he heard about the new album slot, he pitched in for the band. They performed 'Cherry Red' with Tony singing live over a remix of the backing track – he looks suitably embarrassed. Ken caused the crew more than a few headaches. He was digging his heels in over being forced to mime and he was adamant that the band should play live. The plan was for Tony to sing live over a pre-recorded backing track. For playback purposes, they had a one-and-a-half-foot square speaker set up on a chipboard support – hardly hi-tech. They ran through the song and it seemed okay, but when the audience came in, there were a lot of problems with the sound. The noise of their dancing feet seriously compromised the track.

It was at this point that Ken Pustelnik took things into his own hands: 'I told the producer I wasn't happy so I made my way to the executive bar.' What else could a disgruntled rock star do? On his way, he had a stroke of luck as he saw John Dummer, who was doing a lot of work for the BBC. Dummer was able to sign Ken in and he confronted the producer, who must have had a bit of a shock. The upshot was he got his way, but when they sat down to watch the program, all they could hear was Ken's hi-hat. He failed to hear it during recording because he had his headphones on.

Pete Cruickshank has different memories of their time at *Top Of The Pops*, as he recalls that there was a lot of hanging around, during which time, he was looking out to see if he could see Pan's People (girl dancing troupe) – he never did.

Tony's version of the day is slightly different again: 'I was given the job of picking Ken up; he lived in Chiswick High Street, above a butcher's shop (which was empty 'cos the butcher had done a runner). We hired a Transit and driver to pick me up and then Ken up on the way to the studios.' (Tony knew it would be difficult to wake Ken due to him being a heavy sleeper and had previously had the manager of a bed and breakfast demand that we vacate him from a room. The manager eventually had to open the door with a pass key, as there was no way he could wake him up from their hammering on the door.) Tony knew there would be no point in knocking on the front door to the flat, but there was an old broken greenhouse just below his bedroom window: 'So I risked life and limb and climbed up this rickety structure. Fortunately, it was a casement window and it was open. I climbed in and he was lying there completely comatose.'

Another thing about Ken was that he never undressed to go to bed; consequently, there was always an accompanying odour: 'He was lying there fully clothed and stinking! I shouted and kicked the bed until he stirred. When he woke up, I told him that the van was outside to take us to the studio and left. I went to the van, opened the passenger's side window fully and sat in the middle seat next to the driver to protect him from the smell! When we got there, we watched Pan's People rehearse; it sounded like a herd of galumphing elephants, stomping and counting in time to fit the choreography. I really used to fancy one of them, but I wasn't impressed.'

'At our soundcheck, we knew we had to mime to a backing track, which Martin Birch had prepared.' Tony's monitor was on the dance floor some feet away: 'I was singing live and Ken couldn't help but hit his bloody drums. I was already having difficulty hearing the backing track in front of me and Ken's erratic drum hits behind were making it worse. I asked an engineer if the audience would be between me and the monitors, and he said they would. It was no good; I had to get them to move the monitors closer, and although they complained about possible feedback, they gave in in the end. We were introduced by Ed Stewart. He virtually apologised for us being there, saying something like, 'Now, boys and girls, we are going to bring you something a little different tonight'. I thought, 'wanker'! I played my Zemaitis on the show, but it was one of those wiped by 'Auntie'; just as well as I was sporting a full beard, which seemed like a good idea at the time.'[28]

The strange thing about this was that they never released any singles from the album. The strategy, hitherto, had been to release singles for airplay. But then, when they appeared on the premier singles show, nothing materialised. This was a strange time for album bands. This was compounded by the wacky editorial policy of some publications. The teeny bop magazines like *Jackie* were regularly featuring bands like the Groundhogs and this will remain a mystery as to why.

In the early part of the year, the subject of touring the States came up on more than one occasion. The band archive of 29 April gives a confident message from Roy Fisher's diary: 'See Tony for Amps for US tour – size and weight'. However, by 14 May, there was a negative, less sure air about things: 'Pat Meehan said get Vince Romario – NY agent to call him – put a good word in for US tour'. Even as late as May, in an interview with *NME,* Tony reported that the tour's structure was not quite right: 'We weren't happy about the tour anyway because we had dates that would be either Sacramento or San Francisco and we've learnt the hard way that you have to have something definite on paper.'

Ken elaborates as to why they were not happy with what was being done: 'Roy Fisher told us he had got us a tour in the US. But the problem was that it was with The Beach Boys! I like them but to tour with them would have been a complete mismatch. We all felt the same way.' Roy Fisher recalls it differently: 'The idea of a tour with The Beach Boys never existed as far as I am concerned. I would have obviously known they were not compatible. The tour I arranged for the US with the United Artists president and CMA booking agency was to be with Johnnie Winter, a massive rock/blues act at the time.' Pete recalls the several misfires on foreign trips: 'We would have our passports ready only to find out the trip had been cancelled. So, by the time we started to talk about the US, I was in half a mind it wasn't going to happen.'

In June/July, the band embarked on a headlining UK tour of concert halls and Universities. The gigs took up most of the month and it was a sign of the band's growing profile. It was an indication that the days of roughing it were over, as Tony related to Jerry Gilbert of *Sounds*: 'I'm finding now that the concerts we do are much more satisfactory. The clubs are hot and cramped, and although I'm nostalgic about clubs, there comes a point where you need the comfort of the concert halls.'

On 4 August, they travelled to Holland to support Canned Heat at the Paradiso, Amsterdam. They were getting paid £150, plus hotel and transport costs. However, the main attraction was that they were going to be part of a film that was being shot there. The scenario was that a girl goes over to Amsterdam and ends up 'finding herself' in a hippy community. She goes to several venues and sees many bands. According to Andrew Lauder, the rushes were not too good and the scenario was corny. It was also the first time dry ice had ever been used at a Hogs gig, but Ken hated it as he thought that was more like Pink Floyd. Pete remembers it was a bad gig and the audience were so stoned that they were lying on the floor. For some reason, the film was shelved. However, Tony mixed the tapes of the gig at Pye Studios in late September and the soundtrack album was released in Holland. The only Groundhogs track used is 'Still A Fool', running at over eight minutes.

On 28 August, the band played at the little-remembered Weeley festival, held at Clacton On Sea. It was partly organised by the Clacton Round Table in order to raise funds for charity. For them, this was on a much bigger scale, as their previous attempts to raise funds were limited to Donkey Derbys! The Groundhogs appeared low down the bill, and yet, on the advertising poster, they were second to The Faces. This was odd, as they had just had a top-five album that was still selling well – over 40,000 copies and counting. A fan called Rich provides details of the calibre of artists performing: 'I arrived just after the trouble with the angels as they were being taken off the site in police vans. Myself and six mates made our way straight to the front, but trying to wade through 20,000 people wasn't a good idea. We made it to about 20 feet from the stage, where we tried to sit in a space about three feet square. From what I can remember of the music, it was the Groundhogs (brilliant), Mott the Hoople (good), Barclay James Harvest (too long to set up), King Crimson (21st-century schizoid brilliant).'

In the first weekend of September, the band had a doubleheader of Festivals abroad – one in Germany (Speyer) and one in Austria (Vienna). Two of the bands on the bill were Black Sabbath and Gentle Giant. Patrick Meehan, who, at one point, had been gainfully employed as John Lee Hooker's driver, managed both these bands with his son, who was also called Patrick. In the main, these kinds of events blend in with all of the others, but on this occasion, it was to have far-reaching consequences for Tony. It was on the plane to Vienna that the problems started. Tony recalls what happened when they boarded an old Viscount: 'This thing started whirring away up the runway and took off and stayed three feet above the ground for about five minutes. I've never experienced anything like it before because you think this is really it … And you look at the other people sitting there with glazed eyes … Then this voice comes across saying, 'We are returning to Frankfurt airport, we have a little trouble, nothing to worry about'. He then banks so sharply that suddenly he's heading for this fucking plane taking off, and by this time, we thought, well, what's the difference – either we hit the ground or the plane.' From this time, he really hated flying; it was an experience that Tony took a long time to get over and was always in the back of his mind when US tours were mooted.

On 10 September, they headlined the Buxton Festival, which was actually held indoors at the Pavillion Gardens. The following day, they played at the Queen Elizabeth Hall in London and received £500, which was one of their biggest pay cheques to date. Tony Stewart of *Melody Maker* was there: 'Out of the many gigs I've seen … this was easily one of the best … Tony, Ken and Pete still follow and work well with each other. The arrangements are again loose and so include a lot more of Tony's guitar improvisations … Ken drives hard in his kit with some complicated rhythm patterns, which often build the number up to a fever of excitement, blended with some persistent bass runs by Pete.' They still played old favourites from the first two albums, like 'Still A Fool' and 'B.D.D'.

In fact, Tony was keen to put the record straight and he did so to James Johnson of *NME*: 'We are still playing the blues, really. It is only on record we have changed. On stage, 50% of our numbers are blues and the ones we play off the album are those which have a blues feel to them.' However, Tony admits that the switch away from their roots opened up the band's potential – not to say his songwriting – because he felt that the blues was a little bit 'restrictive'.

Following the aborted movie gig, they flew out to Germany to support John Mayall for eight gigs. The tour started at Munster on the 12 September and included shows in Munich, Dusseldorf, Berlin and Frankfurt. The Berlin gig turned out to be lively. The gear van was stopped on the autobahn because it was travelling in the outside lane – apparently, the outside lane was hardly used, as the speed limit was then so low. Before going to the Deutschland Halle, which was a big sports stadium, they did a radio interview and it went really well. A girl from UA accompanied them down to the gig, but that's when the problems started. They tried to get through the stage door on the side of the theatre, but they were told to go through the front. They couldn't get in the front either, so the UA rep tried to explain that they were the support band. Roy Fisher takes up the story: 'Ticket prices in Germany then were high and there were a lot of militant students milling around. They were protesting about the prices. When they let us through, the students surged through as well and we were carried along with them. It wasn't long before we met some more security, but these had batons. Tony got lifted by both arms, kicked up the backside and thrown out. Ken got his hair pulled, but Pete managed to get through; I also had my hair pulled and I was hit over the head with a baton. I couldn't understand what the security man was saying to me. It was only the girl that saved me.' When they did get in, they saw scores of Police drinking coffee under the stage, looking smug. When the band went on stage, Tony explained to the crowd what had happened. The crowd reacted to this and they were right behind the band, riding on the buzz; they played a great gig that night!

Ken wasn't happy with Tony on that tour and the feelings were mutual. Back in the hotel, Tony spotted an old valve radio by the wooden cover of the radiator in Ken's room. As usual, they couldn't wake him up so Tony turned the radio on as it was right behind Ken's head. It took a while to warm the valves up, but when they did, the volume came in like a ton of bricks. Ken sat up and then went back in the prone position! He wasn't too happy with that prank. The band had been together for a long time now, and from time to time, the tensions rose.

After the tour, Ken gave his first solo interview to Tony Stewart of *NME* (he had argued for some time for this). It appeared to be routine, but it ruffled a few feathers in the camp: 'We enjoyed the tour because it is too easy to play in England and get encores … making it routine. In Germany, we meant nothing at all and it has got to be good to be appreciated.' Okay so far, but then he decided to fire off a few bombs: 'We could have blown them (Mayall) off stage any night; we did blow them off.' It must be said that Ken was aware of what he was doing: 'A lot of those interviews are very much the same. The journalist is looking for something extra, so I gave it to him.' Tony was furious, although he never said anything at the time, as he recalls: 'You don't do that if you want to get more work. I don't like that sort of thing; it disparages another artist.' Ken antagonised Tony further by referring to him as 'our guitarist' and saying that he 'has got an inflated ego'. To Tony, that was a wounding remark: 'I have never had an inflated ego!' But Ken also realised where the inspirational element of the group is located: 'I'm not trying to kid myself that it's a three-piece co-operatively written thing, and whether I agree with that doesn't matter. My only job is to have a good time on stage and just hope everybody else does.' Ken wouldn't be speaking to the press again.

The idea of a US tour was still being worked on. In early September, Roy Fisher was talking to Pat Meehan regarding the tour. They then spoke to Joe Smith of Elektra Records (part of Warner's) regarding them releasing the *TCFTB* album in the US, but Martin Davis had already done a deal with UA for the US. On 4 October, it was noted in the band archive 'Vincent Romario – CMA agency of New York – interest to book US tour.' On 17 November, Roy Fisher heard from Mike Stuart of United Artists US and had agreed to a six-week tour of the States and major promotion starting on 1 March 1972. The new album was mooted for release on Groundhog Day in February, but as far as America was concerned, for the time being, it all came to nought. Recently, Roy Fisher put the record straight: 'I did get agreement from Mike Stuart, president at UA, to financially back a tour of the US with a big radio promotion. The reason this did not happen was because, by the time I came back with this deal confirmed, the group had already gone to Wilf Pine at WWA.'

Right: Seneschals Tony, Dave, John and Ray Wade, with Cakey on drums, at the Castle, Tooting, 1962. (*TS Personal Collection*)

Left: One of a series of very silly publicity shots as The Dollarbills. Tho shiny suits woro tailor-mado. From left to right: Tony, Dave Boorman, John Cruickshank (on the floor), Jack (sax) and Pete. (*Pete Cruickshank*)

Right: The first publicity picture of the Groundhogs. Clockwise: John Lee (John Cruickshank), Bob Hall, Tony McPhee, Dave Boorman and Pete Cruickshank. (*TS Personal Collection*)

Left: Tony, Bob Hall, Dave, Pete, John Lee and John (seated). (*Roy Fisher/TS Personal Collection*)

Above: The Groundhogs during their 'big soul band' era. From left to right: Pete, Fred (sax), Colin Huntley (drums), John, Mick Humbey (keyboards), unknown (brass), Tony. (*Pete Cruickshank*)

Right: This turned out to be an eventful gig on the John Lee Hooker tour for less than appropriate reasons. (*Pete Cruickshank*)

Below: Released on Shel Talmy's Planet label, 'I'll Never Fall In Love Again' had a positive reception. (*Pete Cruickshank*)

DISC weekly

JANUARY 15, 1966 6d

WILL PAUL JONES GO SOLO?

see page 3

THE UNTAMED
breaking in the charts with
"IT'S NOT TRUE"
c/w
'Gimme, gimme some shade'
PLF 103

PLANET
34 GREEK STREET,
LONDON, S.W.1.
REGENT 2148

JOHN LEE'S GROUNDHOGS
first release on Planet next week
"I'LL NEVER FALL IN LOVE AGAIN"
c/w
'Over you, baby'
PLF 104

Left: In order to get a gig, Roy Fisher suggested they `dress up' ... so, as Herbal Mixture, they did! (*Roy Fisher/TS Personal Collection*)

Right: Pete, Mike Meekham and Tony in a publicity flier for their first single. Regency jackets were high fashion. (*TS Personal Collection*)

Right: The band with John Lee Hooker during their tour. Being from the American South, John was always complaining about the cold. (*Michael Hasted/TS Personal Collection*)

Left: A rare early live picture. Ken's bass drum has future Genesis artist Paul Whitehead's Groundhog. (*Andrew Lauder*)

Right: A signed publicity photograph. (*TS Personal Collection*)

Left: Pete Cruickshank in deep concentration. (*TS Personal Collection*)

Below: Eyes up, lads, you never know what will come down.

Right: A press advert for *Thank Christ For The Bomb*. (*TS Personal Collection*)

Above: The band with Andrew Lauder in the UA offices. (*Andrew Lauder*)

Left: Press promotion for *Split*. (*TS Personal Collection*)

Below: The band on stage at the Krumlin Festival. This photo was taken at the same time as the one used for the back of the *Split* album. (*Christopher Richardson/ TS Personal Collection*)

Right: Ken seemingly squashed between his cymbals. (*Terry Aldridge/ TS Personal Collection*)

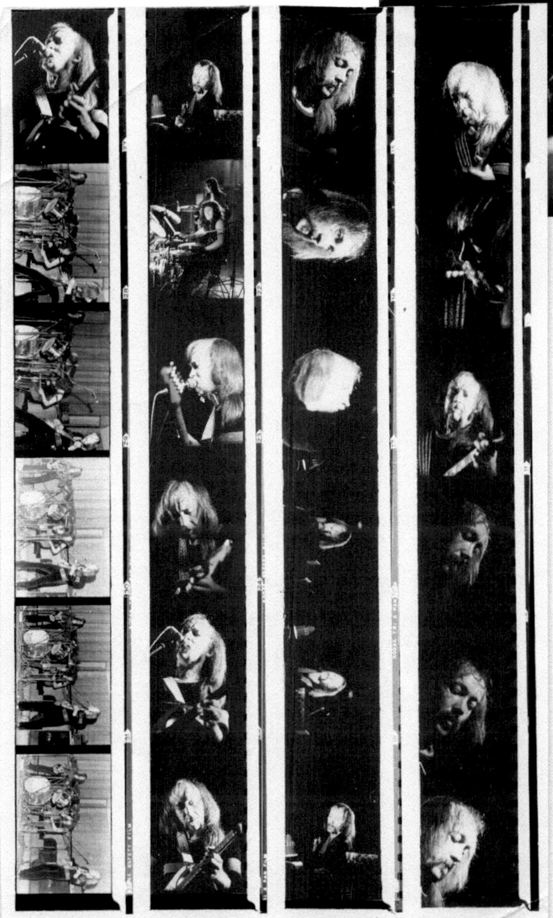

Left: In action at the Rainbow Theatre, Finsbury Park. (*TS Personal Collection*)

Left: Tony having great fun at the Mellotron. (*TS Personal Collection*)

Right: A picture from the *Hogwash* tour with new boy Clive in the middle. (*TS Personal Collection*)

Right: This *Hogwash* advert didn't quite tell the truth, as neither Pete nor Tony used plectrums. (*TS Personal Collection*)

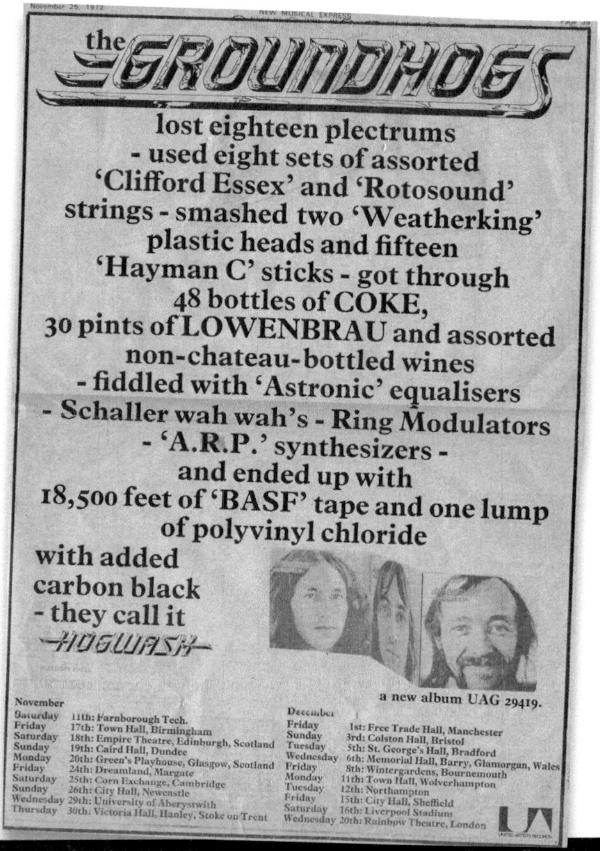

November 25, 1972 NEW MUSICAL EXPRESS

the GROUNDHOGS

lost eighteen plectrums
- used eight sets of assorted
'Clifford Essex' and 'Rotosound'
strings - smashed two 'Weatherking'
plastic heads and fifteen
'Hayman C' sticks - got through
48 bottles of COKE,
30 pints of LOWENBRAU and assorted
non-chateau-bottled wines
- fiddled with 'Astronic' equalisers
- Schaller wah wah's - Ring Modulators
- 'A.R.P.' synthesizers -
and ended up with
18,500 feet of 'BASF' tape and one lump
of polyvinyl chloride
with added
carbon black
- they call it
HOGWASH

a new album UAG 29419.

November

Saturday	11th: Farnborough Tech.
Friday	17th: Town Hall, Birmingham
Saturday	18th: Empire Theatre, Edinburgh, Scotland
Sunday	19th: Caird Hall, Dundee
Monday	20th: Green's Playhouse, Glasgow, Scotland
Friday	24th: Dreamland, Margate
Saturday	25th: Corn Exchange, Cambridge
Sunday	26th: City Hall, Newcastle
Wednesday	29th: University of Aberystwith
Thursday	30th: Victoria Hall, Hanley, Stoke on Trent

December

Friday	1st: Free Trade Hall, Manchester
Sunday	3rd: Colston Hall, Bristol
Tuesday	5th: St. George's Hall, Bradford
Wednesday	6th: Memorial Hall, Barry, Glamorgan, Wales
Friday	8th: Wintergardens, Bournemouth
Monday	11th: Town Hall, Wolverhampton
Tuesday	12th: Northampton
Friday	15th: City Hall, Sheffield
Saturday	16th: Liverpool Stadium
Wednesday	20th: Rainbow Theatre, London

Below: A *Melody Maker* profile. Tony's birthday is, in fact, on 23 March. (*TS Personal Collection*)

Melody Maker

The GROUNDHOGS file

EVOLUTION: Guitarist Tony McPhee and, bassist Peter Cruickshank were in the original Groundhogs which worked from about 1962 to 1966.

"We took the name from John Lee Hooker's 'Groundhog Blues'," says Tony. The group then split for two years, "and the members of the band went their separate ways. We were a blues band in those days, it was at the height of the blues boom. But this died off, and the band split."

Tony next went with a group called The Truth. "We had a hit with a Beatles number called 'Girl'. Then I spent a time with a band led by Boz — ex-lead singer with King Crimson. Next I was in a three-piece, Herbal Mixture, with Peter and drummer Mike Meekham. That was a psychedelic-type band, but it folded.

"For a little while I was with John Dummer's Blues Band, which took me up to the re-formation of the Groundhogs, in 1968. Harmonica player Steve Rye was in the band, but when he left we reverted to a three-piece again."

FIRST PUBLIC APPEARANCE: Backed John Lee Hooker on his tour of England '68
FIRST BROADCAST: Sound of the 70's 1971
FIRST TV: Top of the Pops 1971
TOURING MANAGER: Alan Laycock, 58 Cambridge Way, Haverhill, Suffolk.
RECORD PRODUCER: Tony McPhee
RECORD COMPANY: United Artists Records, Mortimer House, 37-41 Mortimer St., W.1. 636 1655
AGENT: Chrysalis, 388-396 Oxford St., W.1. 493 9461
MANAGER: Worldwide Artistes Management Ltd, 39 South Street, W.1. 499 1553
TRANSPORT: Mercedes Truck for equipment, Zodiac Executive for group
P.A.: J.B.L. 1000 Watts P.A. System.
SINGLES: "Eccentric Man" May '70
ALBUMS: "Scratching The Surface" Nov '68, "Blues Obituary" Oct. '69, "Thank Christ for the Bomb" May '70, "Split" April '71, "Who Will Save The World" April '72.
PUBLICIST: Keith Goodwin, 7 Denmark St., London, W.C.2. 01 836 5067/8
FAN CLUB: Alan Laycock
MUSIC PUBLISHER: United Artists Music, 37-41 Mortimer St., W.1. 636 1655

TONY McPHEE, guitar
BORN: Humberstone, Lincs. 22.3.44
EDUCATION: Grammar School, London, 1 GCE "O" French.
MUSICAL EDUCATION: Self-taught
MUSICAL INFLUENCES: John Lee Hooker, Jimi Hendrix, Herbert Sumlin
PRINCIPLE COMPOSITIONS: "Thank Christ for the Bomb," "Split" albums
SONGWRITING INSPIRATION: Random playing with unfamiliar instruments.
FAVOURITE SONGWRITER: Roger Chapman and The Family
FAVOURITE SINGLE: "Lucille" by Little Richard
MOST INFLUENTIAL LP: "Are You Experienced" by Jimi Hendrix
RESIDENCE: Large cottage, Haverhill, Suffolk
FAMILY: Wife Christine and son Conan 1 years old.
AWARDS: 6th in MM International Pop Poll Guitar section
INSTRUMENTS: Gibson SG Electric guitar, Fender Stratocaster electric guitar, Zemaitis electric guitar, Yamaha acoustic 6-string Jumbo, Mellotron, ARP 2600 Synthesizer, piano and plays all keyboard instruments.

PETER CRUICKSHANK, bass guitar
BORN: Calcutta, India, 2.7.45.
EDUCATION: Charlton England Secondary Modern
MUSICAL EDUCATION: Self-taught
CAREER: 10 years ago started semi-pro band called Dollar Bills then joined 'Hogs
MUSICAL INFLUENCES: Mainly modern jazz — Charlie Mingus. Bass player with Grateful Dead
FAVOURITE SONGWRITER: Peter Townshend, Lennon and McCartney.
FAVOURITE SINGLE: "Can't Explain," by The Who.
MOST INFLUENTIAL LP: "Anthem Of The Sun," Grateful Dead
RESIDENCE: House in Bury-St.-Edmunds, Suffolk
FAMILY: Wife Janice and 2 sons, Paul 3, Adam 11 months
INSTRUMENTS: Custom made Tony Zemaitis bass guitar, Gibson EB3 bass, 200-watt Laney amp, J.B.L. cabinets. Also plays piano.

CLIVE BROOKS, Drums and percussion
BORN: London, 28.12.49
EDUCATION: Grammar, London, 4 O's English, Geog., Art and Technical Drawing
MUSICAL EDUCATION: Selftaught
CAREER: Started seven years ago playing with various semi-pro local bands in London. 1st professional appearance with Egg then joined 'Hogs
MUSICAL INFLUENCES: Stem from the blues
FAVOURITE COMPOSER: Stravinsky.
FAVOURITE SONGWRITER: Cat Stevens.
FAVOURITE SINGLE: "Hey Joe" by Jimi Hendrix
FAVOURITE LP: "The Rite of Spring" by Stravinsky
RESIDENCE: House in Dunmow, Essex
FAMILY: Single
INSTRUMENTS: 24" Hayman Bass Drum, 16" x 16" Hayman Tom Tom, 13" x 9" Hayman Tom Tom, 14" x 5½" Ludwig Snare, 20" Paiste Cymbal Ride, 18" Paiste Crash Ride, 16" Paiste 602 Crash. Matched pair of 16" Zyn and Avedis Hi Hat Cymbals

Next week: The Strawbs

Left: Tony flanked by his guitar during the *Two Sides* tour. (*Paul Brears*)

Right: The Roundhouse was the first 'explosive' gig on Tony's solo tour. (*TS Personal Collection*)

Left: Size matters! So they say. (*TS Personal Collection*)

Right: Clive, Pete and Tony waiting for the ferry home. (*TS Personal Collection*)

Left: The winner gets the best seat on the ferry! (*TS Personal Collection*)

Right: UA promo: Martin Kent, Mick Cook, Dave Wellbelove and Tony. (*TS Personal Collection*)

Above: An unidentified picture taken by a fan showing the Synthi Hi Fli in its thin white box at the front of the stage. (*TS Personal Collection*)

Right: All in a day's work for Tony McTrousers... (*Paul Freestone/TS Personal Collection*)

Right: The small council house in Tooting where Tony grew up. (*Joanna Deacon/TS Personal Collection*)

Below: Dave Anderson, Tony McPhee and Mick Jones doing their best 'Hard Men of Rock' pose. (*TS Personal Collection*)

Left: Tony with Gold discs, Zematis guitar and the author. (*MH Personal Collection*)

Right: Tony and Joanna in perfect harmony. (*TS Personal Collection*)

Left: A short reunion in 2003 pleased many and produced a DVD performance at Shrewsbury's Buttermarket. (*Joanna Deacon/TS Personal Collection*)

Chapter 9 - Who Will Save The Groundhogs?

Right, you lot, cop this!
Ken Pustelnik's approach to a resistant audience

A lot of groups are in control, but we're not; it must be amazing to see three very ordinary people crawl on stage and smash into it.
Ken Pustelnik to *Melody Maker*

In early November 1971, the band embarked on their biggest tour of the UK, taking in dates to the middle of December. By then, sales of *Split* had sailed over the 50,000 mark and the band were in the ascendancy. They were supported on the tour by Egg and Quicksand, but there were rumblings in the camp about how the press viewed them. In an interview with *Melody Maker*'s Andrew Means, they had the chance to voice their concerns. The headline was straight to the point: 'Have We Been Fair To The Hogs?' One of the things that precipitated this was Roy Fisher's open letter to the music press. In the letter, he accused the press of ignoring his men and even floated the word conspiracy!

However, Means was at pains to point out that the band were partly to blame for any indifference by pointing the finger at too many one-word answers and showing a distinct lack of enthusiasm. Ken admits that they never went to music business functions and kept themselves to themselves, as he sums up: 'Everyone knew everybody else, but we were in a bubble!' However, this was actually one of the strengths of the band. They never exposed themselves to trends. They just went out and did their own thing. This was ever apparent in their approach to live shows. The Groundhogs did not interact on stage like other bands. Sometimes, Pete Cruickshank would follow Tony, leaving Ken out on a limb and free to do his own thing. As Ray Telford noted in *Sounds*, it was this 'off the wall' approach that attracted the most criticism. Terms like 'self-indulgent' were bandied around, but to the band, their attitude to playing live was their strongest card.

Tony McPhee outlines the fluid nature of the band on stage: 'It depends who was on a good night. I might find a riff, but Ken could get a good rhythm going and we would follow him. Hopefully, we would come back as one in the end.' It didn't always work out like that, but they never believed they should recreate the record note for note on stage. Tony told *Zig Zag*: 'Ken just wallops everything in sight and sometimes I lose him completely. Like I often come back during a solo and can't work out where he is – so I just have to play a note.' And he really did wallop them, as there were many times when he cracked the cymbals! Ken acknowledges his matter-of-fact approach: 'I hate the drummers who come to me and say, 'Have you seen the latest pedal? It goes 0.3 seconds through the air faster.' My answer is, 'I just play them, mate.'' Ken was a unique drummer and he gave *Melody Maker* a clue as to how he achieved it: 'I listened to other people's styles – which helps to expand technique – but didn't incorporate these elements into my own style. This destroys one's natural talent.' It could be said that the Groundhogs, in a way, were two bands. In the studio, Tony had more control over what was played, at least on bass, but on stage, Pete Cruickshank recalls that 'those bass lines were my own.' It is this democratic situation that made them such an exciting and unpredictable live act.

There was, however, one major factor that gave this interaction tension on stage and an edge over most other bands. They hardly ever rehearsed and to take this restrained approach exhibited a tremendous confidence in their stagecraft. As they always seemed to be gigging, there didn't seem to be any need.

But the band were not on stage in a bubble. How did they interact with the audience? The idea of a band doing a big tour today with the same set is pretty commonplace. But the fact remains that audiences vary over the world, and in the old days, some had strategies to cope. Ken gives an insight into the nuances of the art form of winning an audience over: 'Sometimes, it's 'Oh Christ' they're not into it, we are going to have to work with this. Let's get it by the throat and shake it, or 'My goodness', it was so easy that we didn't have to work at it. I like it when they are a little bit resistant and when there is a bit of friction. That's when I say, 'Right, you lot, cop this!' Or what I like to call our oral chaos.' Looking back, Ken is convinced that this is a big challenge to take up as it is a complex interaction: 'You have to hit the audience at the level they operate rhythmically and emotionally and that's what we did!'

Tony had a slightly different attitude to this, as he told Chris Welch of *Melody Maker*: 'The Groundhogs today go out and play and we don't force anything. We hope that it works out. If it's a duff audience, nothing happens. But we play to enjoy ourselves. What's the point of playing otherwise? You might as well dig holes in the road.' An important part of their strategy for Pete Cruickshank was to hit them from the first number. It was this that set the tone for the rest of the gig. To him, 'Split Part One' was a vital weapon: 'It was my favourite number and it opened the show for a long time. It had so much power and it set the pace for the rest of the show.' This is yet another exciting aspect of the band on stage; they all had different insights into what they were doing and how to achieve their goals.

Audience interaction itself was on more than one level. As a band, they had done more than their fair share of supporting other top acts. On the surface, it seems that a support band can't lose, but Tony recalls the recent Stones tour where things can get confusing: 'If a supporting group muffs up something, it is very easy to lose the audience completely. Actually, on this tour, the audiences were very attentive; so attentive, in fact, that they were almost too cool. At the end of every set, everybody clapped politely, which was okay, except that we never knew whether they were being polite or actually enjoying what we were doing. In some ways, it is always better to play to a more critical audience with a few hecklers because then you've got something to play at, something to draw you out and then the end result is musically much better.' Of course, the support slot is really for a band trying to get a foothold and not for an established act, although there are times when the support gets a better audience reaction. On a tour of Germany Free agreed to let Colosseum play last as they were going down better.

Well before the November tour, United Artists were banging on the door for another album (UA had decided to discontinue Liberty Records and merge everything into one label). The problem was that Tony didn't have any new material. In an interview with *Sounds* in late May 1971, he admitted that he did not have a clue of what the next album was going to be about. However, the original idea for the cover came from the band's love of Marvel Comics. Roy Fisher suggested it would be a good idea to have a Marvel-type album cover. Their favourite hero was Silver Surfer, which was drawn by Neal Adams. Pete recalls this period: 'Even though we were all into Marvel Comics, it was Ken who was into them in a big way. He used to collect them on the road.'

Roy Fisher traced Adams down and secured his services by August. It wasn't long before the idea of portraying the band as superheroes, taking on the world's problems, was brought up. But things didn't initially go well for Adams, as he fell asleep with the finished artwork in his briefcase on the New York subway. When he woke up, it had been stolen! Finally, on 17 November, the re-drawn artwork was sent to London from New York. With the artwork in hand, Tony set about creating the music and lyrics for the album. The trouble was that they didn't finish their UK tour until mid-December! Tony was a man who worked best under pressure, but there was a limit to how far this method could work before burnout.

When they perused the artwork, Tony was 'Marvellous' McPhee, Pete was 'Quick' Cruickshank and Ken was 'Powerful' Pustelnik. As far as they were concerned, Adams had delivered the goods. Our heroes are seen at various dramatic stages trying to save the world against pollution, warmongers and overpopulation. But these storylines are injected with a degree of humour, especially as 'Quick' Cruickshank accidentally sends the mother of overpopulation to India! There's some sharp political comment, too, when 'Marvellous' McPhee fails to stop the polluting factories. Adams pictures an unholy triumvirate of the Church, the Army and a corrupt politician, with the Church mouthing: 'Yes, Yes, my boy! Pollution is the small price we pay to stave off the Godless Communists!' The punch line of the story is the lads are hopeless in the superhero stakes, so they are transformed into the Groundhogs, where they can accomplish more with their music. It's a pen that is mightier than the sword analogy.

The band were seriously overworked, as the archives make clear. Their winter tour finished with the last gig at Reading on 13 December 1971. Yet, they were ensconced in De Lane Lea Studios just nine days later. They even reconvened three days after Christmas Day. After the last two years of hard work, the band needed a break. Even by the standards of the day, they were one of the most hardworking bands! The continuity that Tony had sought for so long was broken, but there was nothing he could have done about it. De Lane Lea had been relocated from Holburn to Wembley. The new studio was state of the art and they were the first rock band to use the facility. In theory, it was going to make the recording process even better.

Even though the studio was state-of-the-art and had 16 tracks, Tony thought it was sterile. Furthermore, he was far from happy about the circumstances surrounding the whole concept. As far as he was concerned, *Split* was still selling well, so he couldn't see why this album was needed so soon, but the record company wanted another big seller. As luck would have it, there was an array of instruments in the studio, but one in particular caught his eye. Sitting in the corner was a

Mellotron (this was a keyboard instrument that recreated the sound of an orchestra). He was keen to use it, as he explains: 'Ken was listening to a lot of Yes (this would have been the *Fragile* album) and I quite liked the sound of the Mellotron. I liked that idea of different chords, so I thought I'd try it.' On the other hand, Pete was listening to a diet of mainly American bands like The Grateful Dead, Frank Zappa and Spirit. He was strangely disinterested in British bands then. This probably explains why he was repelled by the Mellotron: 'I felt it was a gimmick or even a toy. I was concerned because it was such a departure from our usual sound.'

In the past, Tony had been the only person contributing material. As a result of their yearly album contract with UA, Tony had to leave it to the last minute to write the songs, so Ken decided to start writing himself, as he remembers: 'I had a guitarist friend called J. D. Fanger and I took him to the studio. I told Roy Fisher that I had a song – 'Let's hear it', he said. I thought, 'Good old Roy." So they ran through the song and it seemed to sound good. It was suggested to Tony that they use it, to which he replied, 'I don't play other people's songs!'

As Ken recalls: 'It had the desired effect as, within a week, he'd written half the album.'[29] Tony was forthcoming about the problems he had on this album: 'I came along to rehearsal and Pete and Ken just sort of gave me a blank stare and I just sort of gulped and said, 'Let's try them again' ... what I'd done on tape I'd taken along to them, but what came out of there wasn't the same to what I'd intended.' Pete recalls: 'Tony would write the song and then we'd record it straight off there and then as there was no time to develop it.' This had been the perennial problem after *Thank Christ For The Bomb*!

It was this pressure that provided the background to the opening cut 'Earth Is Not Room Enough'. The title came from the sci-fi book by Asimov and is another one of those familiar word plays that Tony loves. It inspired him to set the story from the inside of a gas chamber somewhere in the US. He especially concentrated on the American fixation on ritually executing its citizens. He makes his case against the death penalty clear, recalling his childhood: 'This was the 1950s and they were still stretching people's necks on gallows; there was a lot to change and most of the worst would eventually be outlawed in the next couple of decades.' It's clear that this had stuck in his mind when writing the album, but he also related it to how mankind is gassing itself globally with pollution.

Locked in a room, strapped to a hollow chair,
Faint musty smell, odour of stale air,
Sealed from the outside in a cage that is six-foot square,
Eyes that are fixed in a glazed, disbelieving stare.

Cyanide pills dropped in an acid bath,
Froth forms a cloud as deadly as death's own staff,
Lungs start to burst trying to hold your breath,
But have the last laugh 'cos Earth is just a cage seven thousand miles wide!

The inventive Mellotron opening is used to great effect and continues throughout. As Ken comments: 'The Moody Blues never used it like this. Tony used it originally and gave it an almost mournful, no hope feeling.' The most amazing thing is the different amount of sounds he gets out of the unreliable machine, known for repeatedly breaking down! The opening track is amongst their finest, with plenty of light and shade. The second cut is 'Wages Of Peace' and it brings the mood down but is an effective rocker about the ways in which nature can have harmful effects on mankind. 'Body In Mind' picks up on the subject of pollution but concentrates on the human mind as something that can be infected. It's quite catchy, too, with a great solo from Tony. The band are rocking on this one. 'Music Is The Food Of Thought' is a reflective song and tells the story of how mankind has the potential to save itself. Tony particularly liked this one because it's reminiscent of the material they played in the early blues days. It has a grave ambience to it and is heightened, again, by some supporting Mellotron:

To save the race
We need to trace
The source of power and fuse it…
Enlightened minds
All seem to find
The vehicle is music

In contrast to Tony's aggressive playing on the first side of *Split*, his guitar playing is more restrained thus far on this album. The opening track on side two is the wonderfully named 'Bog Roll Blues' – this one was written on the toilet! The guitar intro was culled from a tape of bits and pieces that Tony worked from, and this one just happened to fit. The band's raunchy sound here is punctuated by some tasty work from Tony. Pete loved the comedy of the lyrics, offset by the dark undertones present in lines such as 'There's too many people nowadays who just want to wipe their ass of the whole affair'. 'Death Of The Sun' rattles along at a good lick and it showcases two sped-up guitars, one twice as fast as the other.

Tony bought a secondhand harmonium from an East End market and thought it would fit for 'Amazing Grace'. It was a song he had liked for a long time. It ends with a scorching guitar riff. The album closer is the barnstorming 'The Grey Maze' and is a return to the old days. Ken remembers this track very well: 'The new studio was fitted upstairs with a bar and café. We were the first rock band to use the studio. When we started playing, we had loads of complaints about the noise from upstairs.' The band are in truly inspired form as they, at last, have a chance to let rip. It's probably two minutes longer than it should be, but it provides a fitting counterpoint to the rest of the album.

The sessions also created a few problems regarding the dynamics within the band. One track in particular stood out for Tony and Pete. For 'Music Is The Food Of Thought', Ken had an intense discussion with Tony regarding his uncertainty of being able to drum on it. In the end, it was worked out and 'Music Is The Food Of Thought' did have Ken on. The way they usually worked was that Tony worked out both guitar parts and then Ken would come in with his part. However, as Tony explained to *Sounds,* it sometimes didn't work out the way he wanted: 'I won't say to Ken the same because I know that what I'm thinking is a funky sort of drumming which he doesn't play. So, I just hammer away on chords and Pete will do his bass bit and Ken will get some idea … As I said, this album has been a bit of a strain, but on the last two, it's worked okay because I was doing something that they could accept, but this one was different.' However, as Tony admitted to *Melody Maker*'s Tony Stewart, the root cause of the problem was that they didn't have enough preparation: 'With this new one, because of the weight of work, I didn't get time to relax and write songs. In effect, I'd used up the sort of formula I had for writing songs … so I had to try and rethink the whole outlook.' By the end of it, the innate skill that Tony McPhee had of working under pressure took its toll to the degree that he wasn't happy with the work. For the time being, Tony had been wrung dry of inspiration!

Looking back on the album, Ken had this to say: 'It was too rushed and we were overworked, but I like the sparseness of it, the depth and the weirdness. It suffers a bit from the ambitious notion that you have complicated ideas but are forced to approach them simply. In other words, things don't go as planned when put to practice. The lyrics float nicely, though. The energy was phenomenal, but it didn't come across on the record. There's a certain limpness about it.' Certainly, an example of this is on 'Earth Is Not Room Enough'; when Tony's guitar comes in after the Mellotron opening, it does sound a bit feeble. However, the album takes the band into new musical territory and it sits nicely coming after the more rock-orientated *TCFTB* and *Split*. The album could be looked at as their most eclectic and there's a large chunk of Hogs fans that rate it highly. For Ken, it was to be his last album and it's incredible to think of the musical journey they had made from *Scratching The Surface* to *Who Will Save The World*!

As was the norm for most bands then in the middle of making the album, they were back gigging and played four concerts in rapid succession. On 8 January 1972, they played Leicester, and two days later, Jo Ann Kelly joined them at their Chatham gig. The day after they played Cheltenham Town Hall, *Disc*'s Andrew Tyler was there. After the support band Writing On The Wall had finished their set, Tyler describes the proceedings: 'They open with 'Mistreated' and the eyes immediately fall on Tony. On stage, he is a transformed man – all energy and showmanship … By far, the best thing of the evening is his solo in 'Groundhog Blues'… Cheltenham has gone wild. Several girls seem to be banging their heads against the front of the stage. Everyone is on their feet and the aisles are packed tight.' They ran through the gamut of their best material, but they didn't include anything from their new album; it was the shape of things to come.

The album was finally finished on 6 February, with the master cut the following day. In mid-February, Roy Fisher went back to the States in the hope of finally securing a US tour. However, by the time he got back, things had slipped from his grasp. For quite some time, Tony had been dissatisfied with Roy Fisher's managerial performance, but it wasn't going to be easy to break ties with him: 'We went to a solicitor because we (Tony and Ken) wanted him out. They told us you couldn't break a contract just because you think someone is bad at their job.' By now, Tony had built up a catalogue of grievances against Roy Fisher's performance. The John Mayall tour of Germany in 1971 is an example.

He recalls the details: 'On that tour, we played eight shows and we got £750 between us. But Mayall used our roadies and our PA! I felt that we should be getting more money. I thought The Stones support tour was a good move but I wasn't happy supporting as we'd had a top-five album. We did another short tour of Germany later on supporting Gun and I wasn't happy with that either because all they had was a hit single called 'Race With The Devil'.'

Roy Fisher recently had this to say in response: 'Regarding Tony's grievance over £750 for eight shows with John Mayall, I did not fix the price – the agency did. I always discussed offers with the group first, so they had the option not to do it.' It was clear that Roy Fisher had made some smart moves in the early days, but Tony was now looking for someone to take the band to another level. He believed the band had more to give. In fact, Tony had already come into contact with his future management on a previous foreign trip. However, it's not that Roy Fisher didn't think that the band had more to give, as he recalled: 'Of course they did, which is why I arranged the tour in the US! But the group were totally paranoid about flying and America. The CMA agency, which would have handled the tour I arranged, was one of the biggest and most powerful in America at the time. In reality, if they had stayed with me and gone to the US on the tour with Johnnie Winter, they would have had a very good chance of success and would have been elevated to the position they had worked so hard for.'

On the way to Vienna and Frankfurt with Black Sabbath and Gentle Giant the previous year (this was the trip that had cemented Tony's hatred of flying), they had come into contact again with Patrick Meehan, who was the manager of both bands. Wilf Pine was a salaried associate of World Wide Artists (the Meehan family company). It was his son, Patrick Meehan Junior, who was to play an ever-increasing part in proceedings. Wilf Pine had started out in the music business as an odd job man for tough-guy manager Don Arden.

Later on, he worked for Arden's former assistant, none other than Meehan Senior. But it was Meehan Junior who had a talent for spotting bands that had the potential to reach the top and had the management that could convince musicians that they could take them to great heights. One of the early bands he poached was Black Sabbath. In Wilf Pine's recent biography, *One Of The Family: The Englishman And The Mafia*, a conversation is described with Meehan Senior: 'Listen, Wilf, there's a lot of talk going on in the record industry about Black Sabbath.

Take it from me, they're going places, and although we know that Jim Simpson's a lovely human being who managed the group from the day they started … Sabbath won't stay with him forever.' This was how the Meehan's generally acquired their roster of bands.

On the plane to Vienna, Tony got talking to Wilf Pine and expressed his dissatisfaction with Roy Fisher. Pine was a fast worker; he impressed the band at Frankfurt because he got them higher up on the bill than Fleetwood Mac, much to John McVie's chagrin! But at that stage, Tony was not looking for other management because they were contracted to Roy Fisher, so he wasn't thinking along those lines. Wilf later attended a Groundhogs gig at the Queen Elizabeth Hall. He was there because Gentle Giant (a WWA act) were supporting, but he stayed on to watch the Groundhogs' set. He describes it in his biography: 'But although musically they were wonderful, they were not so exciting to watch as Sabbath and they struck me as a very odd collection of individuals.' He goes on to describe Tony: 'He just stood there in the middle of the stage, in a pair of old tatty jeans, with long hair hanging down … But he had a great blues voice and what he could do with a guitar was incredible … I knew one day I was going to steal the Groundhogs.' That day was fast approaching! The next job for Wilf was to think of a strategy to oust the current management.

Roy Fisher's company was called Zak Management and he was in partnership with ex-John Lee's Groundhogs frontman John Cruickshank. John joined the company just after *Thank Christ For The Bomb*. Zak Management also had Egg and Cochise on their books. They also promoted the first Alice Cooper tour of the UK – before they made their name. They had a bit of bad luck with the New York Dolls because it looked like they had secured them when, suddenly, one of the band members died – so they went back home. It was later on that Cruickshank became a director and ploughed some of his own money into the company. Obviously, this was a difficult situation for John, as his brother, Pete, was in the band. Losing the Groundhogs would have particularly disastrous consequences for John Cruickshank. He recalls these events: 'We were initially approached by Patrick Meehan Junior, who suggested they combine forces, but, in reality, I think he was trying to find information about us.'

It was early March and things were moving fast. When Roy Fisher returned from America, he got a shock: 'Got a call from Wilf Pine. He said, as of now, we are managing the Groundhogs. I hung up.' That was all that was said. A few days later, Fisher phoned Pete Cruickshank, who told him he didn't know what was happening. One of the things that had happened was that Wilf Pine got wind that Wilf Wright of Chrysalis was being considered (they were the Groundhogs booking agents), but Pine's advice to Tony was succinct: 'Don't go with Wilf Wright; you might as well stay with Roy Fisher.' He never did find out why he said that about Wright.

Shortly after this, Tony, who was in Haverhill, had a visit from Wilf Pine. They drove to Ken's flat in London, where Wilf made a pitch for them to join WWA. In reality, it probably wasn't your usual business meeting, as Roy Fisher opined: 'Wilf picking up Tony with two heavies and then going to talk to Ken was typical of the way they did business.' However, Ken was also impressed, as Tony recalls: 'After Wilf had gone, Ken said to me, 'I'm worried as I can't see anything wrong.' I didn't know Pete's opinion on this as he was always reticent in coming forward.' However, Ken recalls it slightly differently: 'I wanted to go with Chrysalis, but when Tony turned up at my flat with Pine and two big guys, I could see he was already sold on the idea. I thought I'd try and change it from the inside, so I went along with it.' Pete Cruickshank confirms Ken's story: 'I was surprised when Ken changed his mind as I would have gone with Chrysalis if we had to change. I could see that a big management could open doors but I didn't know anything about WWA, who were only talking to Tony.'

As their first act, the new management took the band off the road because they needed a break. In an interview with *NME* later that year, Tony outlined the relief this brought: 'It had almost become a vicious circle. We needed the money from gigs to simply stay on the road at all. It became a very sad state of affairs. There were times when we'd go on stage sick of the whole set.' It was agreed that, up to the US tour, the band would be paid £70 a week each. On 8 March, Chrysalis (booking agents) were instructed by the band's solicitor (Canter & Martin) to work with World Wide Artists. The letter also instructed them to pay all indemnities that might arise from Zak Management. The same day, Roy Fisher took an injunction against World Wide Artists on advice from his solicitor, Tony Russell. Roy Fisher and John Cruickshank met with Patrick Meehan Junior and Wilf Pine on 12 March. By now, Roy Fisher was 'persona non grata' with the band. A few days later, he spoke to Pete Cruickshank, who told him: 'I'm not supposed to speak to you.'

Suddenly, it was all over and Roy Fisher noted: 'I agreed settlement out of court with Pat Meehan as I felt too much personal involvement to fight the Groundhogs in a long legal battle. I did not get or feel threatened by Wilf Pine, but maybe this would have come if I had not agreed to settle for relative 'peanuts' as compared with what the band could have made in the US in 1972. The new recording contract I negotiated and agreed with Mike Stewart – raising royalty from 3% to 8%, plus 2% for Tony as producer – for the UK, US, Canada and Japan was never signed. *Who Will Save The World* died a death as it was not promoted. My only regret was the Groundhogs not making it big in the US. This would have put Tony up there with Clapton and Beck. And Wilf Pine getting my fucking gold disc is still a sore point.'[30]

According to Tony: 'We only got our gold albums for *Split* sometime after Roy left us. Fisher was aggrieved because he had steered the band to the success of *Split* and Wilf Pine had arrived at the tail end of it all. But Wilf had to fight to get us the gold disc because we were a little short of the 100,000 required.' However, Roy Fisher put the blame on this farce somewhere else: 'In reality, if the UA distribution had not been screwed up at the time of release, *Split* would have sold a lot more and, therefore, we were entitled to the gold disc earlier on when I was still with the band.'

John Cruickshank had this to say about the end: 'Roy accepted £2000 as a payoff, which was a ridiculous amount of money. As for me, when we lost the Groundhogs, our company was in trouble and I ended up losing my house. When we met Pat Meehan, it was clear we were not in their league. Roy wasn't dominant enough, but he worked hard for the band and he had that personal touch, which I think they lost.'

The finances for the band were organised in an odd fashion. The original contract they had with Roy Fisher stipulated that all performing record royalties be paid to him and not individually.[31] This meant that the band never received individual royalty statements. It was Liberty's policy, in order to avoid confusion – for them at least – not to send out multiple statements. They received their royalties from Roy. Their regular monthly payments, made up of mainly gig money, were a curious mix, too, as Tony explains: 'I lived in Haverhill and I had train bills to pay. So, Roy totted my travel expenses up and paid Pete and Ken half of the total. The truth is, I just went along with it like I did other things.' Roy Fisher elaborates on this: 'Ken and Pete did not feel that Tony should get more expenses than them just because he moved out of

London. Giving them half of what he got was my compromise to try to keep all happy. It's a pity Tony did not air this problem at the time. But this was typical, and I had to be a mind reader on most points as they rarely spoke up, not even Ken.'

The trauma that was unfolding behind the scenes belied the public face that the band had to present to the world. *Who Will Save The World* was released during this time and Tony had to do a string of interviews, showing that it was business as usual. In an advance preview of the album, *Melody Maker's* Andrew Means was positive about the new direction: 'The Mellotron translates McPhee's musical ideas onto a different plane. While his lead guitar work is directly stimulating and intensely subjective at times, the Mellotron gives the music more expanse.' Across the pond, the Groundhogs were quietly building a reputation for themselves. Writing in *Rolling Stone,* the volatile Lester Bangs was more belligerent for the cause. His opening gambit in his review was uncompromising: 'It's about goddam fucking time these Groundhogs started to get some recognition.' He even gets some comparisons in with the two previous albums and, perhaps, anticipates the future: 'Those two albums were just good run of the racks heavy grunge. *Who Will Save The World* is that much more. McPhee's guitar work is as frenzied as ever but much denser and more complex than before.' The contemporary internet *Allmusic* guide took an interesting, if not a retrospective, view: 'McPhee took the unusual step of adding progressive rock elements on this album, especially in his use of Mellotron and harmonium. Blues-rock and progressive rock is not exactly a fashionable combination among critics these days, but McPhee at least deserved credit for trying something a little bit different instead of endlessly recycling the blues-rock clichés he'd mastered. Lyrically, he reached back to the socially conscious (if not terribly clear) musings on war, peace and philosophy that had preoccupied him on the *Thank Christ For The Bomb* album. It wasn't gripping enough to add up to something notable.'

The new album also caused some confusion in the press about the inspiration behind Tony's music. In an interview with *MM*'s Chris Welch, he baulked when it was suggested to him that he made *Split* for the heavy hard-rock audience: 'We never aim our albums. The music is not premeditated like that. As far as possible, the album represents what we've been playing on stage. After *Split*, we got fed up with hearing that type of sound, so we utilised ideas from the new album in our stage act, which has always been standard. The music is very free and we get completely involved in every number. Every night, it comes out different.' It illustrated the enigma that surrounded the band; there were many journalists who didn't really understand them.

One of the most pressing questions that Tony was being forced to answer was the accusation that the band were being pretentious with their superhero image. Pretentious was, at the time, a very dirty word. Groups like Jethro Tull and Yes were bearing most of the flak. However, as Keith Emerson noted: 'You have to be musically pretentious to do something original.' Tony's answer to *Sounds* was very effective: 'I think a pretentious statement is something that's not quite so obvious. But it's so obviously pretentious that it's not.' For those who bothered to read the cartoon strip, they would have seen that, in the end, they were not very good at saving the world anyway! When asked if this was going to be the start of a new phase in the history of the band, he was non-committal.

The truth is that the album didn't appear to have many tracks that would translate live. Even though Ken was keen to play them, it never really happened. Later on, Tony was asked why they never really played the new album on stage. His reply almost consigned the album to oblivion: 'I made the album at the behest of UA. After it was finished, it kept them quiet, so we went back to playing *Split*.' While it's true they didn't feature the album much in their shows, they did relent at a few gigs and played a couple of them. The album got to number nine in the charts but it quickly disappeared without trace.

They flew out to the States in early June for their debut tour of the US. The tour was a curious mix of headline gigs and support slots for big names from both the UK and USA. The bands they were due to appear with were such luminaries as The Faces, Black Sabbath, Edgar Winter, Humble Pie, Black Oak Arkansas and Alice Cooper. In spite of Tony not being keen on touring there, he knew the States was very important in terms of potential album sales. That never really bothered him, but there were a couple of problems he anticipated. The first one was that he truly detested flying and this tour was going to have a lot of that – he wasn't the only one in the band. The second reason was he thought that, in some ways, the country was quite backward. He didn't like the way they were treating black people. It appeared to him, plus a lot of other people too, that some parts of America were pretty much like apartheid in South Africa.

The journey to the first port of call at Memphis was a baptism of fire and the shape of things to come. Arriving there via Washington was a mammoth 19-hour trek. In customs, they confiscated Tony's oranges, which his mother had packed for him, due to the danger of disease, so he was annoyed about that. Pete had taken his wife, Jan, to Thunder Bay, Canada, to her parents' house. He was making his own way to Memphis and found it daunting, to say the least. He takes up the story: 'My wife's parents told me to be careful of all the rednecks; to be honest, I was shit scared. I was travelling alone in a country I didn't know. When I arrived at Memphis Airport, it was baking hot. I made my way to the Holiday Inn and promptly locked myself in. It was only later I realised that all the horror stories were wrong'. Not only did he like Memphis but he also liked the people, too!

On 8 June 1972, a guy called Dave (Black Sabbath roadie) took them to the hotel in readiness for their first performance at Stax Radio, Ardent Studios. It turned out to be rather embarrassing, as during the show, Tony couldn't remember the arrangement for 'Still A Fool' because it had been so long since they'd played together.[32] They soon got into it but something else happened that Ken remembers very well: 'Almost as soon as we started playing, the audience started clearing out. I thought, 'We can't be that bad!'' He later found out that this was one of the first stereo radio stations in America and they had gone out to the car park to listen to the gig on the radio. They were actually applauding in the car park!

After the recording, a guy called Rusty, who was the rep for UA, asked them if they wanted to go to a club that night. They were all game, so they went with him. It looked rather seedy outside, but Rusty knocked on the door and a sliding panel opened. In the gloom, Tony could just make out that it was a black guy – 'Yeah?' – to which Rusty replied, 'We got UA artists here'. With that, the door was open and they made their way in. Tony remembers hearing Dave the roadie as he walked in the opposite direction – 'You must be fucking mad!' – they didn't see him again that night. They were ushered to tables on the periphery of the stage. Tony heard a voice say, 'Sit down whitey!' It was then that he realised the whole audience were black. It was a big club and Solomon Burke was performing on stage. He also remembers seeing Wilson Pickett there!

It was only when they were led to the side of the stage, where they met fellow UA artists, that the ice was broken and they were able to mingle without any problems. They had their photo taken with Booker T's horn section, and in the end, the evening was a success, but Pete was under no illusion that if they had been white Americans, it could have been different. America was in racial turmoil at that time as black people were determined to claim their constitutional rights. Pete recalls that, at another club, it got around that they were a blues band. It wasn't long before they had a visitation from a group of large black gentlemen who shook their hands in a peculiar way: 'They twisted their hand round and gripped my thumb. It was only later I found out it was a Black Panther handshake. I thought, wow!'[33]

Two days after the radio show, they made their long-awaited US debut supporting Edgar Winter at Overton Park Bandstand, Memphis. It was a mini Hollywood bowl-type arena but the band, even though they hadn't fully recovered from the travelling, had to contend with the stunning heat and stupefying humidity of 80% – even 60 is considered high. Ken recalls the gig: 'Edgar Winter was great. They jammed in the dressing room all day and then went on with boundless energy. I watched them from the side of the stage.' But he had a surprise when they went on stage: 'One of the first things that struck me about the States was how many people knew our stuff.'

They played a memorable gig with Black Oak Arkansas at Vets Memorial Coliseum, Jacksonville, Florida. They were escorted to their hotel by the police and told to stay there until the gig. Ken recalls the weird events as the police – who took a high-handed attitude to things like gigs back then – accompanied them to the venue: 'We got on stage with house lights on and they stayed on. The police flanked both sides of the stage and they looked menacing in their shades and arms folded.[34] It was the worst atmosphere I have ever played in. In the front row, there were a few Groundhogs fans from Chicago, and when we started playing, they started freaking out. By the end of our set, they'd encouraged the rest of the crowd. That was one thing the police couldn't control. These people were seriously repressed.' He loved headliners Black Oak Arkansas – they were just a bunch of hillbillies – and when they travelled, they took their own little town with them on the bus with lots of hangers-on ready to sample the delights of being around a rock band. They were a great act, too.

Early on the tour, they had a few days to break, so they decided to do their own thing. Pete went to Canada to see Jan. Tony decided he'd go back to Memphis as he had befriended local celebrity and DJ Jon

Scott and had been made very welcome in Scott's home at 3744 James Road! Tony takes up the story: 'I asked Ken where he was going and he told me he'd come with me. I was hoping he would have stayed with the roadies. I thought, shit! I told him he'd have to fly, but he was determined to come.' Both Tony and Ken hated flying but it was the latter who was suffering the most now. When Tony arrived, he found out that Stax Records (the famed soul label) was having an outdoor party; he knew Ken would have problems: 'I was having a bad time, but Ken was much worse. One of the things that annoyed me the most about him was he wouldn't admit to anything. He'd never admit to disliking flying, which I knew he hated. He was claustrophobic and agoraphobic. In fact, he was everything! The problem for Ken was that Stax had set up in the middle of a field. So I watched him go round the perimeter of the hedge until he got to the shortest point, then he made a dash for it.' It must have made an odd sight for anybody witnessing proceedings.

They flew to New York, where they stayed at the plush City Squires Hotel. This hotel was notable for having their doorman kitted out in what they thought was typically English garb – red jackets and riding boots. In fact, it was quite embarrassing, as Tony remembers: 'He asked us if he could take our luggage, but everything we had was in two plastic bags! As he carried them through the foyer, you could see him squirming as the other bellhops (this was the US name for hotel porter) jeered.' In the evening, they went to see a Canadian rock band called Mama Lion. The following day, they were reunited with Pete, who arrived from Canada. They were booked for a photo shoot just across the road from the hotel, but there was a snag in getting there, as Tony recalls: 'Ken couldn't cross the road, so we had to get a taxi to take us round the block. I remember he had got some pills from the doctor and his hands were shaking so much that he could hardly take them. He was in a really bad way.' Pete recalls those depressing events: 'I remember the photo shoot very well. Ken was on his knees; he was holding my ankles and he looked up at me and said, 'Pete, I can't cross the road."' In the end, they had to take a taxi around the block just to cross the road!

Ken's problems had been evident to Pete in New Orleans at the very early part of the tour: 'We were playing gigs in intense heat and we had a lot of outdoor gigs. But in New Orleans, we played in a big warehouse and it was very hot. At one point, he collapsed over his kit and a roadie had to help him. I knew then he was in a bad way.' Pete mused about the usual pitfalls of the road: 'Being on tour is bad enough. Your points of reference blow out of the window, especially in a place like the States, which is a foreign country. We all went off our heads to some extent. But Ken's problems were self-inflicted. He was taking a lot of things; I don't know how he got through those gigs as he was very shaky.' Tony confirms that Ken had always been pretty reckless: 'He told me he took a sweet off a guy that had some acid in. He couldn't have known what was really in it. He didn't even know the man.'

As far as Tony was concerned, coping with Ken wasn't improving. Tony recalls a pivotal moment on the Gun Germany tour in 1971 as a watershed regarding Ken: 'I remember we played a gig where there were these plastic-backed chairs stacked up at the back of the dressing room. After we played our set, Ken decided to go and see Gun's act. I don't know whether it was because he had to stand on the balcony to see them but he came back in the dressing room with his hands on his head. When Ken was having a bad time, he thought his head was coming off. He called our roadie, 'Alan (Laycock), help me'. So, the two of them were wrestling each other with Alan trying to get Ken's hands off his head. The result was they fell backwards into the piled-up chairs. I thought, 'Great, that's all I need. I knew then he would have to go.'

They moved on to Florida, but if they thought it was going to be a holiday, they had cause to think again as they were rudely interrupted by Agnes. Her full name was Hurricane Agnes and she had already started to rip her way through the United States. People coming from the UK were, in the main, cosseted by such natural phenomena. On one of the band's days off, they visited the Everglades. Agnes was still in full swing, so they were some of the hardy few who ventured in. As they were going across a bridge, they noticed a beautifully coloured bird by the water's edge. They went down for a closer look, and when they got down there, they came face to face with a baby alligator that had its mouth wide open. It was a timely reminder that they were in a dangerous place and, in fact, they did see some of the bigger variety from the safety of their craft later on. Due to the extreme conditions, they got a drenching, but when the sun emerged as they made their way out, it revealed three steaming Brits! It wasn't all play, though, as they were doing a fair amount of radio promotions. They were getting the Groundhogs' message across, but the tour was short and the country was vast.

It made sense to fly wherever they could, but when they left Florida for a gig with Black Sabbath in Virginia the following day, they soon realised that going by air didn't provide all the answers. Even though it was only a few hundred miles in distance, they made several stops to the extent that it seemed, to them, more like a gloried bus route. Furthermore, landing and taking off in the wake of the Hurricane exacerbated everybody's frayed nerves! Tony remembers he was in the toilet of the plane when he started hearing a harmonica: 'At first, I thought, 'ah fuck, I'm really losing it', until I heard the pilot say, 'I'm going to stop playing now as it's a bit turbulent up ahead and I might knock my teeth out' – his humour helped take the edge off the discomfort.'

The next stop was Washington, which was 200 miles away, and because both Tony and Ken were not really up to flying, they decided to ask Dave to drive them (by this time, the storm has passed). They hadn't travelled far before encountering flooded roads. At one point, the water was getting too high for comfort and a policeman approached their car and said, 'That dam up there is ready to blow', and directed them out of the area. They later made their way to Pittsburgh for the Three Rivers gig supporting Alice Cooper. Ken recalls the misery: 'We were stuck there for three days; the water came up to the fourth floor of our hotel. Luckily, our van with the gear was in a high-rise car park.' The Cooper gig was pulled and so was the following day's gig with Black Sabbath and Humble Pie in Akron, Ohio.

A few days later, they made their way to Canada, where they played the famous Maple Leaf Gardens, Toronto, with Humble Pie. They also played The Forum in Montreal with Marriott's men. They finished off their mini-tour of Canada with a headlining gig at St Katherine's Ice Hockey Arena. Ken was glad to get to Canada because the food improved dramatically. As luck would have it – or not, as the case turned out – the tour was extended in order for them to appear at the Pocono Music Festival in Long Pond, Pennsylvania. Appearing with them were such luminaries as ELP and Three Dog Night (who were massive in the US), as well as old friends Edgar Winter, Humble Pie and Black Sabbath. An estimated 200,000 people gathered for the event. The crowds were so great that they could only get in by helicopter, so they had all their first experience in this mode of transport. It was the biggest gig they had ever played.

This time, Mother Nature worked for them. They were booked as the second act on the opening day on 8 July. Claire Hammill's low-key opening worked perfectly for the band – Claire is a singer-songwriter from the UK and, at the time, had just released her first album on Island Records. As they went on stage, the vastness of the crowd had a positive effect on Pete, who was glad that the din drowned the sound of his knocking knees. By now, they had relented and started playing material from *Who Will Save The World* such as 'Music Is The Food Of Thought' and 'The Grey Maze'. The set was well received, but as they came off, Tony felt a drop of rain on his head; strangely, the stage was uncovered. Within minutes, the heavens opened and it wasn't long before the festival was stopped until the evening. This was a stroke of luck for the band because the controversy over this event led to the band appearing on news broadcasts, so it was good publicity they didn't expect, all over the States – with respect to Claire Hammill, the Hogs were more representative of the festival. However, that's when their luck ran out!

The day after the festival, they stayed over and went horse riding at the suggestion of roadie Dave. There was an Indian Reservation shop at the stables and it had long lines of cowboy hats and riding boots. Tony treated himself to a Native American hat. He had never actually been on a horse before and the whole band were shocked when they saw them. They were huge beasts! Ken opted out, but Tony, Pete, Pete the roadie, Dave the roadie and a woman from the stable climbed on board their mounts. In the cold light of day, it was a dangerous thing to do, if only because a horse can sense when there's a novice aboard. They broke into a canter and Tony's hat went west; however, it cannot have been too bad an experience, as the next day, they went again.

Tony realised after a while that the horse he was riding (Senator) was mates with the horse that roadie Pete was riding – he relates what happened next:

> Pete's horse was always lagging behind and Senator would wait for him; then, when the others had gone on ahead too far, he would rush to catch up. Pete's horse was lagging and I noticed that the others had gone around a tight bend in the track. I thought, 'I know what's going to happen next'. As I turned around to tell Pete to hold on tight around the bend, I managed to hold on as they cantered round the corner, but Pete fell off. I had no control of this animal, but the others were waiting and I managed to tell them Pete had come off. They all went back, but Senator had different ideas. He started to bolt towards the direction of the freeway and I was getting battered by all the branches of trees along the way. I decided to jump off. I waited as long as I

could for my horse to slow and then I leaped off. When I hit the floor, I heard a crack. I looked up and my wrist was at right angles; I thought I'd dislocated it. I put my elbow around a tree and gave the hand a pull, but it hurt like fuck.

In fact, he'd broken his wrist. They made their way to the General Hospital of Monroe County, unaware that, due to the extension of the tour, Tony was not covered by medical insurance. It never occurred to anyone in the new organisation to renew it. Tony stressed to the doctor to do a good job and he ended up with plaster up to his shoulder. During his two-day stay in his double room, he was entertained courtesy of his roommate, who had paid extra for a television set. The bill came to $237 and the tour that they had sought after for so long was prematurely ended in the worst of circumstances. The plaster was so comprehensive he could only walk with the support of a broom handle!

The rest of the tour was cancelled and it denied them visits to big cities like Chicago and Detroit. As Pete recalls, things might have gone better: '*Who Will Save The World* was just outside the Hot 100 of albums. It just needed more touring and we might have got into it. After that, who knows, but we should have done more to promote the album.'

As he flew home, Tony had something else on his mind – what he should do with Ken.

Chapter 10 - The Emperor's New Clothes

> The time with Ken was special because it was three people with different ways of doing it, but doing it together.
> Tony McPhee describing the unique chemistry of the band

> It is an extraordinarily good record that covers a wide expanse of ideas and sound.
> *Melody Maker*'s review of *Hogwash*

The first thing that Tony did when he got back to the UK was go to Addenbrooks Hospital. He simply couldn't live with the plaster job that the Monroe Hospital had done. They reduced his plaster to more manageable proportions, at least to the point where he dispensed with the broom handle. The question of Ken's tenure in the band was uppermost in his mind. In the weeks to come, he constantly wrestled with the problem.

Tony's broken wrist didn't completely incapacitate him, however, as he was offered the chance to produce an album. Wilf Pine had signed a group called Dancer to World Wide Artists. Wilf had heard some of the material that would make up the album *Tales From The Riverbank* and he was impressed. In typical style, he drove the band in his white Rolls Royce to Olympic Studio. The band recall that Tony 'imposed strict discipline' in the studio. They recorded a 15-minute version of Soft Machine's 'Why Am I So Short?', which features Anthony Minghella on Mellotron.[35] Wilf came up with the idea of naming one of the tracks 'Mac's Café'; this was intended as the single. But there were issues with the album. Wilf Pine went berserk when he heard they had taken 22 hours to record just the title track. But the final straw in cancelling the album's release was that, soon after it was finished, the band split up. On the positive side, it was the first time that Tony had access to a synthesizer, part of the equipment Dancer had been using before the band fell apart. Being unable to play his guitar, he started dabbling with it and he was impressed. This would prove to add another string to Tony's bow.

The Moog synthesizer was very popular in the early 70s and it was the only brand on the market. However, by 1972, other makes of synthesizer were readily available and Tony started investigating them, especially ARPs, as he felt more comfortable with them over Moogs.

Even though he wasn't a keyboard player, he was fascinated by the array of sounds that could be made. Furthermore, it had completely altered his way of creating music, as he told Ray Hammond of *Melody Maker*: 'I like to write my material on keyboards rather than guitar because I'm so familiar with the guitar that I find it limiting.' He still retained his method of looking for unusual chord sequences, though.

By the summer of 1972, Wilf Pine was the sole manager of the band. Patrick Meehan Junior had negotiated a deal which saw WWA go public. They were now part of the Hemdale Leisure Corporation, which was owned by actor David Hemmings and a producer called John Daly. Hemdale had become the biggest independent group in the UK entertainment industry.[36] The Meehan's offered some of the top bands around, including Yes (not for long) and Black Sabbath. They were now seriously wealthy and it was decreed that WWA would have autonomous status within the Hemdale Empire. Meehan Junior decided that Wilf Pine would become manager of the Groundhogs, Gentle Giant, Stray and the Edgar Broughton Band!

Meanwhile, Tony returned to the problem of whether Ken would stay or go. This was further complicated by Ken's several bust-ups with Patrick Meehan after the American tour. On one occasion, Meehan was giving the road crew grief at a gig before Ken told him to back off. Another time, Meehan had a go at Ken for wandering around New York. He told him: 'You don't do that, just call a limo.' His riposte was succinct: 'Listen, mate, I come from Bristol. Heavy people don't worry me as we have plenty of those back home.'

The tension between the management and Ken settled the score for Tony, who concluded that Ken had messed up and completely blown it in the States. A brief conversation between Tony and Wilf settled it. Tony recalls: 'I told Wilf that I couldn't handle Ken anymore – he had to go. I knew the drummer from Egg and said we might be able to poach him!' Thus began a big scramble to get him! In fact, Tony had already sounded out Clive Brooks as to whether he would be interested. It was good timing as Egg had already split up. It was down to Wilf Pine to tell Ken: 'We think you should leave the band.' Pete Cruickshank wasn't in the office that day, but he recalls conversations with Tony on the subject: 'Tony did mention Ken's possible departure several times. I recall that the doctor told Ken he shouldn't be on the road when he got his medication on the US tour. In that final period of the US tour, he was difficult to handle; nobody wanted to travel with him and even the roadies avoided him. I agreed he had to go.' It was clear to all that Ken wasn't going to make a miracle recovery. But what did he think about Ken's replacement? 'I wouldn't have considered Clive, not because he wasn't a good drummer, but because he was too clockwork.'

Once back home, it wasn't long before Ken started having visitations from the road crew, who were trying to get some of the gear back that he had 'stored'. He knew his days in the band were done, so he kept some bits and pieces he thought he was owed. He was holding back the gear as a negotiating tool, but didn't withhold enough to keep the band off the road.

In spite of the tough reputation of the Meehan and Pine organisation, Ken Pustelnik was surprised with what happened next, as he remembers: 'The next thing I know, I got a letter from their solicitor demanding money from me. I ignored that crap. I thought if a lightweight hippy could put them down, their reputation would be shattered. The truth is that, by then, I didn't care. We had all these ideals and it was reflected in our lyrics, but as far as I was concerned, we were running with the enemy.'

It's true that Ken wasn't always the easiest person in the band to get along with and he could be awkward – he was the first to admit it: 'People would come up to me and ask me to sign things. I'd tell them to go away as I wasn't working. I knew they'd think, 'What an unfriendly bastard!' When I'm off duty, nobody owns me, so if they queued up outside the stage door after the gig, I'd sign all the things they had. No problem. I will not compromise my morals for anything.' It was clear that Ken was into drugs and the rest of the band weren't. But he was disciplined in his drug use and felt that it had nothing to do with the band as long as he still performed on stage: 'Drugs were part of the hippy scene. I thought acid was evil. I couldn't have played while taking bad drugs. I had to be healthy. Drugs were a token. My music was serious and I lived for the few moments it all clicked into place.'

There is still no doubt that he was a powerhouse performer and that nobody quite played the drums like him! Pete Cruickshank is very grateful for the part that Ken played in the Groundhogs: 'My playing would never have been the way it was if it wasn't for Ken. His approach to the drums made me go places I had never gone before or since!' Tony McPhee had another way of saying the same thing: 'The time with Ken was special because it was three people with different ways of doing it, but doing it together.'

The management put out a cover story that Ken's departure was due to 'musical differences'. Thus began the three decades of stories that Ken didn't like the *Who Will Save The World* album and yearned for the return to *Split*! In September 1972, headlines appeared in the music press along the lines of 'Groundhogs Split Amicable'. For Pete, this was a dark period: 'I thought the band were in deep trouble. Tony couldn't play for three months, we had changed management, a large chunk of the American tour had been blown away by the weather and Ken had left the band. All of a sudden, I was on my own and it had a huge impact on me. It felt, to me, like impending doom. It's the kind of thing that was on my mind every day when I woke up. I realised I had to make a big decision about staying in the band. But I had nothing else to go to, so I stayed and bit the bullet. I know that changed me a lot inside.'

That this classic lineup had something unique cannot be disputed; Tony himself had spelt out the consequences of a parting of the ways sometime before. In an interview in *NME* with James Johnson in 1971, he was quite candid: 'At the moment, we have a kind of unwritten rule between us so that we have a way of dealing with each other. If one of us left, the group would collapse because nobody could fill in. We could only reappear as something completely different.' Tony's words turned out to be prophetic; the Groundhogs never had another purely instinctive lineup that had such commercial success, but there's no doubt Tony played/recorded good music with the Groundhogs afterwards. *The Virgin Illustrated Encyclopaedia Of Rock* flies the flag for later lineups of the band: '(I) prefer Anderson/Jones for the live lineup … I heard Tony play some Hogs numbers with The Gibraltans & Fish the other day and they were rocking … better than the original lineup by loads.'

Tony McPhee first met Clive Brooks on the Groundhogs' late 1971 tour of the UK when his band Egg supported them. He got on well with him, so it was no surprise when he suggested to Pete that he be Ken's replacement (no other drummer was considered). Tony had a good laugh with Egg and he recalls a trick he played on their bass player because he consistently got on everyone's nerves: 'We were playing at some gig where there was an internal telephone system. So I phoned up the room where the band were. Clive answered the phone and passed it to Montgomery Campbell, Egg's bass player:

'Is Montgomery Campbell there?' I asked.
He passed the phone to him. 'Hello', said Campbell.

I said, 'Are you Montgomery Campbell?'
'Yes, I am', he replied.
'Are you known as Mont?'
'Yes, I am' came the reply.
So I said, 'I am going to break your fucking legs!'

Clive told me later that he really believed it and was shitting himself for the rest of the tour.'

At the time of joining the band, Clive Brooks had played the drums for eight years. Egg had been his first name band and he was in that band for three years. He told Ray Telford of *Sounds*: 'My style developed itself fully when I was with Egg. Everything was on a fairly rigid musical level and I reckon only about 10% of the material had any room for improvisation. Basically, the group broke up when the bass player (Mont) decided he couldn't work any longer in a rock group.' Obviously, it was going to be a different proposition playing in the Groundhogs as they were a completely different type of band. But Brooks was ready for the opportunity of more musical freedom and the space to breathe. For the record, he played a Hayman kit both live and in the studio.

Tony liked Clive Brooks' style of drumming. His reason was crystal clear: 'He was a very basic drummer. It was different to Ken, who used to fly all over the place. I wanted to change the direction of the band. It turned out he was a little bit too basic, but he was very good.' Pete Cruickshank recalls that the choice of Clive Brooks was a strange one: 'I didn't really like Egg, though they were good musicians. They were into time signatures and everything worked out beforehand and we were the complete opposite.' It was obvious that Tony was fired up again and relished the challenge. Brooks didn't have much time to prepare after he accepted Tony's offer to join the band. It was hard for him despite the fact that they musically gelled. Brooks told *Penetration* magazine how he found it at the time: 'It was awkward at first because the first thing we had to do when I joined was an album and it was very difficult. I wish that we'd done a tour first.' After the struggle of recording *Who Will Save The World* at De Lane Lea, Tony decided to record at Advision Studios. The change meant the relationship with Martin Birch was ended. However, the studio engineer there was just as good. His name was Martin Rushent.

Tony's arm was in plaster for a total of three months. He had already started writing the new material before the plaster came off with the help of the Mellotron. And to his immense relief, he felt the wrist had made a good recovery. With his songwriting approach being slightly atypical due to his arm, he also chose a novel approach to writing subject matter. When a journalist asked Tony what the next album was going to be about, he got a strange reply: 'It's going to be about rubbish.' Tony had always been into puns and wordplay, but this album was going to be the mother of them! The title of the new album was to be *Hogwash*! It was going to be his desired follow-up to *Split*.

In September 1972, they entered Advision Studios to record the new album. The opener is important as it sets the tone for the rest of the album. The intriguingly titled 'I Love Miss Ogyny' had its origins in Tony's dictionary surfing, as he scanned for interesting words. The moment he saw the word misogynist, he realised he could use a lot of puns: 'I thought it's strange that the word isn't 'Mr Ogynist'. I got an idea and I rattled off a lot of contradictory lyrics. As a result, it was easy to write.' The subject matter inspired Tony to go deeper and darker to the point where he even references murder. The delivery is so convincing that one may mistake it for being autobiographical. The first four lines set the tone:

The days that you're gone, I can't stand the silence
The hours that you're here, I can't stand your presence
The starlight that shone from your eyes in the beginning
Now blinds me with hate for you and all women

To accompany these brooding lyrics, he found some great licks on his famous tape library of bits and pieces that he had accumulated. The opening has a particularly haunting and mournful quality to it. They seemed to have lost their improvisational element somewhat, perhaps as a result of Clive Brooks steadying the ship, so to speak. Interestingly, Pete's Zemaitis bass exhibits a lot more high-end than had been discernible on *WWSTW*. He loved that instrument, as he recalls: 'It had such an individual sound and was very easy to play. Furthermore, I bought it for cheaper than a Fender Jazz bass and another bonus was that mine was custom-made. My bass also looked very different to all the others. I don't have it anymore as I gave it away to my son, Paul, as an incentive for passing his O and A levels.' The opening track is especially poignant for Pete as he explains: 'The bass behind the opening vocal is lovely and also Tony's patterns in the middle give the bass more of a free rein. I just went for broke.' But these moments were few and far between: 'On the whole, I thought we were getting too technical, whereas before, we had done a lot of things on instinct. Until recently, we were a blues band and now we were playing on technique and not feel.'

The next track is 'You Had A Lesson', also known to Tony as 'You Adolescent'. The song is about Tony's brother-in-law, Daryl Payne: 'He was a typical teenager with the whole world on his shoulders.' Tony had frequently borrowed Daryl's white Fender Stratocaster when he started playing *Split* live. Daryl was a part-time roadie with the band, but he fell in with a bad crowd and died very young a few years later after he injected strychnine-laced heroin. The track was destined to be a live staple and features some punchy Mellotron from Tony.

Tony's word games continue; the 'Ringmaster' is, in fact, one of the new toys that Tony had discovered. The ring modulator is an electric device that is good for creating percussive noises like clanging bell sounds. He was keen to use it on the album: 'I asked Clive to play a drum solo. He was surprised by my request, as he didn't have one. He said, 'Fucking Hell' – it's just about audible on the album. So he played one there and then and Tony added the ring modulator sounds to it.' Tony's love of gadgets was coming into its own with the plethora of electronic devices that were being invented at the time. One critic even called it the first 'space-age' drum solo.

The next track is straight down the line with no puns, word games or hidden meanings. Tony hadn't forgotten the house in Memphis that he kept returning to on days off during the US tour. '3744 James Road' is his tribute to Jon Scott and his generous hospitality.[37] But it's also about the trip in general, with its trials and tribulations. Tony's manic count-in belies the way in which the music starts off sedately. The main riff was another from his famous tape; he decided to make things more interesting by playing it live in the studio without overdubs: 'I'm in awe of guitarists who play riffs with their thumb and do other things with their fingers (Bert Jansch and Blind Lemon Jefferson are two that he admired). I could never figure it out properly. But what I could do was a simple thing with my thumb.' The opening sounds a little plodding, but becomes more anthemic when the main infectious riff kicks in.

The track didn't completely win over the band because Pete Cruickshank felt that he didn't have much to do in the plodding sections. Also, lyrically, he wasn't wedded to the house like Tony because if they had any spare time, he would go back to Canada to Jan. There are some great moments on this one, including the fantastic guitar solo from Tony. But he was concentrating on the drum sound just as much as the guitars when they recorded it: 'I always wanted to get a drum sound like John Bonham. He had the best drum sound I ever heard in my life – it was in your face! The drummer in the pit at the London Palladium had a fabulous sound. It was just two stereo microphones and that's what we tried to do on this track.' Out of all the tracks on the album, this was the track that worked best in a live setting.

The opener on side two is 'Sad Is The Hunter' and it's interesting to note that the first six letters spell 'sadist'. This song is a born barnstormer for live performance and features two guitar solos. The song reflects Tony's anti-fox hunting stance. He first put down a moral stance on 'Junkman' on *Split* and was keen to carry on the trend with this album. It brought out his playfully devious side: 'I like to put things in that might not be seen at first but are there to be discovered later.' His old friend Dave Wetton was heavily involved with the fledgling Hunt Saboteurs, who were yet to organise nationally. The general public thought this was both disgusting and cruel, and this sentiment was growing. At an anti-hunt meeting that was reported on television, Tony noticed that somebody had 'Sadist The Hunter' on his t-shirt. Perhaps he was a fan of the track? The first and third verses are worth quoting in full as the first verse gives a historical base before the third verse likens hunting to a game:

Read about the Spanish Inquisition,
Read about the witch hunts of those days,
Things have only changed in outward appearance,
Cruelty is integral in man's ways.

Hunting is the vehicle for some men,
To satisfy their baser needs,
Sport is the label for this depravity,
A distortion of the need to feed.

'S'one Song', or its alternative title 'Swan Song', is split into two, and in the first part, Tony 'dies', thus making the raunchy second part his swan song. The lyrics reveal a deep resentment of his school days. Implicit in this is the fact that Tony was bullied at school. These lyrics can pretty much be read at face value as they recall those unhappy days.

The penultimate track on the album is the moody and magnificent 'Earth Shanty'. It's a curious title and came about when Tony thought, 'There's a sea shanty, so why isn't there an earth shanty?' It's a question that he was so convinced about that he created one. The big Mellotron opening creates a stunning ambience and this is supplemented by the rushing of the wind, a sound that Tony achieved on the ARP synthesizer. In fact, it's one of Tony's best melodies. Martin Rushent suggested that Tony use the Yamaha acoustic guitar on this one, working effectively in providing a gentle backing to the vocal as the wind effect dies down. Along with 'I Love Miss Ogyny', this track is one of Pete Cruickshank's favourites because of the more organic feel to it: 'I played the intro with the Gibson and got a nice, rounded sound. After that, I used the Zemaitis with a lot more high-end. With regard to the album, I thought, playing-wise, it was less of me.'

Towards the end of the album, Tony started to think in *Split* mode. He had ended that album with an acoustic blues, but this time, it would be different. He decided to write an original song. His thoughts turned to John Lee Hooker, so he set about writing a song about him. He called it 'Mr Hooker, Sir John'. Back in Detroit, Hooker's hometown, they called him Sir John Lee Hooker, so Tony decided to rearrange it. The song is a moving tribute to him and it is delivered with conviction:

> Your music is timeless as a mountain and as earthy as the clay.

However, as a general point, some people were still hearing things that were not there. The word games were beginning to have an effect on some fans. Tony was told by one, 'I didn't know Hooker was a surgeon.' On the meanings of the lyrics, he was just as forthright: 'It's like saying that people mean every song they sing. That would make it too limiting if true.'

Tony was still applying his technological knowledge to further the band's sound, as well as making life easier. One of his favourite guitars was a very early Gibson SG. The original model was fitted with a side-action tremolo arm, which he decided to remove. In its place, he fitted a re-designed scratch plate in order to include some effects of his own. One of these ideas was a pressure switch that enabled him to achieve a wah-wah effect. Another was to use one channel of the stereo output jack in order to control a special effects unit. This enabled him to operate the special effects locally and do without foot pedals. It was called a Synthi Hi Fli and it was situated on top of the amp. It was marketed to guitarists and consisted of a main processing unit mounted on a stand. It had an impressive complement of effects, including a ring modulator, a vibrato, two phaser modes, three wah-wah modes and several other controls. He would soon have a chance to test his new equipment. A big tour was beckoning!

Wilf Pine organised a big tour of the UK to promote the new album and full-page adverts were placed in the music papers.[38] Fellow World Wide Artists Gentle Giant and Stray were appearing at most gigs, with Badger also appearing for selected dates. The tour was timed to fall in nicely with the release of the new album. *Hogwash* was released on 10 November, just in time for the fans to get their hands on it before the first gigs.

The press were very positive about the album. *New Musical Express* called it a 'fine album' and heaped praise on the new dimension of the band: 'Tony McPhee has really come to terms with both Mellotron and synthesizer and knows how to use them to dynamic effect.' 'I Love Miss Ogyny' and '3744 James Road' are cited as outstanding tracks. Even the more pop-orientated papers were positive. '*Thank Christ* is still the best album the Hogs have made. But *Hogwash* comes a close second. The addition of synths and Mellotrons has made the band far more palatable than they have been for the past couple of albums, and if they keep this up, there's a good chance that they will add thousands to their current horde of worshippers', gushed *Record Mirror*. *Disc* paid the band a decent compliment: 'You can never predict which way the music is going to go next. I think the Groundhogs are searching for something different.'

Across the pond, *Rolling Stone* was equally praising, and like Lester Bangs before him, Gordon Fletcher was just as mystified: 'Why have the Groundhogs yet to make it big in America? Bands with half their talent, taste and heavy-metal intensity seem to be top billed at Madison Square Garden every weekend.' Fletcher was convinced that *Hogwash* was their best album.

On the eve of the tour, Tony told James Johnson of *NME* that the addition of Clive Brooks had injected a fresh enthusiasm (as far as Tony was concerned) into proceedings: 'I'm pleased with the way the new album and the new numbers have worked out. On *Who Will Save The World,* I was really striving to write lyrics – when, obviously, I'd prefer it if they came naturally. This time, though, I got out that notion I'd had about discarding anything that sounded remotely like anything we'd done previously. I found that the album didn't take very long to make.' The confidence in the album clearly translated to the prospect of the tour working out just as well. For the first time, Tony was touring with a Mellotron and ARP synthesizer and he had ideas on how to project them properly – he wanted them to be put through the PA rather than a guitar amp. As a consequence, there was going to be more variety and textures projected to the audience.

The opening gig of the tour was at Birmingham Town Hall on Friday 17 November 1972. Jerry Gilbert of *Sounds* was there to witness proceedings: 'The crowd surged to the front of the hall to greet the new Groundhogs, just as they would be doing at all the other venues on the tour … For Tony McPhee – notwithstanding all those fan letters that constantly exult his talents on a comparative level with Hendrix and Clapton – is the new brains behind British rock music. And in a day when such accolades are two a penny, I would add that I do not make such a statement lightly.' They presented their most blazing material: *Split* in its entirety, '3744 James Road', 'Soldier', 'I Love Miss Ogyny' and 'You Had A Lesson'. They ventured and prospered with 'Earth Shanty' and 'Mr Hooker, Sir John' reaffirmed their roots, changing the mood nicely. Clive changed the band dynamic on stage for the better, again from Tony in *Sounds*: 'In this band, because Clive is a clearer drummer, the lyrics seem to be clearer. In rehearsals, I've managed to hear every word and people are beginning to take notice.' Gilbert wrote a very positive piece on the band, but the headline, 'The Emperor's New Clothes', was puzzling to some.

Wilf had taken the initiative and instigated something that Tony had probably never thought about; it raised eyebrows in some quarters. The Groundhogs had stage clothes! All the band members had boots custom-made at Granny Takes A Trip in the King's Road, London (Pete still has his!). Unfortunately for Tony, his pair never fit properly. Pete Cruickshank had a cream suit made, as the colour always worked for him. Pete recalls the choice of stage clothes was a strange one: 'I wore a frilly shirt from Geoff Banks, London. I thought the management were trying to make us something that we weren't. I never felt comfortable with them. This concept didn't suit us, as we were not an image band; the whole thing confused me. It seemed to me they were trying to make us into pop stars.' Tony had a velvet shirt and trousers. They never fitted either, leading to some hairy moments on stage.

It was at Brunel University where the stage was so high a chair was used as an impromptu leg-up: 'I put my leg on the chair and heard a ripping sound. I thought maybe it didn't split, but when I got up on stage, I felt a draught. I nodded to the roadie and backed up to the amplifier so he could put a safety pin in. But velvet doesn't lend itself to that very well and it quickly ripped some more.' The shirt was no better because there were no buttons on the front, so he had to put it on over his head. By the end of a gig, the shirt had practically stuck to him with all the sweat, so Pete and Clive would have an arm each in order to pull it off. At least the most undignified moments of the tour went, in the main, unseen by the fans.

On 1 December, they played at the Manchester Free Trade Hall. Lifelong fan Steve Thompson was there and he vividly recalls the excitement of the event:

> The electric hiss and humming coming from the speakers and the power of the amps were just awesome. On they came to rapturous applause: Tony, Pete and Clive. I moved to the front to get some close-ups of Tony in full swing. Tonight was the first time I'd heard the haunting song 'I Love Miss Ogyny', which had the theatre spellbound with its lyrics, especially as it merged into 'You Had A Lesson', a medley of 'Thank Christ For The Bomb' and the *Split* suite. My personal moment of the night was the rendition of 'Earth Shanty' with Tony playing his synthesizer like a god on stage. This was the Groundhogs at their best and, I think, the best concert ever. A final encore brought them on for 'Cherry Red', of course, and as we left the theatre, everybody was stunned by the power of the performance.

The tour was turning out to be a value-for-money trip. Stray were getting good reports and the prodigiously talented Gentle Giant would have given anybody a run for their money. There was no taking it easy on this tour for the Groundhogs. But things got a lot harder for Tony at the Greens Playhouse date in Glasgow. The dressing rooms were directly below the stage and got very warm. It was just the sort of area that gave a birthday or two to vermin. Tony noticed there were heaps of raw rat poison in all corners of the room. It wasn't the best of atmospheres before going on stage.

However, Tony's pre-gig preparation was interrupted by a loud bang. He takes up the story: 'There was a raked stage and our PA was quite high; I noticed in the sound check that it was leaning over a bit. I thought the whole lot had gone over, but it turned out that Stray had set off a thunder flash in a dustbin for maximum effect. Our roadies, Charlie and Pete, came down with my Mellotron and all the keys were black. All the soot from the ceiling had rained down on the keys.' Luckily, after much cleaning and testing, it worked, but no thanks to Stray, who were oblivious to all the problems they had caused.

Tony had been keen to bring the Mellotron to the live arena, but it gave him constant technical problems – soot raining down from the ceiling notwithstanding. The original models had eight-second tapes. The idea was that the springs in the workings pulled the tape back down again at the end of the cycle. However, this didn't happen every time, so he had to take the front off in order to pull the string back whenever it got stuck. He even had the manager of the Mellotron come down, but when Tony demonstrated the problem, it worked perfectly! But everybody who ever used one cursed its unreliability.

One of the key numbers that showcased the Mellotron was 'Earth Shanty' and it was one of the highlights of the show. But Tony suffered a crucial lack of timing with the new technology at the Caird Hall, Dundee. It was clear that it was one of those moments of reflection, as he told Jerry Gilbert of *Sounds*: 'I couldn't quite get the synthesiser together – there was a slight mismatch between synthesiser and amp, and in 'Earth Shanty', just as it went down to the quiet bit, someone shouted in a broad Dundee accent, 'Have you finished tuning up yet, Jimmy?' It brought me right down. I didn't know I could be deflated so easily, although it's a good thing really because it gives you something to strive for.'

While on tour, there was a strange incident that is burned in Pete's memory: 'Clive got on well with us, but one day, he did something really stupid. We were travelling in the Zodiac somewhere in Wales. Alan Laycock was driving with Clive in the front seat. Tony was in the back and I was reading *Lord Of The Rings*. Suddenly, we spun round, hit the kerb and we finished up on the other side of a single-lane road. Our wheel was buckled and we were all stunned.' Tony also remembers the event: 'I heard Alan say to Clive that the handbrake was useless to stop the car in an emergency. I knew what Clive was going to do next; he put the car in neutral and pulled the handbrake up.' When they got out of the car, Clive just said: 'Don't say anything!' If a vehicle had been coming the other way, they could have been badly injured or even killed. But Clive was unpredictable. On another trip, Tony remembers an incident when a crow hit the windscreen and was obviously killed – Clive just laughed. It just seemed a callus thing to do.

The tour came to its conclusion with a gig at the Rainbow, London, on 22 December. The year 1972 had been one of considerable difficulties for the band. However, by the end of the year, most of those problems appeared to have melted away. The new drummer had settled in well and they had recorded an album that was up there with their best. Furthermore, the release was met with enthusiastic reviews! It was depressing, though, when it failed to chart – the band were extremely disappointed. Tony put the failure down to *Who Will Save The World* because, even though it made the top ten, many of their fans melted away after buying it, not liking the new direction. The album did, however, make it into Kid Jenson's chart on the famous Radio Luxemburg.

Even though the band were doing well, it was clear to Pete Cruickshank that this was a different band without Ken Pustelnik, as he recalls: 'I got used to Ken's unconventional way of playing and it was difficult to get used to Clive Brooks. In the old band, I was like a hinge on the door between the other two. On stage, somebody would instigate a speed change and the others would be into it instinctively. I think we lost a lot of spontaneity with Clive.'

As they went into 1973, the band had something they could build on, but Tony was already laying down the foundations for something else that would take him away from the band, albeit temporarily.

Chapter 11 – The Studio That Mac Built

> Out of all the artists I managed, Mac was the most outstanding. He played better guitar than Clapton, Iommi and all the others.
> Wilf Pine

> I feel that I have something valid to say outside the framework of the Groundhogs and I want to get it out of my system.
> Tony McPhee in 1973

During the recording of *Hogwash*, Tony had been very impressed with the overall sound of the album. So much so, he told engineer Martin Rushent: "I'd love to get this sound at home.' Rushent's reply was, 'Why don't you then?' That's when I decided to buy the setup at the old De Lane Lea studio, which I had heard was up for sale. It cost me £5000. I got a lot of equipment and some of it was historical. Included in the deal was the original machine that The Animals' 'House Of The Rising Sun' was recorded on.' He heard that the equipment was being sold off, so he went for it. He had some recording facilities before this, but they were limited to Revox machines that could only deliver to demo standard. The deal for the 8-track equipment was done, and in January 1973, the roadies were ferrying parts of it to his house in Haverhill for installation in his garage-turned studio. His ambition was never to record a Groundhogs album in London again!

Usually, Tony was quite a mild-mannered, unassuming guy who just got on with being the leader of a rock band. However, in January 1973, he gave a remarkable interview to Jerry Gilbert of *Sounds*. Perhaps Tony was still smarting from the disappointing sales of *Hogwash*. But when the name of Eric Clapton was mentioned, he went out of character: 'I get the feeling I'm just a nuisance; that nobody wants to admit that I'm here. I know full well I can match any of those guys and that what I'm writing about is above it in a way because I'm trying to get across something that's veering away from the normal and I'm just getting the feeling that not many people will accept it … I'm being dismissed on all counts because it's just down to trendy names.' It was clear that Tony was frustrated by his lack of credit: 'When people said to me that they liked the Groundhogs' music, I thought, yes, Pete and Clive/Ken played on it, but it's my music!' It's now a question of whether being in a band could satisfy Tony's ambitions.

In February, they started gigging on the college and smaller venue circuit on the home front. It was on this tour that their relationship with some sections of the press turned sour. Previously, Tony's main complaint about the press was being ignored. Contrary to myth up until then, the coverage they received had been almost overwhelmingly good, certainly from *Thank Christ For The Bomb* onwards. However, it was around this time they started to receive negative, even vindictive notices. *Melody Maker* sent Geoff Brown to review the gig at the Stevenage Locarno. Although he was there to review the gig, he even found time to criticise their back catalogue! But it's hardly constructive stuff and is based on clichés: 'Their live programme has the consistency of a sea of wet cotton wool.' In one particularly destructive section, some good work from Tony is used to attack the fans by suggesting that the band's fans were lacking in ambition: 'But the Hogs devoted are faithful and several brief flashes of Tony McPhee's best guitar work gave ample evidence of just where their loyalties lie.' Wilf Pine became frustrated that his band were not getting a fair shake of the dice when it came to the press.

In early April, Tony appeared as a solo artist on the *Old Grey Whistle Test*. He was booked to fill in for the Country Joe McDonald, who cancelled at short notice. He played two acoustic blues numbers: 'Me And The Devil' and 'Write Me A Short Few Lines'. The latter was written by an early influence of Tony's – Fred McDowell. It was odd that Tony should have been on the show because, up to that point, the Groundhogs had never appeared on the show. Shortly after, they embarked on a short tour of Europe. The tour took in Denmark, France, Holland, Germany, Norway and Sweden. The tour was quite novel for Clive Brooks as he hadn't been abroad all that much. When they were in Norway, Clive was so excited by the huge amounts of snow, he frolicked in it. One local looking out at Clive turned round to Tony and said: 'Tourist!' But even Tony and Pete succumbed to the atmosphere as the band had a photo taken with snowballs in full *Gunfight At The OK Corral* pose.

The Groundhogs' new rock management, who were very much part of the show business elite, wasted no time in spending their money and Patrick Meehan Junior and his ex-employer Don Arden were no exceptions. It was visitations to their houses that Tony remembered very well. The self-made millionaire John Roles had previously owned Meehan's house. His bankruptcy enabled Meehan the chance to buy it and Tony was glad of it – he loved that house. The house was in Coulsdon, just south of Croydon and Tony's big night out was to play on the full-sized snooker table and slowly get pissed. Arden's house was called Shalom. One night, Tony was drinking Pernod and someone was spiking it with vodka; needless to say, Tony soon began acting the arsehole and became uncharacteristically aggressive, even offering John Fiddler of Medicine Head a fight 'outside', although he can't remember why. It was at this time when he first met Arden's young daughter for the first time. Sharon Arden later married and managed wildman Ozzy Osbourne and went on to become a big celebrity.

The touring was completed at the end of April and Tony took the band into his studio to do some sound checks for future albums, but he was also preparing to record his first solo album. Tony was very happy with the management situation: 'Being with Wilf was loads of fun; you felt impregnable with him. Nobody would mess you about while he was around. He was really sharp and he could suss situations very quickly. He wasn't popular with everybody, though. I remember we were playing a gig in Wales and I got to know Andrew Lauder, but he never came to see us. It was because he didn't like Wilf and he didn't like us going with him.' Wilf Pine thought Tony was a tremendous talent and he started to think of ideas to promote him. One of these ideas was to form a supergroup around Tony. No names were discussed because Pine soon had another idea and it concerned going out on his own, as Wilf recalls: 'I suggested that he do a solo album and tour. I told him he could do something with the blues and synthesizers. It was my idea to do something about fox hunting, as Tony was passionate about it. I wrote a cheque to cover four ARP 2600 synthesizers for him.'

With Tony about to embark on this ambitious project, it's incredible to think that he had a certain level of scepticism about synthesizers. In an interview with *Zig Zag* just after *Split* came out, he answered a question about bringing synthesizers into the act: 'I'm not really a weird noise freak. I think it's much better and cleverer to get a strange sound out of an ordinary instrument, which is why I admired Hendrix so much. He could make Moog noises with a guitar.' It would be easy to be critical of Tony, but the truth is, at that stage, not many could see the potential of the synthesizer. In fact, on all their early albums, Queen put 'No Synths Used' somewhere on the cover. It was only later they embraced them fully.

Tony's solo project more than troubled Pete Cruickshank; he was still reeling from all the changes initiated over the previous year: 'I thought the Groundhogs were being marginalised. It seemed to be going all one way as Wilf Pine seemed to concentrate on Tony. I wasn't too keen on Tony's project as the band would be off the road for a while.' It was also clear that he saw Ken as a counter-balancing force in the band: 'It was good to have everything not going in the same way. It's a healthy alternative.' During the coming solo period, Pete and Clive were put on a fixed fee, so they did have some money coming in.

Around this time, Tony was offered a session with an important singer/songwriter. His proficiency with a synthesizer was becoming known in the music world. The gig was with Donavan at Morgan Studios, London. The session was for his *Cosmic Wheels* album. Tony always demonstrated synthesized wind noises to illustrate the capabilities of the ARP. However, while he was waiting in reception at the studio, he heard a woman on the pay phone say, 'Rick (Wakeman) can't get his synth working, can you come down?' Tony thought, 'He's supposed to be a wizard! I should have told her I'll fix it for £100.'

However, Tony's knowledge of other synthesizer players was limited. He hadn't heard what the other trailblazers were doing with them. The only synths he'd really heard before were from pop bands like Chicory Tip. There was one thing he was certain about: 'I was positive a lot more could be done with them.' In retrospect, it was a good thing he had little idea what others were doing because he could make his own mark with it. To say that Tony was a little insular was an understatement. When somebody asked him if his album was going to be like Mike Oldfield's *Tubular Bells*, he would say he'd never even heard of it! However, Tony was not only going to play all the instruments on his album but he was going to produce and engineer it, all in a studio that he had built himself. It was going to be a true solo album and one that a major artist had never attempted before.

The benefits of owning a studio were many. It's certain that without his homespun facilities, the project would never have happened in the first place. But this way, Tony could get fully acquainted with the studio sound and even improve it before recording commenced. With expensive studio hours, that wasn't always possible. There was also an elimination of the embarrassment factor, as there were things he was loathe to try out in a foreign environment. This factor illustrates that sometimes he wasn't as confident in a studio as you might expect somebody with so much experience. At home, he could experiment to his heart's content. But probably the biggest factor in all of this is that Tony was the only one in the studio and was in complete control of things.

As Tony started to think about how to record the material he'd written, his inability to play the drums prevented him from fulfilling his dream of filling every musical role. When the Groundhogs had soundtested the studio in early May, Clive Brooks kept his drums set up in the studio for quite a while. During this time, Tony tried to get to grips with them. He did learn how to play the intro of Stevie Wonder's 'Superstition', but he gave up after that. He decided he would use a drum machine. The actual machine was a Bentley Rhythm Ace Drum Machine. These machines were in their infancy and they were crude things. The fact that he had never had any keyboard training was much less of a problem.

The centrepiece of the album was the 25-minute, four-part concept called 'The Hunt'. Apart from the obvious, the track imagines that man has failed to shake off the barbarism required to survive in the stone age. Additionally, hunting is seen as a ritual and portrayed as a sport, often 'played' by the wealthy gentry. It was this pomp and its service to those at the top of the British class system that Tony hated the most. While dabbling with the ARP, he found the perfect way to start the piece. 'The Hunt Part One' begins with the sound of yelping hounds. One thing is clear from the outset: the incredible atmosphere that's created. When the fanfare of the 'hunting horns' ushers in Tony's narration, then you know this is going to be special. The narration is important as it hits the listener on different levels about fox hunting but is also transfixed by the storyteller's delivery.

> Yelping hounds pack to form a Gorgon's head of gyrating tails ready to turn a stag's heart to stone at a single glance.
> Each dog has a pedigree that would fill a ream of paper as have their masters boasting generations of good breeding.
> Family trees with branches laden with the names of past landed gentry, their greatest contribution to the land being when they fall in their Autumn years, providing the earth with the same humus as their mongrel serfs.

The spoken section ends with the word 'lethal', which acts as the trigger for a huge synthesizer gambit. It's all very dramatic stuff and a fittingly aggressive synthesizer sound. The last section of the first part has Tony singing, including the line, 'No words could ever describe the hate I feel for these men'. At this stage, the drum machine comes in and the tempo increases. Tony explains: 'With the drum machine, I got a different rhythm by mixing 3/4 and 4/4 time signatures, which triggered the synths to follow that rhythm because they were all linked up.' The first part concludes with a good solo on the ARP. The first part didn't come easy or quickly, as Jerry Gilbert of *Sounds* outlines: 'Mac admitted that laying down the initial track was fairly boring, as well as being the hardest part of the exercise since the musician was working blind.' But Tony McPhee was a fast learner! 'The Hunt Part Two' starts off more laid back, but the ambience is no less sharp. Tony's narration is more inquisitive in nature. A welter of cascading synths accompanies this to mournful effect. The penultimate part begins with a most infectious riff and it also contains one of the most interesting sections, as Tony explains: 'I used the synths to sound like bongos, but by chaining the other synths, it had them at a tone just higher and lower to increase the effect.'

The final part is the most musically effective. This is mainly because Tony is really getting to grips with playing the ARPs, enhancing his technical ability, as opposed to using them for effects and soundscapes. As he admitted to Jerry Gilbert: 'There was a lot of trial and error, like deciding whether to put the synthesizer through an amplifier. But the last track only took me about a day, and by then, I felt the sound was right on every part as opposed to the initial part of the track, which took quite a while, so I ended up editing a bit on tape.' The synths are cleverly used as Tony builds layer on layer. Tony used the National Anthem at the end because he believed the Royal Family instigated the whole class system. However, he decided at the last minute to cut it down to a snippet because he didn't want to be in the listener's face. Wilf Pine wanted the longer version, but Tony won that argument!

With 'The Hunt' in the can, Tony set about recording the blues side. During the early part of the recording, Wilf phoned Tony and asked him for the titles of the songs. At that stage, he only had 'The Hunt' as a title, so he went into the garden and plucked the titles out of thin air there and then. He phoned him back to relay the information. However, he hadn't written any of the songs at that stage! So, he set about writing the music and then the lyrics around the titles he'd made up.

The first track is 'Three Times Seven' and it splits the path to adult life at 21 into three sections of seven. The first seven years is the child stage.

Years eight to 14 are adolescence and the final years end in adulthood. 'All My Money, Alimony' is another one of those interesting McPhee wordplays. The title was purely accidental and wasn't incriminating, as at that stage, Tony's marriage was okay. But another interesting aspect is that alimony – having to financially support an ex-wife after a separation or divorce – is an American word and wasn't very well known in the UK at the time, but, again, it's one of those word games. Perhaps Tony had a crystal ball, but the line, 'It didn't seem fair I should spend all my time working for you', seemed to foreshadow the breakdown of his marriage! The third track is titled 'Dog Me Bitch'. It features electric guitar. It was unfortunate because, for some McPhee watchers, the use of the word 'Bitch' in the title – a derogatory word for a woman – evidence that Tony didn't like women. In fact, they couldn't have been further from the truth. The final track is the curiously titled 'Take It Out'. This one is the weakest of the side and it's significant because Tony couldn't think of any words – which didn't happen very often – so it remained an instrumental, albeit a fiery one. The outstanding track of the blues side is 'Morning Eyes', a love song for a deceased girl. There's some great slide guitar on this one.

The synthesizer created possibilities unimagined before and yet there was an element of uncertainty that Tony had never faced previously in a studio, as he told Jerry Gilbert of *Sounds* when it was all over: 'I tried to keep it melodic in essence and to give it form and shape because it's easy to use the synthesizer purely to create an electronic sound.' The first few minutes of 'The Hunt' prove beyond doubt that Tony did exactly that. From start to finish, the whole album took less than six weeks. In retrospect, the album marshalled all of Tony's technical knowledge and ingenuity. He had always maintained he worked best under pressure. Jerry Gilbert brilliantly summed up the album as '1965 meets 1973'. The album was called *The Two Sides Of Tony (T.S) McPhee*!

Tony was happy with the music, but the sleeve wasn't totally to his liking. The inner sleeve featured a photo of a mother and a baby clutching a pound note – it clearly alluded to 'All My Money, Alimony'. Many people thought it was Tony's wife and son, but, in fact, they weren't people he knew at all. The other idea was the design by his eyes. One side of the cover has 'tears' coming down his face, which was supposed to represent the blues side; the computer printing on the other side represents the new technological side. Only the picture of the messy wiring on the inside irked him.

While Tony had been recording his solo album, Wilf Pine came up with a couple of stunts to garner some press attention to counter some of the negative coverage. The first one concerned Tony going to the US to make a movie with two major established stars. One of them was rumoured (by Pine) to be Dustin Hoffman. The film was going to be about a 20th-century wandering musician and was provisionally titled *The Wandering Minstrel*. The story appeared in several music papers. The second stunt concerned the alluring headlines in the 8 September edition of *Sounds*: 'McPhee Quits Groundhogs'. Wilf Pine is quoted as desperately trying to patch up the 'terrible disagreements' between Tony and the rest of the band. This particular story was clearly just a short-term stunt to keep the Groundhogs' name relevant; but it perhaps had some negative fallout. When the paper came out, Tony was in rehearsals for his solo tour. But amazingly, the Groundhogs had performed at the recent Kendal Festival (26 August). It was their first gig since April and they were rusty. Irene Reed of *Melody Maker* picked up on it: 'Tony's voice didn't carry much at all, and at times, he and Pete Cruickshank seemed to be having difficulty in staying in the same key.' It's incredible to think why Tony would want to fit in a one-off date for the band while in the middle of hectic preparations for his solo tour, other than the need for money. The album was released to coincide with the tour and *Melody Maker*'s Tony Stewart was enthusiastic: 'The album, in conclusion, is something of a minor masterpiece.'

On the eve of the tour, *Sounds* ran a punchy article with Tony that reiterated the headline of the previous week: 'Prisoner Of His Own Castle? Jerry Gilbert looks at Tony McPhee's decision to split the Groundhogs'. However, when perusing the article, the reader realises the headline overstates the situation, as it mentions future Groundhogs plans. The solo tour was limited to ten dates, with the opening gig at the Roundhouse, London, on 16 September. The format of the show was as follows: Tony would play on various guitars for the first hour, with the next hour showcasing his array of keyboards, which included the four ARPs and an RMI Electric piano. The centrepiece of the second half was 'The Hunt'. There wasn't much room for props, but Clive Brooks loaned Tony a shop mannequin on a turntable with mirrors on it. Tony thought the lights would have a positive effect, so it was placed behind him at all the gigs. The opening night was not without incident, though. Just after Tony had finished the first number in the first half, there was a bomb scare and the place was evacuated; the police let the audience come back in after 15 minutes. Tony is also pretty sure he knows who the culprit was and is still not amused.

It was at the Roundhouse that fans had the chance to experience the sheer intensity of 'The Hunt'. Tony used a touch plate on the drum machine to trigger the synthesisers, and during the first part, when he got to the word 'suffer' – which is the last part of his narration – he hit the plate and the synths and drums came in like a ton of bricks. Tony recalls the effect it had on him: 'When that happened and I heard the synths, I thought, 'Fucking hell!' Things went so well that there were times when I would have loved to have been in the audience myself!' Ray Telford of *Sounds* was there and he corroborates the excitement generated: 'T.S seems to utilise every aspect of his synthesizer and all the other boxes of tricks he plugs in and switches on. 'The Hunt', the longest piece performed of the set, drew possibly the most positive reaction and rightly so, for it demonstrated McPhee's complete mastery and unbounded possibilities of the synthesizer. Neither was there a feeling that technology was being substituted for music. He can sound tender, soft and melodic one second, and the next, punching out heavy riffs.'

Melody Maker's Dave Lewis was also at the gig: 'After the unscheduled interruption by the demon bomb hoaxer, McPhee launched dramatically into his electronic wizardry, strutting like a mad professor from one control panel to the other.' But there were some things he didn't like: 'There were some melodic moments, but some of it sounded like a jet plane passing low overhead and the glittering window-dresser's dummy with a spear revolving in the background was really very ham.' It seemed as if the reviewers were tripping over themselves to write a good review and *Record Mirror* hit the floor first: 'Those who had never seen him before were whispering what to expect. There was total respect. It was the sort of atmosphere normally reserved for legends of our times: a height that Tony is fast approaching. He is a really fine blues performer and the songs from his new album prove that he can compose good blues as well as perform them … Definitely one of the best acts I have heard for a long time.' Tony encored with a version of Cream's 'Crossroads' and everybody went home happy.

In the main, things went well, but not always. At one of the gigs, just before showtime, Tony was shaving, but he forgot to tighten the razor down and he ended up cutting himself several times. There was nothing else for it but to do the gig with plasters on his face. It was hardly the classic rock 'n' roll scenario! The final gig at St Albans was especially emotional and several fans told Tony later that it was very intense. Pete Cruickshank was at the gig: 'I was quite impressed with the show; it was very powerful. I didn't like the entire album, but I liked the first part of 'The Hunt' and it was well worked out. Looking back, I was surprised he never did another solo project.'

Tony played all parts on the tour; he set up all the gear and he had been in complete control of the proceedings so that nothing major went wrong on the whole tour. It was a complete success, but many Groundhogs fans were biting their nails because of Wilf Pine's bogus headline about Tony going solo. They didn't need to be worried as he was itching to get back to the Groundhogs!

Chapter 12 – Groundhogs Blues

I don't believe you have listened to the album
Tony McPhee's expunged line in a letter to *Melody Maker*

Some people thought Ken was crap because of his unique style. I wasn't conscious of it at the time, but we lost a lot of identity after he left.
Pete Cruickshank in 2004

With his solo tour completed, Tony started to think about getting the band back together again. It wasn't long before they went into his home studio to record the follow-up to *Hogwash*. It was the first Groundhogs album he engineered. As usual, Tony had no completed songs and the material was written at the last minute. He did have his tape of riffs that he could delve into. He also had a new innovation for the album: a Synthi Hi Fli. Tony had used it on the *Hogwash* tour and now he was keen to use it fully in the studio. This was a particular era when new equipment was coming onto the market all the time.

This was an important album as it was coming on the back of Tony's very good solo work. He had to prove to some of the fans that the band had a future. The album's opener is 'Light My Light', which conveys a world that is dark with death and decay. The Synthi Hi Fli is in evidence right from the off but the music came from an old influence, as Tony recalls: 'I like progressions; that's the blues in me. There are certain progressions that go up and down; this one goes down. I also used some unusual chords again.' Tony's voice sounds earthy and led some to believe he was having problems, but, in fact, it was a deliberate ploy to explore a new vocal timbre.

'Free From All Alarm' opens with a solo acoustic section from Tony. His atypical vocal delivery makes this blues track sound better. For those who perused the album sleeve while playing this would have been confused as it stated that Pete Cruickshank and Clive Brooks appear on the track. Just when you think it must be wrong, Tony's elongated final 'alarm' is the signal for the rhythm section to kick in, as they navigate between 7/4, 6/4 and 5/4 time signatures throughout the remainder of the track.

The third track and future live staple is 'Sins Of The Father', which mocks Chicory Tip's big hit 'Son Of My Father' (this is the track that

Tony had considered to be one of the worst uses of a synthesizer). The restrained use of the Mellotron illustrates that Tony knew when to use it most effectively. As usual, he was looking for any opportunity to involve wordplay and the next track, the album's single, provides one of his most inventive. 'Sad Go Round''s title was influenced by science fiction writer Ray Bradbury. Bradbury had written a story about a merry-go-round that de-ages people as the ride spins. Tony liked that idea and developed it so that the opposite happened: on the 'Sad Go Round', in which a ride leads instead to negative consequences. What makes the track even more interesting is the dreamy quality of the main riff, which, coincidentally, came to Tony while he was in 'the land of nod'. It's a pity it didn't get anywhere as a single because it's one of the band's finest moments.

The flip side opener showcases the Synthi Hi Fli the most. Out of all the tracks on the album, this one also has the most interesting music. 'Corn Cob' was another of those titles plucked out of the air by Tony. An interesting aspect of this is that Pete and Clive do not feature on the track. It was late one night in the studio and Tony laid down the guitar part and carried on with the bass part, too. He also decided that the drum part would be minimal, so he put a bass drum on it. 'Plea Sing, Plea Song' is simply a play on pleasing. There's a phased echo behind the guitar that sounds great.

By this stage in their career, a Groundhogs album wouldn't be complete without a Mellotron classic and 'Snow Storm' provides it. The title came from Tony 'painting pictures in his head'. He also plays the bass on this one and his style immediately differs from Pete's bass style – Tony plays a lot faster on this one. The reason why he took Pete's place is that he knew what he wanted, so he reeled it off. But it does seem odd when perusing the inner album sleeve. It was clear that Pete had his own thoughts on this. Tony had never played bass before on a Hogs track.

The final track is a reference to *Joker's Wild* (TV show), so Tony called it 'Joker's Grave'. The intro of 'Hello there' and the manic synthesizer run was left in to reflect the madcap spirit of the title – interestingly, Tony's voice sounds jocular but threatening. This is an apt pairing for a song about how stupid people are – especially *Melody Maker* reviewers! Another interesting aspect is the use of bongo drums on this one. Tony got the idea when he listened to the intro of 'Time' from Pink Floyd's *Dark Side Of The Moon*. And with the sound of bongos, we come to the end of a very good album and it is highly rated by many fans. This was very positive as they had now made two good albums with their new drummer.

Tony decided to call the album *Solid* for no other reason than it sounded catchy. To many fans, it was a most apt name, as it seemed to capture the spirit of the music. It was rumoured that the original title was *Phart* and some stores had indicated they would refuse to stock the album. In fact, it was another Wilf Pine stunt – the whole thing was a fabrication. It was a humorous way for the band to have one over on the press. However, on a negative note, the production falters in certain ways. The guitars, for example, sometimes sound too 'toppy'.

In the past, Tony spent a lot of time on the album sleeve. It was clear from *Solid* that he had run out of ideas or had decided to take a back seat. Gered Mankowitz took the cover shot in his studio in London. It was Mankowitz's idea for the whole concept. The band are pictured looking mean, moody and enigmatic. The back cover shot of the vacant chairs is even more puzzling. In fact, there was no rhyme or reason for the vacant chairs other than it was something to photograph. Pete Cruickshank recalls that the whole thing was unprofessional: 'We never actually saw the finished work; we only saw slides and you couldn't really get an idea of things.' Suffice it to say that when the band saw the sleeve, they were disappointed. It's easily their worst cover.

On the surface, things were fairly upbeat, but below the surface, things were in bad shape, as Pete Cruickshank recalls: 'I thought *Solid* was a good album, but, to me, it seemed more like a solo album. I liked 'Light My Light' and 'Sad Go Round', but on the whole, it was another step away from the Groundhogs for me. When Tony played bass on two of the tracks, I thought to myself, 'What's this?' I think anybody would have thought that. 'Corn Cob' didn't seem right for us. 'Jokers Grave' starts off well but it goes on far too long and ends up a din. It seemed to me this new material offered a lot less scope for live development. Tony was experimenting a lot and was more into his own thing than before. In the studio, he was becoming more insular. Everything was Tony and it seemed to me that it wasn't a healthy atmosphere. I didn't feel involved anymore.' Pete never felt connected to the new management, and by this time, he was feeling distant from Tony, too!

In November 1973, the band started an extensive UK tour supported by another of Wilf Pine's acts – Jonesy. Prior to the tour, Wilf was leading the press another merry dance by stating that Tony was not interested in being in the Groundhogs, so incorporating a synth and acoustic slot in the show was making up for it somewhat. Of course, it was all rubbish, as Tony had no intention of permanently going solo. It was also rumoured that the band had to scrap some recording sessions, but this was untrue. It was, therefore, disappointing that the band only released the single 'Sad Go Round' ('Plea Sing, Plea Song' was also released as a single b/w 'Dog Me Bitch'). For some reason, the album was delayed. Tony was determined to use a new track for the flip side; he developed a basic riff, lacing it with plenty of synth. The track was completed very quickly and he called it 'Over Blue'. It was later included on the CD format of the album, although it was written as a B-side and never intended for inclusion on an album. The single was released just in time for the tour.

Just before the tour, the band spoke to Jerry Gilbert of *Sounds*. Clive Brooks was asked what he thought of Tony's solo tour and the Hogs being halted for the time being: 'I think we both thought, 'blimey' – we weren't expecting this. I think the problem was that my joining the band was a step in the right direction but not a big enough one – I slotted into the old style instead of creating a new one.' Brooks admitted there had been a breakdown in communication and a lot of things went unsaid. That was definitely a problem of the old lineup. A good example of this was Ken's interview when he claimed they blew John Mayall off the stage. Tony was seething, but nothing was aired on the subject. The interview ends with a reference to how Pete and Clive's inactivity in recent months had made them raring to go.

The tour comprised over 20 shows at medium to large venues. Tony decided it was the time to develop some theatrics, so they used dry ice, but they had a few problems. It was difficult to predict the direction of it and sometimes it could even have a comical effect if the mist went the wrong way, so it didn't always have the dramatic impact they had hoped for. With regard to Tony's solo spot, Wilf Pine's original idea was to do part of 'The Hunt'. A special rack was made to house the ARPs, but in the end, Tony went off the idea, as it was far too complicated to attempt live. Anton Matthews, who was the engineer on the solo tour, was drafted in. One of the things that Tony was concerned with was the sound. In those days, there were plenty of bands that played far too loud – Deep Purple proudly entered the Guinness Book of Records in 1972 as the loudest band, a record they still hold. Tony explained in an interview: 'Recently, we've been cutting down on the volume at gigs. When we do this, Anton has a chance to pull the vocals through. The louder you play, the more chance you have of losing the vocals somewhere along the line.' Matthews was really a recording engineer from Olympic Studios in Barnes. He was in control of the equipment that the band used on stage at that time, which included ten Quad 303 amps (five on each side) with 900 watts in total, controlled by a 20-watt channel Alice mixer desk.

On the tour, they premiered 'Light My Light' and 'Sins Of The Father' from the new album. It went well, but Tony was quite perturbed by the behaviour of the support band, Jonesy: 'We played the Sheffield City Hall and the dressing rooms were downstairs in one big room. All that separated the bands was a curtain. They never stopped arguing on that tour. I thought that's silly because if you do a bad gig, so what?' It gives a clear indication of his outlook on live performance: from time to time, mistakes are made, but life's too short to dwell on them. In spite of the success of this tour, there were no foreign gigs. This was worrying for a band that had always gone down well in parts of Europe.

By this time, Pete Cruickshank was thinking a lot about how different the scenario now was: 'I related to the people who came to see us in the sense that they were seeing a different band. Tony was using Mellotrons and synths more and more in the new material, but the crowd were still shouting for cuts from the old days, such as 'Cherry Red' and 'Split Part One', when the lineup of the band was different. As a result, some people thought Ken was crap because of his unique style that didn't seem to fit with what punters expected to hear from their nostalgic favourites. I wasn't conscious of it at the time, but we lost a lot of identity after Ken left. But the band then were more like some of the other bands.' For Pete, they lost the congruence that had brought success. Furthermore, Roy Fisher recalled recently: 'Ken said what kept them really glued together in the past was constant work. One of their reasons for breaking from me was they were working too much!' The opposite of this transpired in the Clive Brooks era; their workload was nowhere near the same as when Ken was in the band.

The early part of 1974 saw the Groundhogs play low-key gigs all over the country. Nothing much seemed to be happening other than waiting for *Solid* to be released – pencilled in for June. It's a salient point that, under Roy Fisher, they ended up being overworked, but now they were moving in the opposite direction. Pete recalls those days with WWA: 'We seemed to spend a lot of time hanging around. I did feel they only took us on because it looked good on paper along with the rest of their other bands.' However, the Groundhogs had another album released before then. It was an album that Tony McPhee didn't even know was coming out. The simmering dissatisfaction towards the media – *Melody Maker,* to be precise – that Wilf Pine felt came cascading to the surface when United Artists released *Groundhogs Best 1969-72* in April. It was an album review that Jeff Ward probably wishes he'd never written! Incensed, Tony tried to phone Ward on numerous occasions at the office and at home, but his mother always answered at home and said he was not in. One day, Tony got Clive to phone and he pretended to be Steve Lake (another *MM* reviewer). Ward came to the phone and Clive put the phone down, but when Tony called back immediately, he got the same response from Ward's mother.

Re-reading the review after all these years, one is struck by the sheer venom and negativity of the piece. It begins with: 'When this bulky double album dropped on my desk, promising more than 80 minutes of Groundhogs sound, my first reaction was, 'Oh my God! What have I done to deserve this?' It concluded with: 'It's just an offensive noise and deadly dull. Sleeve notes indicate another 'best' album in a couple of years. Save us!' The middle section wasn't much better either: 'Although the tracks are not in sequence, certain stages of the band's, err, development can be witnessed.'

Steve Lake reviewed *Solid* in June 1974. The headline didn't bode well – 'Solid Boredom' – and he even accused Tony of stealing TS Elliot's moniker! Here's just a sample: 'I don't for a minute believe that anybody in the band takes this kind of conveyor belt, neo-sociological pop cum-heavy-metal at all seriously… *Solid*? It should be re-titled 'Squalid'. Or better still, 'Stale'.'

To say this was the straw that broke the camel's back would be an understatement. Wilf Pine's initial reaction was to suggest they go down to *MM*'s office in Fleet Street and throw the phones through the windows! The seriousness of this suggestion cannot be underestimated, as Tony recalls that it was only his assistant, Clive Jenkins, who persuaded him that it would be a bad move. Wilf's next course of action was to phone the *Melody Maker* offices, and luckily, depending on your point of view, Jeff Ward answered the phone (remember he'd been ducking Tony's calls). Wilf could be quite charming and he asked Ward if he had ever seen the band live and why he didn't like them. Ward was clearly on the defensive and his main resistance seemed to be that he wasn't the only one in the office who didn't like the band. Tony recalls that Wilf ended the conversation by advising Ward to look over his shoulder when leaving work because, one day, Wilf would be there to break his legs!

Wilf wasn't totally unaware of the implications of what he'd done, as he contacted one of his employees straight afterwards for advice. *Sounds* scribe Jerry Gilbert was doing some work for him: 'I got a phone call from Wilf. He told me he'd just made the mistake of threatening a journalist.' No one knows whether Wilf Pine's actions are unprecedented. What can be said is that journalism was moving away from reviewing the album or the gig and moving towards a cliché-ridden style where personal insults were the order of the day. Lester Bangs was the king of this new approach, but he was not the only purveyor of this; at one point, Ian Anderson of Jethro Tull threatened to retire because of the onslaught. Pete Cruickshank hated the reviews as much as anybody, but he thought the whole thing had gotten out of control. He felt that it wasn't the thing to do to retaliate in such an aggressive fashion. The next thing they knew, Wilf had a phone call from solicitors representing Ward. The solicitor stated that the telephone conversation had been taped (which was most unlikely) and that if anything happened to our client, etc. Wilf replied in his most charming manner, asking the solicitor's name and where he worked and then repeated his threat: every night when he left the office, he'd better look behind him.

It's a shame how low *Melody Maker* had sunk and how ignorant some of their journalists were. By this time, it was a full-blown feud between the two camps. However, the Groundhogs were not the only ones getting fed up with the scribes. Patti Smith famously threw cakes at journalists during a press conference. However, it wasn't all bad news, as *New Musical Express* weighed in with a great review of the album. It is heartening to note that some journalists were actually playing the album: 'After a few listenings of this, I've come to the conclusion that the Groundhogs are well back in form … The production on this album is excellent and McPhee has obviously worked hard to achieve a sound that is tight and forceful but with enough area to experiment in.' Beverley Legge of *Disc* also came to the rescue and her review seemed to anticipate Steve Lake's bile: 'If ever a band suffered from prejudice, it must be the Groundhogs. Hopefully, this album will go a long way towards getting rid of that. It's packed with straightforward, down-to-earth, driving rock music with just a dash of blues.'

In 1964, Tony McPhee penned an open letter to the press defending John Lee Hooker and Howlin' Wolf's musical integrity. Now, he would be forced to defend his own because of the criticism also directed at him. In July, *Melody Maker* published his letter under the headline: 'McPhee: I Believe In What I Write'. In the letter, Tony sets out his case logically and effectively. He starts off by stating that the animosity has only become prevalent recently and pinpoints Jeff Ward's appointment as a 'self-styled, tin-god reviewer', but he also accuses Lake of being a 'no-holds-barred-playing-it-dirty-Hogs slayer'. He notes that the nature of reporting has changed: 'Bad reviews are usually like kicks to the rump; they sting for a bit but don't really annoy. Now, these two have aimed their kicks from the front straight to the groin and it hurts; whereas bad reviews are sometimes justified, these two have just been plain vindictive and insulting and I feel I have to straighten them out on a few facts.'

Tony was upset that Lake had taken a line from 'Jokers Grave' as proof that the lyrics were garbage. As Tony states: 'I think you read the lyric sheet searching for fodder for your sarcasm.' The fact that Lake 'declined to name the bass player' is proof that, as it wasn't on the sleeve, he didn't know it was Pete Cruickshank. At face value, it appears that it was a magnanimous gesture for the paper to print the letter. However, they left out one line of Tony's letter: 'I don't believe you have listened to the album'. Why leave that out if it wasn't true?' Also, the paper were keen, if only as a sop to Wilf Pine, to show they were giving the other side a chance to air their views. Their seriousness to this cause can be judged by the fact that they put 'LP Winner' at the end of the letter (funnily enough, Tony never did get his winner's LP!).

Around this time, Tony started to develop the theatrical side more. Wilf Pine had instigated stage clothes, and since then, dry ice had also been incorporated into the show. His idea was to feature one of their greatest numbers, 'Soldier', as the fulcrum. At the end of the number, the band went off stage and Clive Brooks changed into his soldier's uniform. What gave him time was a synthesized tape that engineer Anton Matthews played from Tony's ARP imitating bombers and explosions. Clive would then rush back on stage, and at the tape's conclusion, a spotlight would be trained on his face, and with a starting pistol, he would 'shoot' the light out. But as Tony recalls, there were problems: 'The starting pistol was never really loud enough even when Clive pointed it at the microphone. At one stage, we had a prop – a WW2 Sten gun – but that didn't work properly either.' They persevered with this well into 1975, but at one gig, Tony recalls that Clive exclaimed: 'This is getting boring'. Pete Cruickshank remembers this stunt very well: 'It didn't really work and we were losing our way. People came to hear the music and that was where our strength lay. We were never a visual band as we didn't have a frontman like Robert Plant.'

On the subject of stage work, fans were clamouring for a live album. By 1975, most of the big bands had released one, with the Groundhogs, Led Zeppelin and Black Sabbath being the most notable exceptions. In an interview with *Progression* magazine the previous year, Tony explained why: 'There were a couple of attempts at live recordings that were dire because we're sort of a problem in terms of giving a sufficient sound on tape. At the BBC, whenever we do the 'In Concert' things, it's very easy to blow those big tubes (on the transmitters) they've got, you know, with an overload. So they have to try and limit it, get the whole sound compressed … But there are times when we go very soft and then I come in with a loud chord.' It was well known that, in Tony's opinion, the BBC were very good at recording music, so if they couldn't do it, then nobody could. It was a shame that the band didn't record a readily available great live album in this classic period.

Even though *Solid* had made a welcome return to the album charts, the feud with *Melody Maker* left a sour taste in the mouth. As far as Tony was concerned, there were too many things going wrong and there was more to come. He had felt down for quite a time and it's well documented on the album that the lyrics were depressing, though whether or not the lyrics are meant to be a personal document of this is unclear. Due to all their antics, the show was extended to two hours, but at a gig in Cambridge, Tony decided to curtail some of the theatrics. Consequently, the show was pruned down closer to an hour and a half; he felt that two hours was too long anyway. At the end of the show, the promoter complained vehemently about being short-changed, as he expected the allotted time in the contract. As a result, Tony was doing a lot of thinking and it seemed to him that everybody was having a go at the Groundhogs. The change of management in 1972 didn't really reap dividends overall. Though WWA had plenty of ambition, they didn't seem to have much vision – a malaise that didn't just manifest itself with the Groundhogs.

Just when Tony thought it couldn't get worse, it did! By late 1974, World Wide Artists was in turmoil with Hemdale (their parent company); there was no money coming through to the band. Wilf told Tony: 'Once you stop dealing in readies, you don't know where you are.' Other WWA artists, like Gentle Giant and Black Sabbath, were in a similar position and, for some, it was going to get unpleasant! It got so bad that Wilf Pine advised the band to collect the gig money, so they had to contact all booked venues and ask them to pay the money into a recently created Groundhogs bank account. This created hassle when all they wanted to do was make music. At the same time, the band joined Wilf's own company, Heat Music, but were still part of WWA. It was a situation that later led Tony to sum up the period as everything 'crumbling' as things were getting complicated. Wilf himself was becoming more estranged from Patrick Meehan Junior as he was close to the Groundhogs and Meehan was not doing them any favours; he moved his office away from WWA's Dover Street headquarters.

This was a period of managerial chaos and it couldn't go on for much longer, as Pete recalls an incident in detail: 'We were at the offices and we got talking to a couple of guys from Black Sabbath. They ended up banging on the desk, demanding to see some accounts. In the three years we were with WWA, we had one set of accounts for one tour. At least with Roy Fisher, we had a statement every month detailing the finances. I remember when I wanted to buy a house, I asked them for the money. They said they would deal with it, but I wanted the mortgage in my name. If you asked for anything, they would always say they would get it for you. I did get the house but I moved because I was frightened I would lose the house if anything went wrong. That's when I moved to Bury St Edmunds.' In the end, the band left WWA and they immediately had an injunction slapped on them.[39]

Tony McPhee was completely down about the situation. In February 1975, he came up with a radical solution. He decided to disband the Groundhogs! He called Pete Cruikshank and Clive Brooks to his house in Haverhill and broke the news to them. As Tony recalls: 'Pete took it badly; his chin was on the floor. He was very concerned about what he was going to do in the future. I felt bad about it, but what could I do? Clive didn't say a lot at the meeting.' When the story broke in the press, they were more forthcoming. In an interview with Pete Makowski of *Sounds*, Pete Cruikshank was down to earth: 'We knew it was going to happen, but it still came as a surprise.' Clive Brooks was more quixotic: 'The strange thing is that when we told Tony we were going to do interviews, he said okay, but he was going to lay back and not say anything for a while.' Pete ruminated on Tony's silence: 'This makes the whole thing weird; we can only assume he's going to pursue a solo career or maybe start another Groundhogs with a different lineup. Who knows?' In fact, the only reason why Tony didn't speak to the press was that he didn't trust them anymore as a result of all the attacks.

With gigs to fulfil, the band headed to their final destination. Surprisingly, the atmosphere at these gigs was quite good. On 4 April 1975, at the King's Cross Cinema, London, the band bade farewell to their legion of fans. The only thing that Tony recalls about this gig is how cold the theatre was. Pete Cruickshank recalls the 'crappy' sound. The press were there to hound them into the grave. Alan Jones of *Melody Maker* made sure the band were not going to bow out in dignity – in print, anyway! He started to compare the state of the decaying theatre with the band. At least Tony ensured they would have to find another target for their bile.

The band members parted amicably, but just when the dust had finally settled, the state of the finances was lurking there to haunt them. Just after the gig, Tony had a tax demand land on his mat. The contents portended terrible things and he was shaking as he read it. It was a demand for £10,000! When he pulled himself together, he got an accountant from the West End, London, to try and sort it out. As he recently admitted, when it came to finances, he was naïve, so he left all the decisions to him (he was even unable to pay the accountant as he was so broke). However, it was to create problems further down the line. The seeds of these problems were sown in the early 1970s when Tony, Pete and Ken made the Groundhogs a partnership on Roy Fisher's advice. Each member was an equal partner and the reason was to gain certain advantages, such as fair shares and the avoidance of rancour and developing egos. But in the end, it backfired on them. Amazingly, the partnership was never even dissolved when Clive Brooks joined the band. So, on paper, Ken Pustelnik was in the band until 1975!

Inland Revenue thought that, as Tony was a musician, he was raking money in. In fact, the band parted almost penniless, but it was no consolation to Tony that the Inland Revenue frequently used this tactic of assuming people must be quite rich in certain occupations as merely a starting point for discussion to settle a claim (agreed later as £1200). There were two claims being made. The first was for 1971/72, when they changed management from Roy Fisher to WWA. The second part of the claim was for the three years after 1972 (this meant WWA hadn't paid any tax regarding the band). In the end, the tax losses were written off against Tony's name. But to do this, his accountant had told the IR that Tony was the employer. This now meant Pete Cruickshank was classed as an employee; he was liable to pay income tax and couldn't write any tax losses off as Tony had done that already! It was then that the IR came for Pete (the IR never approached Ken Pustelnik on this matter). He later phoned Tony and asked him why he had said he was the employer. Pete was also in dire financial straits and couldn't pay anything at that time. As he reflects: 'After many static pauses, I put the phone down on him. I was still fighting the taxman well into the 1980s. In the end, I managed to convince them I wasn't an employee, but not before I paid a third of the tax for 1971/72 – the final year with Ken.' Tony had to pay the remainder by selling equipment. Tony remembers that Ken managed to avoid paying anything by disappearing.

Tony and Pete had been through a lot together and it was a sad way to end their relationship. They didn't speak to each other after that for 27 years.

Chapter 13 – Eleventh Hour

> McPhee is one of the original guitar heroes. The master of howling, full-speed runs, clanging chords and high-pitched screaming.
> *Melody Maker* journalist Chris Welch

Even though Tony McPhee was relieved that the Groundhogs saga was finally over, it wasn't long before he started to concentrate on exactly how he was going to earn a living. In spite of his regular publishing money, he realised he was going to have some financial problems. For some time after April 1975, he focused on the idea of having a successful solo band like Rory Gallagher. His public declaration that the Groundhogs were finished depressed the fans, but circumstances were soon to arise that put this 'retirement' out of his control. The plan was to record a solo album and then go out with a new band. The truth was that the Groundhogs had become a millstone for him. However, as the year frittered away, he was faced with a blank sheet of gigs.

It was around this time that he received a call from Richard Cowley of Cowbell Agency (he formed the company with Kenny Bell). Cowley informed him that he was having enquiries about the possibility of Groundhogs gigs; he then asked him to re-form the band. At first, Tony informed him of his solo plans, but Cowley tersely told him, 'You won't get any gigs'. Tony mulled it over for a few days, and slowly, he came round to the idea of reforming the Groundhogs again. The question was, however, who would be in the band? This further alienated Pete Cruickshank as he recalled Tony saying that he wouldn't form the Groundhogs again. But to Tony, the Groundhogs were his invention and he felt he had every right to reform the band.

At that stage, Tony didn't have concrete ideas on who the new band members were going to be, or even the instrumentation for that matter. However, Cowley recommended two bands to him. They were the Pink Fairies and Zzebra. But when he went to see them, he didn't think they were suitable, especially as the latter all had big beards! For a while, Tony hooked up with a keyboard player from a tower block in Essex. His name is lost in the mists of time, but Tony paid him a retainer of £30 a week. The problem was that he was never sure of what Tony wanted him to do. It wasn't long before he realised he was wasting £120 a month. It was then that Richard Cowley recommended another band consisting of Mick Cook (ex-Home) on drums, Martin Kent on bass and Dave Wellbelove on guitar. At first, Tony wondered how it was going to work with a second guitarist. However, the funky rhythm section of Cook and Kent impressed him. Inspired by this and the twin guitar theatrics of bands such as Thin Lizzy and Wishbone Ash, Tony accepted the new challenge of accommodating Wellbelove on second guitar. There was another reason why he wanted a fairly unknown lineup, as he related to *Beat Instrumental* and Chris Simmonds: 'I had the chance of getting known accomplished musicians for the band, but I decided against it as I didn't see the need for people with preconceived ideas about music. This way, I'll be able to mould together a really tight, cohesive band.'

Richard Cowley negotiated a record contract with United Artists. As a consequence, Tony was reunited with Andrew Lauder, who was still their A&R man. He had come full circle; he was back in the fold of Lauder where his incarnation of the band started with Liberty Records. He started to think about making an album with the new boys. He decided he was going to instigate a new style of writing, as he wanted the sound to be funky but still have a healthy slice of blues. It was here that he realised that Mick Cook could help: 'Mick was always going on about 'reverse beats' – playing a groove backwards in a drum fill – which I sort of understood, but I said I preferred them to be forward. At first, it was off-putting but sometimes it would inspire me to come up with a more interesting lick.' By November 1975, they were ready to go into Tony's home studio to record the album that would be known as *Crosscut Saw*.

In early November, Tony got a call from Dave Wetton, who had been the bassist in The Seneschals; the two men had remained friends. By this time, Wetton was more heavily involved with the fledgling Hunt Saboteurs and their movement was gaining not only more members but public sympathy, too. They had written to the BBC asking for a platform for their views. The BBC agreed to give them a 20-minute slot on *Open Door* on BBC 2, but they only had a short time to come up with the film. It wasn't long before Wetton concluded that 'The Hunt' would be the most appropriate music. During his call with Tony, permission to use the track was willingly granted. So Dave Wetton took the album in for the BBC sound engineers to work on. He decided to use the opening section, as it was the most dramatic in the piece. The program consisted of a studio discussion (including Wetton) and a documentary film of a real hunt. It was the first time that the public had ever seen such a graphic illustration of the 'sport' and Tony's music/oratory provided a compelling companion to it. On 22 November, the program was broadcast and it provoked a massive increase in the membership of the Hunt Saboteurs. Tony was credited at the end of the show. It is unknown if he ever saw it.

Crosscut Saw was recorded in a few weeks and is a testament to the new direction that Tony was looking for. This is evident in the first cut, which is the title track, with charming guitar licks that contrast with the aggressive *Split* guitar playing. Dave Wellbelove takes the solo here and it shows that Tony wasn't frightened to delegate. He realised after the trio band split that rushing around, mending everything himself and writing the bass parts, etc., was not necessarily the best thing to do. 'Promiscuity' is next up and continues in the more laidback style of the opening cut. Mick Cook employs some of those reverse beats – Pink Floyd uses these on 'Echoes' from the *Meddle* album. Tony is pleading with girls who sleep around not to (he always thought it was a silly thing to do). Tony also chips in the Synthi Hi-Fli. The third track, 'Boogie Withus', sees Tony on more familiar territory, but this time with a two-pronged guitar attack. It's a rollicking journey and became the opening number of the show. Tony is back on form with his wordplay games. It's actually a play on Googie Withers' (a film heart-throb of the 1950s) name, but isn't about her. Dave takes the solo again on this one. The first side closes with the excellent 'Fulfilment' and it includes some interesting acoustic work from Tony.

The second side opens with the joyous 'Live A Little Lady'. The lyrics are very important to Tony: 'It's about a lady pleading with a young girl not to waste her life. It hurts me when people talk about what my attitude to women is supposed to be. I've been a feminist for years; I've supported equality.' It's a catchy tune and it's no wonder it was chosen as the single. It's laced with plenty of ARP synth to boot! 'Three Way Split' is three bits of music together, giving a nudge in the direction of the classic *Split* album. 'Mean Mistreater' is the album's acoustic blues number. Having said that, it's one of Tony's best. The album closes with the autobiographical 'Eleventh Hour', so named as Tony was always leaving things to the last minute (and always did!). The beginning is very atmospheric and it develops into a showcase for some of his best guitar work on the album.

Tony was delighted with the album. He told Clive Wilson in an interview in early 1976: 'Luckily, it sounded really solid and the whole thing came together within a month. It had to be spontaneous and it was.' But he also made a startling admission: 'I think I'd been trying to a bit too hard with the effects, trying to pull something out that wasn't there. So, musically, I've gone back to basics – there's a bit of synthesizer, but it's mainly a guitar album because I think the thing is to simply be an exciting rock band.' He was keen to have a different kind of sleeve for this album. He had an idea that he described to the artist and left the rest up to him. The artist was Mick Lye of the Blue Egg Studio. On the back cover picture, which was taken at Haverhill, Tony's white cat (called white cat) was the centre of attention.

With this band, Tony had his new sound and he looked forward to going out on the road. February 1976 was a busy month for them as a 30-date tour of the UK had been organised for them. The tour was lower-key than before, with less fanfare surrounding it, kicking off at the Column in Nelson on 20 February. However, Tony confessed to Chris Simmonds that there was a certain degree of the unknown about the situation: 'The whole idea of performing again is very strange because in the past we got used to touring solid, with never a break of more than a couple of months. Now I've been off the road for almost a year, and I have a new band. It will be a completely different feeling. I just don't know how I'm going to take it.' Things appeared to be looking up, as, just before the tour started, the rift with *Melody Maker* appeared to have healed when Penny Valentine tipped 'Live A Little Lady' for the singles charts. In spite of the help, it didn't make much of a dent on sales.

Around the time of the release of the album, *New Musical Express* contacted Tony for an interview. This was rare as, usually, it's the press that need chasing. Tony Stewart was drafted in to do the piece. Sometime later, Mac related to *Newcastle University Magazine* that not much had changed with the music press: 'I've done a few things with Tony Stewart in the past and they have always been alright, but this time … I was feeling a bit merry, having had a few beers, and this guy really started giving me some heavy stuff. In effect, he was saying, 'Who do you think you are coming back and making us listen to your stuff? What gives you the right?' I couldn't believe it. I thought, 'Oh no, don't start this again'. In the end, he wrote this little thing on the Thrills page, which was really objectionable.' What was it with the press and the Groundhogs? It was a question that Tony was unable to answer. It must be said that many of the older bands were suffering around this time. Part of the problem, and it's apparent in Stewart's 'What are you still doing here?' attitude, is that most of the journalists at this time were busy sponsoring the punk bands and they had little time for bands created in the 1960s by then.

Just before the tour started, the band finally got on *The Old Grey Whistle Test*. Tony was still playing the part-time inventor; he was using a cordless guitar by then and he had adapted a transmitter originally bought for his solo tour so that he could go from one keyboard to another. Only the guitarist out of the Swedish band, the Sputniks, had ever used one before. This caused the BBC crew a few problems, as they had no faith it would work. They were concerned it would pick up taxis (as was spoofed later in *Spinal Tap*). Tony knew that, apart from the aerial soldered joint on the transmitter that was prone to coming off, it would work okay.

They rehearsed in the back studio in the afternoon and shot in the evening. They kicked off with the new album's title track. At the conclusion, Tony gave an introduction: 'Hi, welcome to our first gig, that was a thing called 'Crosscut Saw' from our album of the same name. We're going to do another one from the same album. This one's called 'Boogie Withus', where Dave takes the solo.' At the end of that number, Bob Harris remarked on the transmitter in the guitar. The thing that Tony remembers the most is Harris chain smoking and having trouble with the autocue.

The tour went well and Tony ceded a few solos to Dave Wellbelove, although he always played them the same way, which was in contrast to Tony, who never played the same solo twice. Andrew Lauder turned up at the Derby gig and he witnessed a great concert. Tony didn't know it, but the show was taped and it stayed in the can for 28 years. When it was finally released as *The Groundhogs Live UK Tour '76* by MLP, it showcased five numbers from the new album: 'Boogie Withus', 'Promiscuity', 'Eleventh Hour', 'Crosscut Saw' and 'Fulfillment', but also included old favourites like 'Cherry Red' and 'Split Part Two'.

The band played with a lot more discipline than as a three-piece. However, the press were still hanging over the band like a bad stink! Chas De Whalley was there for the Croydon gig. Even though he left a bad review, there are a few surprising admissions. The first was that he liked *Crosscut Saw* and that he didn't actually see the whole gig. But he was still firing off the leaden-foot clichés: 'He (Tony) picks the licks like a Kray brother with a crowbar, puncturing your skull in time with the bass and then working the iron around until you think that boredom alone might want to make him stop.'

Lifelong fan Tony Sherratt witnessed a gig on 1 March 1976 in Quaintways, Chester. He recalled that Tony had a novel way of demonstrating the effectiveness of his transmitter:

> Having seen the hogs in large venues, this was the first for me at a nightclub. The set was a tempest with Tony using radio pickups on his guitar. At one point, he disappeared off to the toilet mid-song, still playing a guitar break without missing a note. The addition of a second guitar gave a totally new dimension to Tony's songs, especially some of the older songs. Although Tony sometimes bounces off the bass, in this concert, he was able to trade payoffs with a second guitar as well. This meant occasionally less adlibbing, but the playing was as inspirational as ever. Even to a smaller audience, Tony whipped up a frenzy of emotion and pulled the fans and onlookers together. After an encore of 'Cherry Red', the Hogs' magic had worked its spell and transformed the room into a pack of 'Yelping Hounds'.

This period was an unhappy time for Tony as his marriage had fallen apart. It had become apparent that he and Christine had been drifting apart from each other for quite a while. The following day after the Birmingham Barbarella's gig (23 March 1976), they had an album signing for *Crosscut Saw* at Virgin Records. It was at the signing that Tony was enamoured with one of the staff – her name was Sue. He hit it off with her straight away and pocketed her phone number when he left. It was the start of a long relationship. Martin Kent, who by all accounts was a charmer, got off with Sue's friend.

Tony had dropped the Mellotron, but he was still using the ARP synthesizer. However, he had another technological trick up his sleeve. He was now using a guitar interface unit. This enabled him to play the synth through his guitar. This was an incredible innovation as it meant he could play the synth better than he could before, as he wasn't really a keyboard player. However, even though he had the imagination to see that this could be achieved, it was one of the few occasions when he required help.

Tony contacted PACE back in the summer of 1975. Tony had a visit from Tony Gipp, who was a celery farmer but who was also involved with a company called PACE Electronics in Cambridge. Gipp found out that Tony lived locally and thought he was loaded; after three hit albums, he was bound to be! He asked Tony if he was interested in buying a share of the company. Tony would have loved to, but he was broke. He managed to get a visit to the workshops at Frenches Yard and met Dick Parmee, their electronics wizard. Dick showed Tony his enormous mixer, which included a number of startling innovations, including LEDs instead of meters. However, as a prototype, it was just too big.

A couple of years later, they brought out the MM (Mickey Mouse) mixers and amps that sold in huge quantities, as they were very good and very cheap, so if he'd had the money, Tony would have been a richer man. PACE built the interface unit that converted the guitar output into voltages required for the keyboard; the note was obtained by using a metal pick and the output of the guitar. The other was wired into the frets of his guitar. In this way, the guitar fretboard took the place of the keyboard, but only single notes, rather than chords, could be played, just like a monophonic synthesizer. Around this time, he was pictured in *Melody Maker* with Gary Moore, who was showing more than a passing interest in this impressive piece of technology.

When you are living in each other's pocket for a long period, as you do in a band, you find out whether you really are a tight unit. In fact, over the eight years of the band, there had been a few rough patches. There had been Steve Rye's drinking that hastened his departure and Ken Pustilnik's complex personality issues. On this present occasion, Dave Wellbelove was becoming a problem for Tony; it was discovered that Wellbelove had an obsession with cleanliness: 'I said it would be great if we hired a Winnebago rather than stay in hotels, as this would give us a lot more freedom. Dave said, 'I couldn't do that; I have to have a shower every day'. It wasn't exactly rock 'n' roll either, as he polished his guitar every day. I called it the immaculate conception.' One day, he turned up in jeans with turn-ups. Tony asked him why he was wearing them. His answer was disconcerting to Tony: 'Because they're in'. Everything he wore had to be pressed and he even used Oil of Ulay on his face and hands! Tony remembers they stayed in a Bed & Breakfast on the tour that had chamber pots under the bed. As a joke, Tony defecated in one and left it outside Dave's door. The owner of the B&B thought it was a complaint against the service provided. It wasn't long before Tony knew Dave would have to go – he just didn't fit in. Just after the tour ended, he was on his way and joined John Miles.

Tony didn't have to wait long for a replacement. Drummer Mick Cook recommended a guitarist he knew called Ric Adams. He was much more to Tony's liking musically as he was much more aggressive in his playing and he was more inventive in his soloing. Ric wasn't totally unlike Wellbelove, however, as his guitar was also treated with more than a little TLC.

The band went straight into the studio to record the follow-up to *Crosscut Saw*, which, due to the expense of studio time, was recorded at Tony's home studio. However, he had to vacate the original studio because the local council found out and informed him he never had planning permission. The result was some invention on the hoof by Tony. He decided to move the equipment into the end room of the house and the band went into the garage, where he rigged up a remote to operate the recording equipment. They didn't have room for Mick Cook, so they put him outside. Tony acquired a canopy from a famous 'Bettabake' van, so the drums were put in there. Unlike *Crosscut Saw*, where the amps were mic'd, the guitars went straight through the desk – he'd never done that before. This would ensure that there would be no overspill from the drums.

Tony was looking for a different sound on *Black Diamond* and it veered more towards country. The new guitarist, Ric Adams, wasn't given as much scope as Dave Wellbelove – he doesn't have any solos on the album. The opener is 'Body Talk' and sets the tone for the rest of the album. It's a more accessible, commercial sound. The track that follows this is the intriguingly titled 'Fantasy Partner', inspired by Tony's idea that the ideal partner was something that was only in your mind and was unobtainable. The last line of the song sums it all up: 'I wish she were alive'. It's certainly an interesting couple of songs to open the album. The next song is one of his favourites on the album and became a live staple. 'Live Right' has a teasing reference to Jesus: 'I was saying you don't have to follow anybody; why not be yourself as long as you don't hurt anybody else.' Tony was proud of the production on this track, so much so that he took the acetate to Andrew Lauder, who was strangely unimpressed. It was clear to him that Andrew didn't like the two albums he'd made for United Artists, especially *Black Diamond*: 'Andrew would always find something that was wrong like 'too much bass' and not enough of something else.' The closer of side one is 'Country Blues' and starts off with a riff that sucks in the rest of the band for a manic few seconds. While it's true that Tony hated living in the city, he didn't like everything about rural life. By this time, he'd become fed-up with farmers, as they were always pleading poverty, even though, to him, they all seemed to be doing pretty well.

The second side of the album has a lot of interesting moments on it. The opener is 'Your Love Keeps Me Alive' and is reminiscent of Wishbone Ash in the harmony guitar parts, according to Tony. He wasn't actually a fan of that style, but he thought it worked on this cut. The next track is especially interesting as Tony lifted 'Friendzy' from Herbal Mixture's 'Please Leave My Mind'. There's a nice 6/4 riff to end this track that bemoans people's inability to get on with each other. The final couple of tracks close out the album in great style. 'Pastoral Future' is one of the few instrumental tracks the Groundhogs recorded and it boasts a beautiful melody. Tony recalls it very well: 'I was in the studio late at night. I just had 'Pastoral Future' and a few other overdubs to finish and we had already booked the cut for the next day, so I spent the night overdubbing and recording, and because I was so tired, it was all nice and laid back. Perhaps I should have done more instrumentals.' Considering it featured no vocals, it was a brave decision to release it as a single (b/w 'Live Right'). Alas, it didn't get anywhere. The final track – 'Black Diamond' – builds slowly to a crescendo after a low-key opening. The structure of the song resembles a kind of rock bolero – it just builds and builds. The lyrics were inspired by the ambiguity of the phrase, 'black diamond', as Tony recalls: 'I loved the whole idea that you didn't need material things. If you squeeze a lump of coal hard enough, it becomes a diamond. It's a reminder that, in the first place, all we had was basics.' It's the best track on the album and a great one to end on.

Looking back on the two albums he made for UA, Tony is unable to choose his favourite. He prefers to pick out tracks from them. He likes 'Eleventh Hour', 'Live A Little Lady' and 'Promiscuity' from *Crosscut Saw* and 'Your Love Keeps Me Alive', 'Live Right' and 'Black Diamond'.

At 6 am the next morning, with the album finished, Tony went right to London to cut the album. After it was cut, Tony met the rest of the band at Gered Mankowitz's photographic studio. When they arrived, they had to shoot the picture that appeared on the back of the album. It was decided to (another good laugh, though possibly a good idea) shoot the band by a pyramid light at the studio, as it was an interesting idea. Tony and Ric Adams had to stand on a block so they would be taller than the light. If Tony looks a bit tired in the shot, it's because he had been up then for over 29 hours and was virtually asleep as he stood by the warm studio light. With the album in the can, the band were keen to get back on the road, and in September 1976, they went to Sweden for a short tour. It was the band's first trip abroad as a four-piece. The show incorporated numbers from both of the UA albums. However, 'Cherry Red' was becoming their nemesis, as Tony explained to the *Newcastle University Magazine*: 'We tried to get rid of that once, but it didn't work ... *Split*, although it was great that it sold so well, became the standard work and now it's very difficult to break away from it.' It had come a long way since it was recorded as a little private joke, but Tony was also aware that, in a way, the band's reputation, to some people, went back a long way. The obligatory US tour was also mooted then, but this time, it failed to come off because Martin Kent had previously been arrested for drug possession and couldn't get a visa.

On 13 September 1976, they played a gig in Stockholm that was also broadcast on the radio. The show went well and was quickly bootlegged – and is still selling! They had a problem with the equipment on the tour. They were now using Orange equipment, but unless the volume was turned right up, you couldn't distort the guitar and this made it too loud, thus restricting what Tony could present to the audience. On stage, Tony had a routine with Ric Adams. He would run his guitar down Ric's for effect, proving to be successful with the crowds, until one night, the routine produced a little scratch on Rick's guitar. This put paid to that routine, as he was, like Wellbelove before him, very protective about his 'immaculate conception'.

The album was released in October to uninspired reviews. Not much had changed, as *Melody Maker* demonstrates, even though Penny Valentine had reversed the trend on the previous album: 'The Groundhogs sound rather tired these days; perhaps it's due to the effort in touting endlessly repetitive riffs to audiences who've heard it all before and demand energy, at the very least, with their boogie. Tony McPhee is, at most, an average vocalist and the occasional synthesizer tricks are just damp squibs in the midst of sluggish mainstream action.' It's a pity that the paper didn't acknowledge the change of musical direction that Tony had taken the band on, in which the cuts were more song-orientated than hitherto. Furthermore, the reviewer acknowledges Tony's prowess with the guitar as that area is left untouched. By their standards, that is gushing praise indeed!

More recently, *Allmusic* made some interesting points, though a bit flippant: 'Riffs galore permeate this LP, with McPhee displaying tons of creativity, and there's no complaint with the music, which is first-rate. Perhaps if they found a dynamic lead singer, this innovative version of the group may have reached the level of success Santana found in the early 1970s. The gruff vocal from Tony McPhee was still a bit beyond the reach of commercial radio at the time. In 'Live Right', he sounds like Mark Knopfler singing about Jesus; a solid track for FM radio, but one that failed to catch on despite its flashes of inspiration.'

The band generally got on well, but by this time, Tony was getting fed up with Mick Cook. He was a good bloke, although Tony referred to him as a 'likeable fool'. Ric Adams lived above Mick, and when Tony visited him, he would sneak up to his flat. Usually, Mick would find out and Ric would tell Tony, 'He knows you're here'. The relationship between Martin Kent and Mick Cook was a bit fraught, too. Kent was going out with Mick's sister and this was a bone of contention with the drummer because he thought his sister wasn't always treated well. They were always arguing about something. Tony recalls one particular night when they were on tour and staying in a B&B. Just before they left for the gig, Tony had 'apple-pied' the bed linen in Martin and Mick's room – they were sharing a double bed. Tony remembers that when they got back in their room, he could hear them arguing, and then a few minutes later, there was laughter. Tony's trick had the desired effect, and for a while, the ice was broken.

They toured the UK on and off into late 1976, but they were facing a crisis. It was not as if they could have taken a break because the finances were always such that this was never an option. However, history was about to repeat itself. In the 1960s, the blues clubs started to go over to soul; at this point in time, a change was happening again. The Groundhogs played Northampton Cricket Club, which was one of Tony's favourite gigs. He got talking to the manager, who told him they had a great band playing at the venue soon. They were called The Sex Pistols and it was the first time Tony had heard their name. By 1977, the club circuit, which had provided a good base for rock bands, suddenly became a desert for them – punk rock had arrived. By the spring, Tony knew the game was up and so the Groundhogs folded.

Chapter 14 - Epilogue

> Tony McPhee made the blues his own and not just a homage. He made it appealing to a young man turned off by every British Bluesman but drawn to this one man's passion to explore and experiment with sound and structure in ways I had never heard before nor have since.
> Karl Hyde of Underworld

> Let's hear it for the Groundhogs, one of the most exciting bands the UK has ever produced and who gave the blues their own particular psychedelic treatment on a bunch of great albums.
> Captain Sensible of The Damned

The end of the Groundhogs was a surprise, leaving fans even more frustrated when their hiatus went on for years. However, the truth was that Tony had simply had enough of the band and the music. It would be seven long years before Tony got another Groundhogs together. Until that time, Tony formed several bands but always steered well clear of Groundhogs material. He was moderately successful in this, first with Terraplane, Turbo (contained Clive Brooks) and The Tony McPhee Blues band in the early 1980s. However, it wasn't long before the latter had 'Blues' expunged from the name, and from that time (1982), Tony was moving towards the band he had spent so much time trying to escape from. He had initially wanted a solo career like Rory Gallagher, but it never worked out that way. One reason for this may be a question of timing. Rory Gallagher launched his career before *Taste* had waned, whereas Tony embarked on his solo career after *Black Diamond*. Had he started after *Split*, he could have reaped more success. As it was, too many Groundhogs fans had seeped away. It was for this reason that non-Groundhogs projects never got off the ground and a reunion was inevitable.

In 1984, the circumstances surrounding the band's reformation and the reuse of the Groundhogs name had its roots in one of the anomalies of the band's career – the absence of a live album. It seemed that the history of the band on record left a few pieces short of the complete jigsaw. Early that year, Tony got a call from a representative of Psycho Records. They wanted to issue a thousand copies of some old Groundhogs live material. Tony gave the go-ahead for the full release – only 100 copies of this was released in 1971 to US radio stations as a promo – of *Live At Leeds*, some BBC stuff and material of the four-piece format from 1976 recorded in Stockholm. The album was called *Hogging The Stage* and was released in the spring of 1984. Much to Tony's surprise, it made a dent in one of the independent charts.

The re-vamped Groundhogs included Mick Kirton on drums and Steve Towner on bass, soon to be replaced by Alan Fish for the album. They went to Alaska Studios, London, in September 1984 to record the first band album for eight years. The engineer was Gary Glitter's son, Paul Gadd. The takes were being fitted into the timetable of the nearby railway line in order to avoid noise leakage during the recording. The album was called *Razor's Edge*. It's a collection of hard-driving, balls-to-the-wall material and stands up very well after all these years. In 1986, Ken Pustelnik briefly re-joined the band. In 1987, the band made another studio album. By now, the band consisted of Dave Anderson (ex-Hawkwind) on bass and Mick Jones on drums. They went into Dave Anderson's Foel Studios in Wales to record the follow-up to *Razor's Edge*. They were signed to Demi Monde, which was actually owned by Anderson. Tony had written the songs in a couple of months, but some of the riffs had been purloined from his famous tape reservoir. The album was a less heavy affair than *Razor's Edge* and it contrasted well against it. It was given the defiant title of *Back Against The Wall*. The album contains some fine cuts but it was to be the last album of original material that Tony would ever record as the Groundhogs. One of the tracks is named '54146' because that was the serial number of his recently stolen Gibson.[40]

In the early 1990s, Tony started playing acoustic blues as a solo artist while still keeping the Groundhogs going. In 1993, he recorded his first solo album in 20 years – called *Foolish Pride* – and the following year, he recorded the excellent *Slide TS Slide*. He also toured Europe with Jefferson Starship. Tony suffered a minor stroke in 1993 when playing at the Robin 1 at Brierley Hill. The band were just starting 'Split Part One' and the members of the band thought Tony had broken a string: 'I couldn't play and I couldn't form the chords on the fretboard. I knew what had happened to me.' He somehow managed to get through the gig and even drove himself home. There were no long-term side effects and he carried on playing within due course.

Meanwhile, the Groundhogs had been through many lineup changes, too numerous to mention here. In 1998, the Groundhogs returned to form with *Hogs In Wolf's Clothing* – Tony's tribute to Howlin' Wolf and a collection of his material. The band consisted then of Eric Chipulina on bass and Pete Correa on drums. The following year, the same lineup recorded *The Muddy Waters Songbook*. With two successful projects, it came as a surprise and shame that their next project was a disaster. They were filmed at the Astoria, London, but Tony caught the flu a few days before and the whole thing fell flat. He felt awful during the gig and disowned the performance.

On 12 April 2003, the classic Groundhogs lineup reformed. The first gig was part of Punk Aid in Brixham, Devon. It was great for the fans to see Tony, Pete Cruickshank and Ken Pustelnik on the same stage together. In Shrewsbury later that year, the gig was filmed and released as a DVD package in 2005, alongside some historical material.
It seems that acoustic blues were closer to Tony's heart during this period, and in 2004, he embarked on a big UK tour with Alvin Lee and Edgar Winter. In late 2004, Tony called time on the Groundhogs and disbanded them forever – or so he thought. They did return briefly with his partner, Joanna Deacon, on vocals as, due to other strokes, Tony couldn't sing. The band carried on until 2014.

It seems appropriate that he released an album of solo acoustic blues in 2004 with Joanna Deacon called *Blues At Ten*, with most of the material being penned by Tony. Joanna co-wrote four cuts with Tony, with the rest of the album being made up of blues standards by John Lee Hooker, Bukka White and Blu Lu Barker. Looking at the great music the Groundhogs made together, it's no exaggeration to say that no rock CD collection, whatever the generation of the collector, should be without *Thank Christ For The Bomb* or *Split*. It's hard to understand why they never got the credit they deserved. Then, as now, they are just not very fashionable. But even the original lineup was never in vogue. There's a lot written now about John Lee Hooker and the British artists he worked with, but it's been conveniently forgotten that the only band to make an album with him was his favourite one – John Lee's Groundhogs!

The same could be said about Tony McPhee as a guitarist. His innovative slide blues style was a revelation in the 1960s and drew admiration from many quarters. From the late 60s, his fingerpick style was one of the major factors in giving the band their distinctive sound when they started to attain a bigger audience. The solid *Scratching The Surface* got the ball rolling. The next effort – *Blues Obituary* – is a fine and vastly underrated album. Their unique sound is most apparent during the first few seconds of 'Strange Town' from *Thank Christ For*

The Bomb, their most satisfying album overall. *Split* is a classic concept piece and is probably the album that the band will be remembered for the most. Even though Tony was not at his most creative when making *Who Will Save The World*, it provides a great contrast to anything they had done before or since, for that matter.

Ken Pustelnik left in 1972 and this was a traumatic period for the band, but there was no discernable dip as Tony kept coming up with good material. First with *Hogwash* and then with *Solid*, the quality was maintained. In between the latter two, Tony made an outstanding solo album in the shape of the eclectic *The Two Sides Of Tony TS McPhee*. Even though he wasn't a keyboard player, he used the synthesiser in his own unique way. The final two albums of the classic period began with the outstanding *Crosscut Saw,* but by the time of *Black Diamond*, the quality of the material was patchy. It proved to be a good time for Tony to call time on the band.

It was at this time that the next generation of musicians came along and some of them loved the raunchy style of the band (it was, therefore, apt that Captain Sensible introduced them on stage at their 2003 reunion gig). This affinity with punks is not exaggerated or even retrospective. It's interesting to note that Terraplane were mistakenly booked for a gig as Terror Plane in 1977 – I'm sure Tony would have been proud of that wordplay mixup. A crowd of punks turned up, but after listening to Tony McPhee's rasping guitar licks, they were won over and they went down a storm. Furthermore, later bands like The Fall and The Datsuns have played Groundhogs material.

Tony had a great career and his music will still be played in the decades to come. The Groundhogs made their mark in a big way. Of course, all of this could have been different if he had accepted the offer from Chris Barber in 1964!

Bibliography

Books

Bacon, *Tony London Live* (Balafoni, 1999)
Brunning, *Bob, Blues: The British Connection* (Blandford Press, 1986)
Driver, J. (ed.), *Sex, Drugs & Rock 'N' Roll* (Constable Publishing, 2001)
Duffy, K., *Mothers 1968-1971: The Home Of Good Sounds* (Birmingham Council, 1997)
Frame, P., *The Complete Rock Family Trees* (Omnibus Books, 1993)
Freestone, P., *Tony T.S McPhee: A Biography And Discography* (Self Published, 1981)
Larkin, C., *The Virgin Illustrated Encyclopaedia Of Rock* (Virgin Books, 2002)
McStravick, S., Roos, J. (ed.), *Blues Rock Explosion* (Old Goat Publishing, 2001)
Paraire, P., *50 Years Of Rock Music* (Chambers Encyclopaedia Guide, 1982)
Pearson, J., *One Of The Family – The Englishman And The Mafia* (Century, 2003)
Shaar Murray, C., *Boogie Man: The Adventures Of John Lee Hooker* (Penguin, 2000)
Strong, M., *The Great Rock Discography* (Canongate Books, 1996)
Wyman, B., *Rolling With The Stones* (Dorling Kindersley, 2002)

Fanzines And Music Papers

The two Groundhogs fanzines, *Hogs Feedback* and *Yelping Hounds*, were used extensively. Mick Stones and Paul Freestone ran these, but, alas, both are defunct now. I found these publications helpful. Tony Sherrat's website, *Squealing Pups*, was also a mine of information.
I used numerous music publications and these were the main ones: *Melody Maker, New Musical Express, Sounds, Disc, Beat Instrumental, Blues Unlimited, Record Mirror, Rolling Stone* and many others too numerous to mention. The internet was very useful in my research.

The Tony McPhee Archive

An extensive array of articles, pictures, contracts and other interesting memorabilia of the music business reflecting Tony's 40-year career.

Gig List

This is not intended to be a full list. Only confirmed shows have been used.

The Seneschals

10-Dec-61 Tooting, Elephant & Castle – possible first gig
28-Apr-62 Nunhead, St Thomas Hall – first Nunhead gig
29-Jun-62 Wimbledon Wimbledon Park – instrumental gig
07-Jul-62 Nunhead, St Thomas Hall – got new outfits 'Hip Time'
14-Jul-62 Ensham Girls School – 'fabulous'
30-Jul-62 Tooting, Conservative Club – 'too loud'
25-Aug-62 Kemsing – Dollarbills also on the bill
02-Sep-62 Audition for a gig at Castle – failed
29-Sep-62 Nunhead, St Thomas Hall – Ray singing at first gig after three rehearsals
24-Oct-62 Tolworth
03-Nov-62 Bermondsey – 'very hip indeed'
11-Nov-62 Tooting, Elephant & Castle – audition for a gig at Castle was a success
22-Nov-62 Tooting, Castle
24-Nov-62 Nunhead, St Thomas Hall – 'exceptionally hip, man'
29-Nov-62 Tooting, Elephant & Castle
08-Dec-62 Bruce Hall – 'hip'
18-Dec-62 Bishop's Grant School
19-Jan-63 Nunhead, St Thomas Hall – bad winter of 1963 'blizzard'
11-Feb-63 Balham, Bedford Hotel – 'rush gig'
14-Feb-63 Companies House, City Road
15-Feb-63 West Norwood, Thurlow Arms
16-Feb-63 Nunhead, St Thomas Hall
23-Feb-63 Streatham, St Andrews Hall
30-Mar-63 Nunhead, St Thomas Hall – 'pretty hip'
06-Apr-63 Bruce Hall – probably Tony's last gig with Seneschals

The Dollarbills

10-May-63 Chelsea, Café Des Artists – probably Tony's debut
31-Aug-63 Cardiff, Sophia Gardens – Vince Hill also on the bill
04-Oct-63 Nunhead, St Thomas Hall
19-Oct-63 London, Kingston Jazz Cellar
14-Dec-63 London, South London Motors
20-Dec-63 Finsbury Park, Crawdaddy

John Lee's Groundhogs

28-Jan-64 London, Jazz Club – supporting The Animals
02-Feb-64 Bromley, Blue Opera Club, Royal Bell
06-Feb-64 London, Jazz Club – supporting Alex Harvey Soul Band
20-Feb-64 London, Jazz Club
27-Feb-64 London, Jazz Club
10-Mar-64 London, 100 Club – club changed the name from Jazz Club – supporting The Animals
17-Mar-64 London, 100 Club – supporting The Animals and The Pretty Things
31-Mar-64 London, 100 Club – supporting The Animals and The Pretty Things
16-Apr-64 London, 100 Club – supporting Graham Bond Organisation
23-Apr-64 London, 100 Club – supporting Graham Bond Organisation
07-May-64 London, 100 Club – with Champion Jack Dupree
14-May-64 London, 100 Club – supporting Alex Harvey Soul Band
28-May-64 London, 100 Club – supporting Graham Bond Organisation
06-Jun-64 London, White Hart Hotel
23-Jun-64 London, 100 Club
06-Jul-64 Manchester, Twisted Wheel – backing John Lee Hooker – to 12 July
08-Jul-64 Blackpool, Cleveleys
12-Jul-64 London, Beat City – end of John Lee Hooker tour
29-Aug-64 Cubiklub, Heywood, Lancs
23-Sep-64 London, 100 Club
01-Oct-64 London, Flamingo – backing John Lee Hooker, two shows each gig – plus John Mayall
05-Oct-64 Beat Room BBC 2 – backing John Lee Hooker
07-Oct-64 Nottingham, Dungeon Club
10-Oct-64 Manchester, Twisted Wheel
15-Oct-64 Double D Club
18-Oct-64 London, Flamingo – plus John Mayall
23-Oct-64 London, Flamingo
24-Oct-64 Windsor, Rikky Tick – 7:30 pm
24-Oct-64 Guildford, Rikky Tick – 9:30 to 1:00
31-Oct-64 London, Flamingo
04-Nov-64 Manchester, Twisted Wheel – final gig backing Hooker
07-Nov-64 London, Flamingo – backing Jimmy Reed – plus Chris Farlowe
13-Nov-64 Richmond, Crawdaddy – backing Jimmy Reed

14-Sep-64 Windsor, Rikky Tick – 7:30 pm – backing Jimmy Reed
14-Sep-64 Guildford, Rikky Tick – 9:30 to 1:00 – backing Jimmy Reed
15-Nov-64 Windsor, Rikky Tick – backing Jimmy Reed – special 6 pm appearance
15-Nov-64 Reading, Rikky Tick – backing Jimmy Reed
18-Nov-64 London, Flamingo – backing Jimmy Reed
21-Nov-64 Manchester, Twisted Wheel – backing Jimmy Reed
23-Nov-64 Harrow – backing Jimmy Reed
27-Nov-64 London, Flamingo – backing Jimmy Reed
04-Dec-64 London, The Manor House
12-Dec-64 R & B Club Romany Dance, Mitcham
18-Feb-65 London, Marquee – with Rod Stewart & The Soul Agents
12-Mar-65 The Manor House, London
14-Mar-65 Hotel Leofric, Coventry
14-Jul-65 London, Refectory, Golders Green
21-Jul-65 London, Refectory, Golders Green
31-Jul-65 London, The Pontiac, Putney
13-Aug-65 London, Marquee
27-Aug-65 Refectory, Golders Green, London
30-Aug-65 London, Marquee
01-Oct-65 Bromley Hill, Bromel Club
25-Oct-65 London, Marquee
29-Oct-65 London, Refectory, Golders Green
04-Nov-65 London, Marquee – with Graham Bond Organisation
14-Nov-65 Hotel Leofric, Coventry
26-Nov-65 London, Refectory, Golders Green
15-Dec-65 Coventry College of Arts
02-Jan-66 Hotel Leofric, Coventry
09-Feb-66 Cheylesmore Hotel, Coventry
05-Mar-66 Hotel Leofric, Coventry
06-Mar-66 Hotel Leofric, Coventry
23-Mar-66 Police Ballroom, Coventry
24-Mar-66 Police Ballroom, Coventry

Groundhogs

09-Nov-68 Boston, Glyderdome and London, Roundhouse – Led Zeppelin – their first gig under that name
09-Nov-68 London, Roundhouse – backing JLH
08-Dec-68 London, Studio 51
07-Feb-69 London, Marquee

08-Feb-69 Blues Scene 69, Festival Hall – tour supporting John Lee Hooker – also on the bill: Champion Jack Dupree, Aynsley Dunbar Retaliation, Jo Ann Kelly
09-Feb-69 Bristol, Colston Hall – Blues Scene 69
11-Feb-69 Birmingham, Town Hall – Blues Scene 69
12-Feb-69 Portsmouth, Guild Hall – Blues Scene 69
13-Feb-69 Croydon, Fairfield Hall – Blues Scene 69
14-Feb-69 Pontypool – backing JLH
15-Feb-69 Manchester, Free Trade Hall – Blues Scene 69
17-Feb-69 Bath – JLH tour continues to 10 March
18-Feb-69 Blackpool
19-Feb-69 Grimsby
20-Feb-69 Leytonstone
21-Feb-69 Leicester
22-Feb-69 Colchester
23-Feb-69 London, Crystal Palace Hotel
24-Feb-69 Newcastle
25-Feb-69 London, Klooks Kleek
26-Feb-69 Portsmouth, South Parade Pier
27-Feb-69 Southampton
28-Feb-69 London, Philippa's, Streatham
01-Mar-69 Bournemouth
02-Mar-69 Nottingham
03-Mar-69 Bishops Stortford
04-Mar-69 Brighton
05-Mar-69 Tolworth
06-Mar-69 Welsh College Of Technology
07-Mar-69 Plymouth
08-Mar-69 London, London School Of Economics
09-Mar-69 Tunstall
10-Mar-69 London, Royal Albert Hall – end of John Lee Hooker tour
17-Mar-69 London, The Resurrection
04-May-69 London, Marquee
13-Jun-69 London, Marquee
27-Jun-69 London, Marquee
04-Jul-69 London, Marquee
22-Jul-69 London, Marquee
09-Aug-69 Plumpton Festival
19-Aug-69 London, Marquee
25-Aug-69 Croydon, Star Hotel

02-Sep-69 London, Marquee
16-Sep-69 London, Marquee
30-Sep-69 London, Marquee
24-Oct-69 London, Marquee
06-Nov-69 London, Marquee
18-Dec-69 London, Marquee
26-Dec-69 Birmingham, Mothers
10-Jan-70 Cardiff
16-Jan-70 Derby
23-Jan-70 Leicester
26-Jan-70 London, Speakeasy
29-Jan-70 London, Marquee
30-Jan-70 Salford
06-Feb-70 Kent
14-Feb-70 Southampton University
16-Feb-70 Sunderland
20-Feb-70 Reading University
22-Feb-70 London, Roundhouse
23-Feb-70 Wolverhampton, Catacombe Club
26-Feb-70 Blackpool
27-Feb-70 Leicester
01-Mar-70 Birmingham, Mothers
02-Mar-70 Richmond Athletic Ground
04-Mar-70 Hampstead
05-Mar-70 London, Revolution
06-Mar-70 University Of Essex Blues Club
07-Mar-70 Bangor
13-Mar-70 London, Marquee
14-Mar-70 Lancaster
18-Mar-70 Chelmsford, Eye's Club
19-Mar-70 Maidstone College
20-Mar-70 Windsor College
22-Mar-70 Bletchley Youth Club
24-Mar-70 Bournemouth Poly
28-Mar-70 Hamburg, Germany
29-Mar-70 Hamburg, Germany
30-Mar-70 Hamburg, Germany
01-Apr-70 Birmingham, Mothers
02-Apr-70 Epping
03-Apr-70 Burnley, Municipal College

04-Apr-70 Bolton, Octogon Theatre
07-Apr-70 Carlisle
08-Apr-70 Derby, New Penny Club
09-Apr-70 Blackpool Technical College
10-Apr-70 Glasgow, Club Maryland
12-Apr-70 Peterborough, Cloud Nine
16-Apr-70 Bristol, Old Granery
17-Apr-70 Sunderland, Fillmore North
28-Apr-70 Wollaston
30-Apr-70 Penzance, Wintergardens
01-May-70 Worcester
02-May-70 Plymouth, Van Dyke
06-May-70 Birmingham, Mothers
07-May-70 Brighton, Big Apple – Ken was hit in the face with a chair
08-May-70 Coventry, University Of Warwick
10-May-70 Southall, Northcote Arms
13-May-70 Canterbury
15-May-70 Derby Art & Technical College
16-May-70 Pershore Horticultural College
20-May-70 Kings Lynn, Corn Exchange
21-May-70 London, Marquee
22-May-70 Leicester, Ll Rondo
23-May-70 Swansea Festival
24-May-70 Manchester, Electric Circus
28-May-70 Preston, Amethyst Club
29-May-70 Maidstone, Technical College
30-May-70 Northampton, Blissworth
01-Jun-70 Wolverhampton, Catacombe Club
03-Jun-70 Richmond, Castle Hotel
05-Jun-70 Sunderland, Fillmore North
07-Jun-70 Birmingham, Mothers
08-Jun-70 Aylesbury, Friars Club
14-Jun-70 Shaftesbury Theatre
17-Jun-70 Camberwell, Fox On The Hill
18-Jun-70 Guildford
19-Jun-70 Maryland Club, Glasgow
20-Jun-70 Malvern, Winter Gardens
21-Jun-70 Croydon, Greyhound
24-Jun-70 Southampton, Floral Hall
25-Jun-70 London, Marquee

26-Jun-70 Walthamstow, Chez Club
27-Jun-70 St Helens Technical College
28-Jun-70 Letchworth, Keys Club
01-Jul-70 Germany Tour – tour ended on 20 July
24-Jul-70 London, Marquee – supported by Supertramp
25-Jul-70 Twickenham, Eel Pie Island
26-Jul-70 Doncaster
30-Jul-70 Worthing, Assembly Room
02-Aug-70 Southhall, Farx
05-Aug-70 Barnet, Resurrection
06-Aug-70 Birmingham, Mothers
08-Aug-70 Plumpton Festival
15-Aug-70 Halifax, Krumlin Festival
28-Aug-70 Isle Of Wight Festival
06-Sep-70 Croydon, Greyhound
13-Sep-70 Manchester, Free Trade Hall – supporting Canned Heat
22-Sep-70 Birmingham, Town Hall – supporting Canned Heat
29-Sep-70 London, Marquee
02-Oct-70 Southall, Farx – so fucking hot that Tony thought he was going to pass out
05-Oct-70 Salisbury, Resurrection
09-Oct-70 Epping, Wake Arms
17-Oct-70 London, Polytechnic Of Central London – supporting IF
18-Oct-70 Southall, Farx
19-Oct-70 Romford, Kings Head
21-Oct-70 Tooting,The Castle
22-Oct-70 Blackpool, Locarno Ballroom
31-Oct-70 London, Lyceum – supporting Free, The Strawbs and Curved Air
01-Nov-70 Birmingham, Mothers
05-Nov-70 Southall, Farx
20-Dec-70 Birmingham, Mothers
22-Dec-70 London, Marquee
30-Dec-70 Bradford
31-Dec-70 Brighton, Big Apple – supported by David Bowie
01-Jan-71 Newcastle
05-Jan-71 Windsor
08-Jan-71 Swansea
09-Jan-71 Bristol
10-Jan-71 Bromley, Bromley Theatre
11-Jan-71 Dunstable, Civic Hall

12-Jan-71 Salisbury, Resurrection
15-Jan-71 Swansea
16-Jan-71 Narbeth
17-Jan-71 Southall
19-Jan-71 Barry
20-Jan-71 Tooting
22-Jan-71 Lancaster
24-Jan-71 Redcar
26-Jan-71 Crawley
27-Jan-71 Liverpool
28-Jan-71 Derby
30-Jan-71 Isleworth
31-Jan-71 Bexley
02-Feb-71 Hartlepool
03-Feb-71 Poole
05-Feb-71 Wallaston
06-Feb-71 Dagenham
09-Feb-71 Southend
10-Feb-71 Repton
12-Feb-71 Preston
13-Feb-71 Colchester
19-Feb-71 Beckenham
20-Feb-71 Bristol
21-Feb-71 London, Roundhouse (Mick Jagger attends and leads to supporting the Stones)
23-Feb-71 Leeds
24-Feb-71 Portsmouth
25-Feb-71 Glasgow
26-Feb-71 Edinburgh
27-Feb-71 East Kilbride and Glasgow
28-Feb-71 Dunfermline
01-Mar-71 Newcastle
03-Mar-71 Sidmouth
04-Mar-71 Newcastle, City Hall – tour supporting Rolling Stones (all two shows)
05-Mar-71 Manchester, Free Trade Hall
06-Mar-71 Coventry Theatre
08-Mar-71 Glasgow, Green's Playhouse (one show)
09-Mar-71 Bristol, Colston Hall
10-Mar-71 Brighton, Big Apple (one show)

12-Mar-71 Liverpool, Empire Theatre
13-Mar-71 Leeds University (one show)
14-Mar-71 London, Roundhouse – final gig of Rolling Stones tour
19-Mar-71 Blackpool
20-Mar-71 Folkestone
22-Mar-71 Cleethorpes
26-Mar-71 Huddersfield
27-Mar-71 Halifax
28-Mar-71 London, Lyceum – with Gypsy and Egg
30-Mar-71 Wood Green
31-Mar-71 Weston-Super-Mare
01-Apr-71 Derby
02-Apr-71 Rickmansworth
03-Apr-71 Plymouth
04-Apr-71 Kinetic Cellar, Chesford Grange, Kenilworth
06-Apr-71 Crawley
09-Apr-71 Abbey Wood, Harrow Inn
10-Apr-71 Nelson
11-Apr-71 Croydon, Greyhound
13-Apr-71 Birmingham
15-Apr-71 BBC *Top Of The Pops* – album slot
16-Apr-71 Leytonstone, Red Lion
17-Apr-71 Aylesbury, Assembly Hall
18-Apr-71 Bexley
19-Apr-71 Nottingham
22-Apr-71 Swansea
24-Apr-71 Bournemouth
25-Apr-71 Taunton
26-Apr-71 Chelmsford, Civic Theatre
30-Apr-71 Hilversum, Holland
05-May-71 Twickenham, Winning Post – supported by Thin Lizzy
07-May-71 Brighton, Sussex Sports Centre
08-May-71 Lincoln Arts Festival Of Music (at Racecourse) – Funkadelic, Arthur Brown's Kingdom Come
09-May-71 Guildford, Civic Hall – with Glen Cornick's Wild Turkey
11-May-71 Newcastle, City Hall
12-May-71 Oxford, Town Hall – with Glen Cornick's Wild Turkey
13-May-71 Chatham, Central Hall – with Glen Cornick's Wild Turkey
14-May-71 Hampstead Country Club
15-May-71 Norwich

21-May-71 York
27-May-71 London, Elephant & Castle
05-Jun-71 Felixstowe, Pavilion
07-Jun-71 Malvern, Winter Gardens – Wild Turkey
08-Jun-71 Bristol, Colston Hall
11-Jun-71 Sunderland, Bay Hotel
12-Jun-71 London School Of Economics
14-Jun-71 Llanelly, Glen Ballroom
15-Jun-71 Manchester, Free Trade Hall
17-Jun-71 Town Hall, Watford – special guests Osibisa
18-Jun-71 Southampton, Guildhall – with Gentle Giant
19-Jun-71 Plymouth, Guildhall – with Gentle Giant
21-Jun-71 Sheffield, City Hall
23-Jun-71 Bristol, Colston Hall
25-Jun-71 Hull University
26-Jun-71 Harrogate, Opera House
27-Jun-71 Croydon, Greyhound
04-Jul-71 Kinetic Cellar, Kenilworth
07-Jul-71 Twickenham, Winning Post – plus Home
09-Jul-71 Newcastle, Mayfair
10-Jul-71 Kilmarnock, Grand Hal
11-Jul-71 Jazz Club, Redcar
16-Jul-71 Birmingham, Kinetic Circus
17-Jul-71 Dagenham, Roundhouse
18-Jul-71 Wolverhampton, Civic Hall
21-Jul-71 Torquay, Town Hall
22-Jul-71 Penzance, Winter Gardens
23-Jul-71 Barnstaple, Queens Hall
24-Jul-71 Dunstable, Civic Hall – plus Egg
29-Jul-71 Boscombe, Royal Ballroom
30-Jul-71 Devizes, Town Hall
31-Jul-71 High Wycombe, Town Hall – supported by Man
04-Aug-71 Paradiso, Amsterdam, Holland
13-Aug-71 Swansea
14-Aug-71 Reading, Town Hall
20-Aug-71 Southport, Floral Hall
22-Aug-71 Public Hall, Preston
27-Aug-71 Harrogate, Royal Hall
28-Aug-71 Wheeley Festival – plus Faces, Colosseum, Rory Gallagher
29-Aug-71 Corby, Festival Hall

04-Sep-71 British Rock Meeting Festival, Speyer, Germany – with Black Sabbath, Rod Stewart & The Faces, Family, Fleetwood Mac
05-Sep-71 Rock Festival, Vienna, Austria – with same as Speyer
10-Sep-71 Buxton Sound 71 Festival – headlined, plus Edgar Broughton, Juicy Lucy, Gentle Giant and East Of Eden
11-Sep-71 London, Queen Elizabeth Hall – plus Gentle Giant
12-Sep-71 Munster, Germany – supporting John Mayall
13-Sep-71 Kiel, Germany
14-Sep-71 Stadthalle, Karlsruhe, Germany
15-Sep-71 Frankfurt, Germany
16-Sep-71 Nurnberg, Germany
17-Sep-71 Berlin, Germany
18-Sep-71 Zafingen, Germany – end of Mayall tour
20-Sep-71 Munich, Germany
02-Oct-71 Sutton Coldfield
07-Oct-71 Copenhagen, Denmark
08-Oct-71 Odense, Denmark
09-Oct-71 Aarhus, Denmark
10-Oct-71 Stockholm, Sweden
15-Oct-71 Stockport
16-Oct-71 Bracknell, Sports Centre
22-Oct-71 Neath, Gwyn Hall
23-Oct-71 London School Of Economics – plus Gentle Giant
31-Oct-71 Gravesend, Civic Hall – plus Egg
06-Nov-71 Barking, North East Polytechnic – plus Egg
07-Nov-71 Hemel Hempstead, The Pavillion – plus Egg and Quicksand
08-Nov-71 Bristol, Colston Hall – plus Egg and Quicksand
10-Nov-71 Enfield, Middlesex Polytechnic
11-Nov-71 Hanley, Victoria Hall – plus Egg and Quicksand
12-Nov-71 Liverpool, St George's Hall – plus Egg and Quicksand
13-Nov-71 Weston Super Mare, Winter Gardens – plus Egg and Quicksand
15-Nov-71 Oxford, Town Hall – plus Egg and Quicksand
17-Nov-71 Manchester, Free Trade Hall – plus Egg and Quicksand
19-Nov-71 Plymouth, Van Dyke Club – plus Egg and Quicksand
21-Nov-71 Westcliffe On Sea, Palace Theatre – plus Egg and Quicksand
22-Nov-71 Southampton, Guildhall – plus Egg and Quicksand
25-Nov-71 Guildford, Guild Hall – plus Egg and Quicksand
27-Nov-71 Birmingham, Town Hall – plus Egg and Quicksand
28-Nov-71 Redcar Jazz Club, Coatham Hotel – plus Egg and Quicksand

29-Nov-71 Sheffield, City Hall – plus Egg and Quicksand
30-Nov-71 Bradford, St George's Hall – plus Egg and Quicksand
01-Dec-71 Newcastle, City Hall – plus Egg and Quicksand
03-Dec-71 Norwich, St Andrews Hall
04-Dec-71 Leeds University – plus Egg and Quicksand
05-Dec-71 Wolverhampton, Civic Hall – plus Egg and Quicksand
08-Dec-71 Aberdeen, Music Hall – plus Egg and Quicksand
09-Dec-71 Dundee, Caird Hall – plus Egg and Quicksand
10-Dec-71 Glasgow, Greens Playhouse – plus Egg and Quicksand
11-Dec-71 Edinburgh, Empire Theatre – end of tour with Egg and Quicksand
13-Dec-71 Reading
01-Jan-72 Dagenham, Roundhouse
08-Jan-72 Leicester
10-Jan-72 Chatham – with Jo Ann Kelly
13-Jan-72 Cheltenham, Town Hall
14-Jan-72 Sunderland
21-Jan-72 Salford
22-Jan-72 Walthamstow
31-Jan-72 Tunbridge Wells, Assembly Hall
25-Feb-72 Lancaster University – plus Alexis Korner and Johnny Johnson & The Bandwagon
25-Mar-72 Boston, Starlight Rooms
27-Mar-72 Birmingham, Town Hall
08-Jun-72 WMC Studios Memphis, Memphis, Tenn – US tour
09-Jun-72 Overton Park Bandshell, Memphis, Tenn – with Edgar Winter
10-Jun-72 Warehouse, New Orleans, Lo – with Edgar Winter
11-Jun-72 The Sports Arena, Atlanta, Go
14-Jun-72 Curtis Hixon Hall, Tampa, Fl
15-Jun-72 West Palm Beach Auditorium, West Palm Beach, Fl
16-Jun-72 Vets Memorial Coliseum, Jacksonville, Fl – with Edgar Winter and Black Oak Arkansas
17-Jun-72 Sportatorium, Hollywood, Fl – with Edgar Winter
20-Jun-72 The Civic Center, Savannah, Ga – with Edgar Winter
22-Jun-72 Rockford Armory, Rockford, Ill
26-Jun-72 Maple Leaf Gardens, Toronto, Canada – with Humble Pie
27-Jun-72 The Forum, Montreal, Canada – with Humble Pie
09-Jul-72 Mt Pocono, Pocono Music Festival – with Black Sabbath, Humble Pie and Edgar Winter
11-Nov-72 Farnborough, Technical College – supported by Badger

17-Nov-72 Birmingham, Town Hall – supported by Gentle Giant and Stray
18-Nov-72 Edinburgh, Empire Theatre – supported by Gentle Giant and Stray
19-Nov-72 Dundee, Carid Hall – supported by Gentle Giant and Stray
20-Nov-72 Glasgow, Greens Playhouse – supported by Gentle Giant and Stray
23-Nov-72 Oxford, New Theatre – supported by Gentle Giant and Stray
24-Nov-72 Margate, Dreamland – supported by Badger
25-Nov-72 Cambridge, Corn Exchange – supported by Badger
26-Nov-72 Newcastle, City Hall – supported by Gentle Giant and Stray
29-Nov-72 Aberystwyth University – supported by Badger
30-Nov-72 Hanley, Victoria Hall – supported by Gentle Giant and Stray
01-Dec-72 Manchester, Free Trade Hall – supported by Gentle Giant and Stray
02-Dec-72 Northampton, Cricket Ground – supported by Badger
03-Dec-72 Bristol, Colston Hall – supported by Gentle Giant and Stray
05-Dec-72 Bradford, St George's Hall – supported by Gentle Giant and Stray
06-Dec-72 Barry, Memorial Hall – supported by Badger
08-Dec-72 Bournemouth, Winter Gardens – supported by Gentle Giant and Stray
12-Dec-72 Hull, City Hall – supported by Gentle Giant and Stray
13-Dec-72 Slough, Community Centre – supported by Badger
14-Dec-72 Chatham, Central Hall
15-Dec-72 Sheffield, City Hall – supported by Gentle Giant and Stray
16-Dec-72 Liverpool, Stadium – supported by Gentle Giant and Stray
22-Dec-72 London, Rainbow Theatre – supported by Gentle Giant & Stray
27-Jan-73 Canterbury, University of Kent
10-Feb-73 Southend, Kursaal Ballroom
17-Feb-73 Malvern, Winter Gardens
02-Mar-73 London, Sundown Edmonton
19-May-73 London, Imperial College
31-May-73 Croydon, Fairfield Hall
11-Jun-73 Summer Rock Festival, Frankfurt, Germany
02-Aug-73 London, Alexandra Palace Festival – supporting Black Sabbath
26-Aug-73 Kendall Pop Festival – also Greenslade, Gallagher and Lyle
16-Sep-73 London, Roundhouse – Tony McPhee solo tour
17-Sep-73 Leeds, Town Hall
18-Sep-73 Birmingham, Town Hall

19-Sep-73 Folkestone, Leas Clift Hall
20-Sep-73 Chatham, Central Hall
22-Sep-73 Barnsley, Civic Hall
25-Sep-73 Harrogate, Royal Hall
26-Sep-73 Southport, Floral Hall
27-Sep-73 Buxton, Playhouse Theatre
29-Sep-73 St Albans, Civic Hall – end of solo tour
05-Nov-73 Portsmouth, Guildhall – tour supported by Jonesy
07-Nov-73 Bournemouth, Winter Gardens – supported by Jonesy
13-Nov-73 Glasgow, Apollo Theatre – supported by Jonesy
14-Nov-73 Aberdeen, Music Hall – supported by Jonesy
18-Nov-73 Oxford, New Theatre – supported by Jonesy
20-Nov-73 Guildford, Civic Hall – supported by Jonesy
21-Nov-73 Birmingham, Town Hall – supported by Jonesy
22-Nov-73 Barrow-In-Furness, Civic Hall – supported by Jonesy
23-Nov-73 Newcastle, City Hall – supported by Jonesy
24-Nov-73 St Albans, Civic Hall – supported by Jonesy
25-Nov-73 Liverpool, Royal Court Theatre supported by Jonesy
26-Nov-73 Brighton, Dome – supported by Jonesy
27-Nov-73 Leeds, Town Hall – supported by Jonesy
29-Nov-73 Preston, Guildhall – supported by Jonesy
30-Nov-73 Sheffield, City Hall – supported by Jonesy
01-Dec-73 Bristol, Colston Hall – supported by Jonesy
02-Dec-73 Gravesend, Woodville Hall – supported by Jonesy
03-Dec-73 Manchester, Free Trade Hall – end of tour with Jonesy
22-Dec-73 London, Rainbow Theatre
16-Mar-74 Bradford University Bradford – warm-ups for *Solid* tour
17-Mar-74 Guildford, Civic Hall
19-Mar-74 Birmingham, Barbarellas
14-Apr-74 Croydon, Fox & Greyhound
26-Apr-74 Ipswich, Manor Ballroom – *Solid* tour
30-Apr-74 Hull, City Hall
03-May-74 North London Polytechnic
11-May-74 Cambridge, Technical College
12-May-74 London, Marquee
17-May-74 Southampton University
24-May-74 Newcastle, Mayfair Ballroom
27-May-74 Spennymoor, Top Hat Club
28-May-74 Leeds, City Hall
29-May-74 Bradford, King Georges Hall

30-May-74 Cleethorpes, Winter Gardens
31-May-74 Sheffield, City Hall
05-Jun-74 Manchester, Stoneground
06-Jun-74 Liverpool, Stadium
07-Jun-74 Newcastle, Mayfair Ballroom
14-Jun-74 Hatfield Polytechnic
15-Jun-74 Reading University
16-Jun-74 Plymouth, Guildhall
20-Jun-74 Penzance, Winter Gardens
25-Jun-74 Oxford, New Theatre
27-Jun-74 Stafford, Top Of The World
28-Jun-74 St Albans, Civic Hall
29-Jun-74 Harlow, Spurriers Park
30-Jun-74 Croydon, Fairfield Hall
04-Jul-74 Portsmouth, Guildhall
05-Jul-74 Swindon College – end of *Solid* tour
04-Oct-74 Coventry
08-Oct-74 Bristol
11-Oct-74 Wolverhampton
16-Oct-74 Greenwich
21-Oct-74 Manchester, Free Trade Hall
24-Oct-74 Blackburn
26-Oct-74 Northampton, County Ground
27-Oct-74 Twickenham, Winning Post
02-Nov-74 Aylesbury, Friars Club
03-Nov-74 Newark, Palace
09-Nov-74 Swansea, Patti Pavillion
10-Nov-74 Croydon, Greyhound
12-Nov-74 Birmingham, Barbarellas
15-Nov-74 Nottingham, Trent Polytechnic
17-Nov-74 Chelmsford, Chancellor Hall
23-Nov-74 Sheffield University
26-Nov-74 London, Marquee
05-Dec-74 Southport, Floral Hall
06-Dec-74 Bath University
07-Dec-74 Dagenham, Roundhouse
10-Dec-74 Hanley, Steam Machine
12-Dec-74 Great Yarmouth, Tiffany's
13-Dec-74 Glasgow University
17-Dec-74 Tunbridge Wells, Assembly Hall

19-Dec-74 Maidstone Polytechnic
20-Dec-74 Slough Community Centre
21-Dec-74 Liverpool, Stadium
28-Dec-74 Folkestone, Leas Cliff Hall
05-Jan-75 London, Roundhouse
10-Jan-75 Derby College Of Arts
11-Jan-75 Leicester
20-Jan-75 Salisbury, City Hall
25-Jan-75 Cambridge, Corn Exchange
27-Jan-75 Huddersfield Polytechnic
31-Jan-75 London, Regent Street Polytechnic
01-Feb-75 St Albans, Civic Hall
02-Feb-75 Westcliffe-On-Sea, Queens
07-Feb-75 Uxbridge, Brunel University
08-Feb-75 Oldham Technical College
13-Feb-75 Metz, France
14-Feb-75 Paris, France
15-Feb-75 Uzes, France
16-Feb-75 Marseille, France
21-Feb-75 Hereford
22-Feb-75 Folkstone, Leas Cliffe Hotel
28-Feb-75 Swansea, Patti Pavillion
01-Mar-75 Hastings
08-Mar-75 Ewell, Technical College
12-Mar-75 London, Marquee
13-Mar-75 Guildford
14-Mar-75 London, South Bank Polytechnic
15-Mar-75 Dagenham, Roundhouse
17-Mar-75 Solihull, Civic Hall
21-Mar-75 Newcastle, Mayfair
22-Mar-75 Peterborough, Technical College
25-Mar-75 Luxumbourg
26-Mar-75 Trier, Germany
27-Mar-75 Saarbrucken, Germany
29-Mar-75 Frankenthal, Germany
30-Mar-75 Ludwigshafen, Germany
31-Mar-75 Kaiserlauten, Germany
04-Apr-75 London, King's Cross Astoria – final gig with Pete Cruickshank – band split-up

Groundhogs As A Four-Piece

28-Jul-75 Sheffield
04-Aug-75 Manchester
10-Aug-75 Lewes
18-Aug-75 Derby
25-Aug-75 Chorley
21-Sep-75 Stockport
17-Feb-76 BBC *Old Grey Whistle Test*
28-Feb-76 Roundhouse, Bristol
29-Feb-76 Croydon, Greyhound
01-Mar-76 Chester, Quaintways
02-Mar-76 Huddersfield, Ivanhoe's
04-Mar-76 Chatham, Central Hall
05-Mar-76 Brighton, Sussex University
06-Mar-76 Manchester, UMIST
07-Mar-76 London, Roundhouse
09-Mar-76 Cardiff, Top Rank
12-Mar-76 Ipswich, The Manor
13-Mar-76 Maidenhead, Fox
14-Mar-76 Twickenham, Winning Post
16-Mar-76 Stoke, North Staffs Polytechnic
17-Mar-76 Plymouth, The Fiesta
19-Mar-76 Brunel University
20-Mar-76 Aylesbury Friars
21-Mar-76 Middlesborough, Town Hall
23-Mar-76 Birmingham, Barbarella's
24-Mar-76 Derby, Kings Hall
26-Mar-76 Lincoln Technical College
27-Mar-76 Northampton County Ground
28-Mar-76 Bournemouth, Winter Gardens
30-Mar-76 Salisbury, City Hall
31-Mar-76 Bradford, Guild Hall
01-Apr-76 Crewe, Civic Hall
02-Apr-76 Newcastle, Mayfair
10-Sep-76 Radio Concert Stockholm, Sweden
08-Oct-76 Liverpool Stadium
09-Oct-76 Newcastle University
10-Oct-76 Redcar, Coatham Hotel
11-Oct-76 Chester
13-Oct-76 Sheffield

14-Oct-76 Stoke
15-Oct-76 London, Woolwich
16-Oct-76 Maidenhead
19-Oct-76 Birmingham, Barbarella's
20-Oct-76 Derby
21-Oct-76 Sunderland
22-Oct-76 Edinburgh
23-Oct-76 Glasgow
25-Oct-76 Doncaster
28-Oct-76 Glamorgan
30-Oct-76 St Albans
31-Oct-76 Croydon, Greyhound – final Groundhogs gig of the 1970s

The Groundhogs Selected Discography

Tony McPhee, John Cruickshank, Pete Cruickshank, Dave Boorman, Tom Parker

1964

John Lee's Groundhogs – 'Shake It'/'Rock Me Baby' – Interphon I-7715 – US only

1965

John Lee Hooker and John Lee's Groundhogs – *And Seven Nights* – Verve Folkway 3003 – US. Released in the UK in 1971 on XTRA 1114
'Mai Lee', 'I'm Losing You', 'Little Girl Go Back To School', 'Little Dreamer', 'Don't Go Messin With My Bread', 'Bad Luck And Trouble', 'Waterfront', 'No One Pleases Me But You', 'It's Rainin' Here', 'It's A Crazy Mixed Up World', 'Seven Days And Seven Nights'

Tony McPhee, John Cruickshank, Pete Cruickshank, Terry Slade, David Ware, Fred

1966

John Lee`s Groundhogs – 'I'll Never Fall in Love Again'/'Over You Baby' – Planet 104

Tony McPhee, Pete Cruickshank, Ken Pustelnik, Steve Rye

1968

Groundhogs – *Scratching The Surface* – Liberty 83199
'Rocking Chair', 'Early In The Morning', 'Walking Blues', 'Married Men', 'No More Doggin'', 'Man Trouble', 'Come Back Baby', 'You Don't Love Me', 'Still A Fool'

The Groundhogs – 'You Don't Love Me'/'Still A Fool' – Liberty LBF15174

Tony McPhee, Pete Cruickshank, Ken Pustelnik

1969

Groundhogs – *Blues Obituary* – Liberty 83253
'B.D.D', 'Daze Of The Week', 'Times', 'Mistreated', 'Express Man', 'Natchez Burning', 'Light Was The Day'

Groundhogs – 'B.D.D'/'Gasoline' – Liberty LBF 15263

1970

Groundhogs – *Thank Christ For The Bomb* – Liberty 83295
'Strange Town', 'Darkness Is No Friend', 'Soldier', 'Thank Christ For The Bomb', 'Ship On The Ocean', 'Garden', 'Status People', 'Rich Man Poor Man', 'Eccentric Man'

Groundhogs – 'Eccentric Man'/'Status People' – Liberty 15346

1971
Groundhogs – *Split* – Liberty 83401
'Split Part One', 'Split Part Two', 'Split Part Three', 'Split Part Four', 'Cherry Red', 'A Year In The Life', 'Junkman', 'Groundhog'

Groundhogs – *Live At Leeds* – Promo
'Cherry Red', 'Garden', 'Split Part One', 'Groundhog', 'Eccentric Man'

1972
Groundhogs – *Who Will Save The World* – United Artists 29347
'Earth Is Not Room Enough', 'Wages Of Peace', 'Body In Mind', 'Music Is The Food Of Thought', 'Bog Roll Blues', 'Death Of The Sun', 'Amazing Grace', 'The Grey Maze'

Tony McPhee, Pete Cruickshank, Clive Brooks
Groundhogs – *Hogwash* – United Artists 29419
'I Love Miss Ogyny', 'You Had A Lesson', 'The Ringmaster', '3744 James Road', 'Sad Is The Hunter', 'S'One Song', 'Earth Shanty', 'Mr Hooker, Sir John'

1973
Groundhogs – 'Plea Sing, Plea Song'/'Over Blue' – United Artists 006

1974
Tony McPhee, Pete Cruickshank, Ken Pustelnik, Clive Brooks
Groundhogs – *Best 1969-1972* – United Artists UDF31
'Groundhog', 'Strange Town', 'Bog Roll Blues', 'You Had A Lesson', 'Eccentric Man', 'Earth Is Not Room Enough', 'B.D.D', 'Split Part One', 'Cherry Red', 'Mistreated', '3744 James Road', 'Soldier', 'Sad Is The Hunter', 'Garden', 'Split Part Four'

Tony McPhee, Pete Cruickshank, Clive Brooks
Groundhogs – *Solid* – World Wide Artists 004
'Light My Light', 'Free From All Alarm', 'Sins Of The Father', 'Sad Go Round', 'Corn Cob', 'Plea Sing Plea Song', 'Snow Storm', 'Jokers Grave'

Tony McPhee, Dave Wellbelove, Martin Kent, Mick Cook
1976
Groundhogs – *Crosscut Saw* – United Artists 29917
'Crosscut Saw', 'Promiscuity', 'Boogie Withus', 'Fulfillment', 'Live A Little Lady', 'Three
Way Split', 'Mean Mistreater', 'Eleventh Hour'

Groundhogs – 'Live A Little Lady'/'Boogie Withus' – United Artists 36095

Tony McPhee, Rick Adams, Martin Kent, Mick Cook
Groundhogs – *Black Diamond* – United Artists 29994
'Body Talk', 'Fantasy Partner', 'Live Right', 'Country Blues', 'Your Love Keeps Me Alive', 'Friendzy', 'Pastoral Future', 'Black Diamond'

Groundhogs – 'Pastoral Future'/'Live Right' – United Artists 36177

Tony McPhee and various lineups
1984
Groundhogs – *Hogging The Stage* – Psycho 024
A mixture of live material including *Live At Leeds 1971*, BBC session tracks from the early 1970s and material from the *Black Diamond* tour.

Tony McPhee, Alan Fish, Mick Kirton
1985
Groundhogs – *Razor's Edge* – Landslide LP 102
'Razor's Edge', 'I Confess', 'Born To Be With You', 'Once More Chance', 'The Protector', 'Superceded', 'Moving Fast Standing Still', 'I Want You To Love Me'

When Alan Fish joined the band, Tony sent him a cassette of some of the new material with his lead parts on and his job was to learn a bass part to go along with it. Fish recalls that when they were recording, he'd think to himself: 'Ah, that's how it goes.' Some of it was like putting a jigsaw together. Tony hadn't written enough material, so he included Muddy Waters' 'I Want You To Love Me'. Mick Kirton recalls this track: 'We never actually played it before we recorded it. It was recorded on the first take. To me, that song is so vibrant and Tony played so well on it.' There's a lot of energy, with Kirton's drums coming across as really powerful. He was using two bass drums and they really thundered. The band also really kicked live as Alan Fish recalls: 'We played at Gillies, Manchester. It was one of those great nights and we played for three hours. Afterwards, we had people come up to us and say they had never heard a band play like that before.'

Tony McPhee, Dave Anderson, Mick Jones
1987
Groundhogs – *Back Against The Wall* – Demi Monde DMLP 1014
'Back Against The Wall', 'No To Submission', 'Blue Boar Blues', 'Waiting In The Shadows', 'Ain't No Slaver', 'Stick To Your Guns', 'In The Meantime', '54146'

Tony had written the songs in a couple of months, but some of the riffs had been purloined from his famous tape reservoir. The album was a less heavy affair than *Razor's Edge* and was better for it. It was given the defiant title of *Back Against The Wall*. In fact, there were a number of cuts on that album that had an element of defiance. 'Blue Boar Blues' was based on the famous motorway service station at the Watford Gap and it's where bands used to meet up and exchange stories of their adventures on the road. Tony remembers gazing in awestruck fashion at Gene Vincent sipping his cup of tea there.

Tony McPhee, Dave Anderson, Mick Jones
1988
Groundhogs – *Hogs On The Road* – Demi Monde DMLP 1016
'Express Man', 'Strange Town', 'Eccentric Man', '3744 James Road', 'I Want You To Love Me', 'Split Part Four', 'Soldier', 'Back Against The Wall', 'Garden', 'Split Part One', 'Waiting In The Shadows', 'Light My Light', 'Me And The Devil', 'Mistreated', 'Groundhog', 'Split Part Two', 'Cherry Red'

The band are in blistering form as they run through a well-balanced selection of material from the history of the band. A real treat is that, on most of the tracks, Tony employs his Zemaitis guitar. This was his frontline guitar back then. He was, however, acutely aware that it was a dangerous thing to take a guitar like that out of his house. *Hogs On The Road* is a practical joke thought up by the band. The album was supposed to have been recorded in Germany but the only audible thing from the tapes was the applause! It was actually recorded at The Old Smithy, Worcester, live in the studio, and was also mixed there. To make things more convincing, Tony apologised during 'Soldier' for using the term 'dirty hun'.

Tony McPhee, Alan Fish, Mick Kirton
1989
Groundhogs – *No Surrender (Razor's Edge Tour 1985)* – HTD LP02
'Razor's Edge', '3744 James Road', 'Superceded', 'Light My Light', 'One More Chance', 'Garden', 'Split Part Two', 'Eccentric Man', 'Strange Town', 'Cherry Red'

Tony McPhee, Alan Fish, Mick Jones
1993
Groundhogs – *Groundhog Night* – HTD CD12
'Shake For Me', 'No More Doggin', 'Eccentric Man', '3744 James Road', 'I Want You To Love Me', 'Garden', 'Split Part One', 'Split Part Two', 'Still

A Fool', 'I Love You Miss Ogyny', 'Thank Christ For The Bomb', 'Soldier', 'Mistreated', 'Me And The Devil', 'Cherry Red', 'Groundhog', 'Been There Done That', 'Down In The Bottom'

The gig only had a dribble of fans because it wasn't advertised properly. *Record Collector* interviewed Tony on the afternoon of the gig and he had a few more pre-gig drinks than usual. It cost £1100 to hire the BBC mobile but Tony was happy with the result.

Tony McPhee, Pete Cruickshank, Ken Pustelnik, Clive Brooks
1994
Groundhogs – *BBC Radio One Live In Concert* – Windsong WINCD054
'Split Part One', 'Cherry Red', 'Split Part Two', 'Groundhog', 'Still A Fool', 'Ship On The Ocean', 'Free From All Alarm', 'Dog Me Bitch', 'Light My Light', 'Sins Of The Father'
Tracks 1-4 from 24/2/72. Tracks 5-11 from 23/5/74

Tony McPhee, Pete Cruickshank, Ken Pustelnik, Steve Rye
1996
Groundhogs – *Four Groundhogs Originals* – EMI CDHOGS1
'Scratching The Surface', 'Blues Obituary', 'Thank Christ For The Bomb', 'Split'

Tony McPhee, Eric Chipulina, Pete Correa
1998
Groundhogs – *Hogs In Wolf's Clothing* – HTD CD81
'Smokestack Lightnin'', 'Baby, How Long', 'Commit A Crime', 'Forty Four', 'No Place To Go', 'Ain't Superstitious', 'Evil', 'So Glad', 'My Life', 'Sittin On Top Of The World', 'Shake For Me', 'Wang Dang Doodle', 'How Many More Years', 'Nature', 'Down In The Bottom'

Tony McPhee, Alan Fish, Mick Kirton
Groundhogs – *No Surrender (Razor's Edge Tour 1985 Part Two)* – HTD CD 86
'Razor's Edge', 'Baby, What Have I Done Wrong', 'I Want You To Love Me', 'Light My Light', 'Split Part Two', 'Superceded', 'Garden', 'Split Part One', 'Groundhog', 'Cherry Red'

Tony McPhee, Pete Cruickshank, Ken Pustelnik, Clive Brooks
Groundhogs – *On Air 1970-72* (BBC) – Strange Fruit
'Garden', 'Eccentric Man', 'Split Part One', 'Split Part Two', 'Mistreated', 'I Love You Miss Ogyny', 'You Had A Lesson', 'Earth Shanty', '3744 James Road', 'Sad Is The Hunter', 'Split Part Four', 'Cherry Red'

Tony McPhee, Eric Chipulina, Pete Correa
1999
Groundhogs – *The Muddy Waters Songbook* – HTD CD91
'Stuff You Gotta Watch', 'She's Alright', 'I've Got A Rich Man's Woman', 'Can't Call Her Sugar', 'Forty Days And Forty Nights', 'Mean Ole Frisco', 'I'm Ready', 'Young Fashioned Ways', 'Hoochie Coochie Man', 'I Feel So Good', 'Mean Red Spider', 'Tiger In Your Tank', 'Mannish Boy', 'Got My Mojo Workin'', 'Country Blues'

Tony McPhee and various lineups
2000
Groundhogs – *HTD Years* (compilation) – HTD CD115
'Baby How Long', 'Dry Land' (demo), 'Soldier', 'Country Blues', 'Shake For Me', 'Down In The Bottom', 'Over Pressure' (demo), 'Garden', 'Evil', 'Never Again' (demo), 'One More Chance', '3744 James Road', 'Groundhog', 'Cherry Red'

Tony McPhee and various lineups
2001
Groundhogs – *3744 James Road* (compilation) – Castle CMDDD 277
Tracks taken from *Hogs In Wolf's Clothing*, *Muddy Waters Songbook*, *No Surrender*, *Groundhog Night* (double CD)

Tony McPhee, Eric Chipulina, Pete Correa
Groundhogs – *Live At The Astoria* – Talking Elephant TECD 026
'Shake For Me', 'Eccentric Man', '3744 James Road', 'I Want You To Love Me', 'Split Part One', 'Split Part Two', 'Mistreated', 'Still A Fool', 'Cherry Red', 'Groundhog', 'Down In The Bottom'

Tony McPhee, Jon Camp, Mick Jones
Groundhogs – *The Lost Tapes Volume One* – Blue Flame BFBL 004 (Italy)
Live In London 1989

Tony McPhee and various lineups
Groundhogs – *The Lost Tapes Volume Two* – Blue Flame BFBL 005 (Italy)
Live In Milan June 1994 & Live In Stockholm ('Cherry Red' only) 1976

Tony McPhee, Pete Cruickshank, Ken Pustelnik
2002
Groundhogs – *The Radio One Sessions (1970-71)* – Strange Fruit
'Garden', 'Still A Fool', 'Cherry Red', 'Eccentric Man', 'Split Part One', 'Split Part Two', 'Mistreated'

Tony McPhee, Pete Cruickshank, Clive Brooks
Groundhogs – *BBC Live In Concert (1972-74)* – Strange Fruit
'Cherry Red', 'Split Part One', 'You Had A Lesson', '3744 James Road', 'Sad Is The Hunter', 'Split Part Two', 'Split Part Four', 'Ship On The Ocean', 'Soldier'

Tony McPhee, Dave Anderson, Mick Jones, Mick Chetwood
Groundhogs – *Tribute To Fleetwood Mac* – Blue Flame BFCD 002
'Stop Messin' Around', 'I've Lost My Baby', 'One Sunny Day'

Tony McPhee, Dave Wellbelove, Martin Kent, Mick Cook
2004
Groundhogs – *UK Tour 1976* – MLP P05CD
'Boogie Withus', 'Promiscuity', 'Corn Cob', 'Eleventh Hour', 'Crosscut Saw', 'Fulfillment', 'Light My Light', 'Split Part Two', 'Cherry Red'

Tony McPhee Selected Discography

1966
'Ain`t Gonna Cry No More'/'Someone To Love Me' – Purdah
'When You Got A Good Friend'/'You Don`t Love Me'
Herbal Mixture – 'Tailor Made'/'A Love That's Died' – Columbia DB8027
Herbal Mixture – 'Machines'/'Please Leave My Mind' – Columbia DB8083
Champion Jack Dupree – *From New Orleans To Chicago* – Decca LK/SKL4747
Tony appears on two tracks – 'Third Degree' and 'Shim, Sham, Shimmy'

1967
Eddie Boyd – *Eddie Boyd And His Blues Band* – Decca LK/SKL4872
Tony appears on two tracks – 'Dust My Broom' and 'Save Her Doctor'

1968
Hapshash & The Coloured Coat – *Western Flier* – Liberty LBF83233
Tony plays guitar on all tracks

1969
John Dummer Blues Band – *Cabal* – Mercury. SMCL 20136
Tony plays guitar on all tracks
John Dummer Blues Band – 'Travelling Man'/'40 Days' – Mercury MF1040
John Dummer Blues Band – 'Try Me One More Time'/'Riding At Midnight' – Mercury MF1119
Big Joe Williams – *Hand Me Down My Old Walking Stick* – Liberty 83207

Tony was a producer
Andy Fernbach – *If You Miss Your Connexion* – Liberty
Tony was only a producer

1973

The Two Sides Of Tony T.S McPhee – World Wide Artists WWA 001
'Three Times Seven', 'All My Money', 'Alimony', 'Morning Eyes', 'Dog Me Bitch', 'Take It Out', 'The Hunt Part One', 'The Hunt Part Two', 'The Hunt Part Three', 'The Hunt Part Four'

1977

Terraplane (Tony McPhee, Wilgar Campbell, Alan Fish) – 'Down In The Bottom'/'Shake For Me' – not released

Tony was now working in his own house producing new bands on his 16 Track Ampex. It was something that he did for fun, really. It was here that he met Alan Fish, who was there with his band called Wedgewood. Tony liked him and it occurred to him that he might be the bass player to fit in with Campbell. Tony called him up and asked him to put some bass on two tracks he was looking to record. The tracks were Willie Dixon's 'Down In The Bottom' and Howlin Wolf's 'Shake For Me'. They were chosen only because they knew them well.

1979

Billy Boy Arnold backed by Terraplane (Tony McPhee, Wilgar Campbell, Alan Fish) – *Checkin' It Out* – Red Lightnin' RL 0029
Billy Boy Arnold backed by Terraplane – *Superharps* (EP) – Red Lightnin' 0027

By dint of good fortune, a friend of Alan Fish had a record label called Red Lightnin' – based in East Anglia – and he was looking for a band to back blues man Billy Boy Arnold on an album. In early October 1977, Terraplane went into Pathway Studios, London, to record the album that was to be called *Checkin' It Out*. For Tony, it was a welcome return to all those sessions in the 1960s with other blues giants. On this project, however, they would have the luxury of two days! The first day was set over for rehearsal, and the next day, they recorded the album. They recorded so many tracks that they had enough for an EP as well. Even though Arnold was not as illustrious as some of the others, Tony thought he was underrated and a good harp player, and like a lot of blues artists, he was very humble and a nice man to boot. It's certainly one of the classiest albums Tony ever appeared on outside the Groundhogs – there's a lot of strong material. Unfortunately, the album was delayed, and when it was eventually released, Tony didn't even know about it. The first time he heard it was when they played a track at Dingwalls, London, in 1979 – it dawned on him that he was hearing his own guitar playing.

Mike Batt – *Tarot Suite* – Epic EPC 86099
Tony plays guitar on one track

Tony was going in another direction by this time. He started writing pop songs, so he thought about whom he could write them for. It wasn't long before he thought Mike Batt would be a good candidate; he'd produced the Groundhogs' first album. He'd had great success with The Wombles in the early 70s and seemed to be plugged into the pop market. But when he spoke to him, Tony had a shock, as he recalls: 'It's amazing that I'm doing this album (*Tarot Suite*) and I was thinking of you because I want you to play on it.' Batt had tried to contact Tony via Rory Gallagher but without success. The session was already booked, so within a few days, Tony went down to London. But he soon found out that Batt had given him a very difficult job. The track that he was to play on was called 'Tarota', but the problem was that Batt wanted some slide guitar,and Tony was convinced it wouldn't work. In the end, Tony turned out to be right. It was the only thing that he recorded in 1979. He never did get anywhere with those pop songs!

1983
Tony McPhee Band (Tony McPhee, Steve Towner, Mick Kirton) – 'Time Of Action'/'Born To Be With You' – TS001

These self-penned tracks by Tony were recorded on 29 March 1983 at Wood Cray Manor Farm in Berkshire. Mick Kirton recommended the studio as he had recorded an album there with his band Roadworks (Steve Towner was the guitarist). Steve Towner, who was a talented artist, illustrated the sleeve with Tony's signature. He decided to pay to have just 1,000 pressed (that's all he could afford) and sell them at gigs.

1993
Tony McPhee – *Foolish Pride* – HTD CD10
'Foolish Pride', 'Every Minute', 'Devil You Know', 'Masqueradin'', 'Time After Time', 'On The Run', 'Took Me By Surprise', 'Whatever It Takes', 'Been There Done That', 'I'm Gonna Win'

1994
Tony McPhee – *Slide T.S Slide* – HTD CD26
'Reformed Man', 'Mean Disposition', 'Slide To Slide', 'From A Pawn To

A King', 'Tell Me Baby', 'Hooker & The Hogs', 'Someday Baby', 'Driving Duck', 'No Place To Go', 'Me & The Devil', 'Death Letter', 'Can't Be Satisfied', 'Still A Fool', 'Write Me A Short Few Lines', 'Down In The Bottom'
Tracks 1-6 were recorded at Tony's home studio in 1994. Tracks 7-15 were recorded on the Jefferson Starship European tour of 1993.

1997
Bleaching The Blues – HTD CD72
'When You're Down', 'All Your Women', 'There's A Light', 'Went In Like A Lamb', 'When Your Man Has Gone', 'Many Times', 'All Last Night', 'When You're Walking Down The Street', 'Meeting Of The Minds', 'Bleaching The Blues', 'If I Had Possession', 'Love In Vain', 'Floatin' Bridge', 'Terraplane Blues', 'Little Red Rooster'

2004
Blues At Ten (with Joanna Deacon) – Blues Matters BMRCCD20042
'Blues At Ten', 'Messin' My Mind', 'I Won't Take Love', 'Strange Place', 'Young At Heart', 'Oh Death', 'Blues Is A Man', 'Devillved', 'PMT Blues', 'Better Off With The Blues', 'Lost Boys', 'Don't You Feel My Leg', 'Single Lives And Family Ties', 'Graveyard Blues', 'Christmas Tree'

Selected Compilations

1968
Blues Anytime Volume 1 – Immediate IMLP 014
'Someone To Love Me', 'Ain't Gonna Cry No More'
Blues Anytime Volume 2 – Immediate IMLP 015
'When You Got A Good Friend', 'You Don't Love Me'
Me And The Devil – Liberty 83190
Tony appears on four tracks – 'Me And The Devil', 'No More Doggin'', 'Death Letter' and 'Rollin & Tumblin''. The latter is a duet with Jo Anne Kelly

1969
I Asked For Water She Gave Me Gasoline (compilation) – Liberty 83254
Tony appears on four tracks – 'Oh Death' (with Jo Anne Kelly), 'Gasoline', 'Rock Me' (Groundhogs with Jo Anne Kelly), 'Don't Pass The Hat Round'
Gutbucket – Liberty LBX 3
'Me And The Devil', 'Still A Fool' (Groundhogs)
Son Of Gutbucket – Liberty LBX 4
'Oh Death', 'Mistreated' (Groundhogs)

1971
Same Thing On Their Mind – Sunset SLS 50209
'Me And The Devil', 'Gasoline' (with Jo Anne Kelly)

All Good Clean Fun – United Artists UDX 201/2
'Cherry Red' (Groundhogs)

1972
Paradiso – United Artists (Holland) 5C 062 93 544
'Still A Fool' (Groundhogs) included.

1986
Blues On Two – BBC REN610
'Express Man' (Groundhogs) radio session with Ken Pustelnik

Moving Fast, Standing Still – Raw Power RAW LP 021
Razor's Edge and *Two Sides Of Tony TS McPhee*, plus the Purdah 1966 tracks

1994
The Best Of A.O.G – HTD CD20
Includes the two Terraplane tracks and two tracks from *Groundhog Night*

1995
Alexis Korner Memorial Concert Vol. 3 – Indigo IGOCD 2025
'I Can't Be Satisified'

Endnotes

1 A participant in the concert was a boy called Mike Scheuer. He was two years older than The Worried Nine. His party piece was an Elvis Presley impersonation. He later changed his name to Mike Sarne and had a massive hit with 'Come Outside' with Wendy Richard (of *Are You Being Served* and *Eastenders* fame) in June 1962.

2 Tony's decision made a big impression on Dave Wetton, who was thinking of doing the same. He noted in his diary on 11 August 1962, 'I'd become increasingly impressed with Mac's moral stance on the subject and had simply been looking for the right opportunity to convince my grandmother, who did all the cooking, that I was sincere. For a while, she saw it as a flash on the pan ... but eventually, she got the message.' Dave Wetton stuck to his principles, and throughout the 1970s, was Secretary of the Hunt Saboteurs Association. He also worked with Tony on a related project in 1975. He is still involved with the organisation.

3 The Seneschals' early repertoire included Duane Eddy's 'Rebel Rouser' and 'Ramrod', The Scorpions' 'Riders In The Sky', The Shadows' 'Apache' and 'The Warlord', The Fireballs' 'Bulldog' and 'Foot-Patter', The Ventures' 'Walk, Don't Run' and 'Ram Bunk Shush', The Rockets' 'Gibraltar Rock' and 'Walking Home', Eddie Smith & The Hornets' 'Up Turn' and 'Border Beat' and The Hunters' 'Santa Monica Flyer' and 'The Storm'. After Ray Wade joined, it was of a more eclectic mix, apart from the obvious ones: Rufus Thomas' 'Walking The Dog', Ritchie Valens' 'La Bamba', Chuck Berry's 'Sweet Little Sixteen' and Eddie Cochran's 'C'mon Everybody'.

4 Cakey lived in Putney, so he had to cart his drum kit on the bus. He managed to get everything in a big suitcase, apart from the bass drum. On one occasion, it even rolled off the back of the bus. On another occasion, he got chatting to a 15-year-old boy who was keen for him to be his drummer. Cakey refused Mark Feld's invitation. Of course, Mark later went on to fame as Marc Bolan!

5 Jo Ann Kelly was inspired by singers such as Memphis Minnie, Robert Johnson, John Lee Hooker and many others. She started out as a folk blues artist playing the local clubs. The blues only had a cult following in those days, so to find a female blazing the trial was rare. As already noted, there were many musicians in the mainstream who had never even heard of the blues. Some of her earliest recordings – which she

hated – were made for Mike Vernon; she bemoaned, like other artists, that she never got any money from those sessions. In September 1968, she took part in the first National Blues Federation Convention at the Conway Hall, London. The fact that she appeared with such luminaries as Stefan Grossman, Alexis Korner and Champion Jack Dupree illustrates the level that she had achieved. She performed with Canned Heat's Al Wilson and singer Bob Hite, who were very impressed.

She had this tremendous ability to get people behind her vision; she was very persuasive. In 1969, John Lee Hooker was playing at the Festival Hall and she managed to persuade him and Big Joe Williams to appear with her at the Bridge House, which was a little blues/folk club. You can just imagine the looks on the faces of the punters when she walked in with them two. The Bridge House was in Borough in South London and was a major attraction to blues enthusiasts. Apart from Jo Ann, other regular performers included Tony McPhee, Dave Kelly, Simon Prager and Steve Rye.

At the second National Blues Federation Convention, she was asked to join Canned Heat but she declined. However, the word had spread across the pond and she was invited to perform at the Memphis Blues Festival. As a result of this performance, she had a few offers but she didn't like the hype that surrounded it, as she related to Bob Brunning in *Blues: The British Connection*: 'They gave me the whole build up, you know. They announced 'John Hammond, the man who discovered Billie Holiday and Bob Dylan NOW brings you Miss Jo Ann Kelly.' And I thought, 'Oh f***.' She was a blues purist and that made her suspicious of the big 'build-up'.

After that, she mainly worked in the UK and was destined to never 'make it'. However, that would be grossly unfair. If ever there was an artist who remained true to herself, it was Jo Ann Kelly. The evidence of her powerful, scintillating voice is there on record. In the 1960s, *Melody Maker* referred to her as the 'mother of British blues'.

It was a great loss when she passed away of a brain tumor on 20 October 1990. She worked right to the end. An obituary noted just where she stood as an artist: 'Unlike such groups as The Rolling Stones, however, or her American contemporary Janis Joplin (who, despite her notoriety, was in no way Kelly's superior), she made no concessions to pop tastes. Throughout her career, she played and sang the blues in a defiantly traditional style, solidly rooted in the idiom of the pre-war Mississippi Delta.'

6 The acquisition of a piano player was not always a bed of roses. Sometimes, they would find the piano at a gig out of tune, in a bad state or even missing entirely! At a gig in Crawley, they found themselves with no piano but, luckily, they located a loan one just across the road. However, they were faced with the perilous job of manhandling it across the busy A23. One of the ways Bob Hall got over some of these problems was to buy a piano tuning kit, which he took everywhere they went.

7 Roy Fisher met Arden's booking agent when he went round to his office in Denmark Street, London. Little Richard was there, too, as Arden was promoting his tour. At the time, they had a temporary secretary working in the office. While he was waiting, a telephone was flung out of the office he was waiting to go into. The telephone landed at his feet. There was a look of horror on the temp's face. The booking agent was Peter Grant, later to find fame as Led Zeppelin's fiercely uncompromising manager.

8 Bob Glass occasionally helped out in the Swing shop when Len Tempan needed time off.

9 Bob Hall met Hooker again in the early 1980s. It was after a gig in California, but Hooker's past shenanigans were, obviously, not far from the surface, as he explained to writer Bob Brunning: 'I walked into the dressing room and there was a sort of sea of people, you know, but Hooker instantly recognised me and I felt good about that because he's played with thousands of people. The first thing he did was say, 'Hey, Bob, don't tell any stories about the old times – here's my new wife!" She was in her mid-20s!

10 There is no doubt that Bob Hall was exceptional and was a great loss when he had to leave John Lee's Groundhogs. This is what promoter Jim Simpson had to say about him: 'The number of (US) blues men who have told me that the pianist Bob Hall is the best piano player they ever worked with and that he's up there with Otis Spann are without number!'

11 Mike Vernon later founded the famous Blue Horizon blues label. He had a knack for seeking out home r&b talent, but he was also able to change with the times. He later produced successful albums from the late 1960s, 1970s and well into the 1980s. These included Ten Years After, Fleetwood Mac, Focus, Dr Feelgood and Level 42.

12 In 1989, Pete Townshend released his *Iron Man* solo album. The guest performers included John Lee Hooker.

13 When Immediate Records was liquidated in 1970, Tony was approached by the liquidators and offered the princely sum of £43 for his contribution. He told them to shove it! However, when Mike Vernon sold these tracks to Sony in 2002, he did get a more substantial sum of money.

14 The tracks recorded were 'Get Your Head Happy', 'No Meat Blues', 'Talk All In My Sleep', 'Easy Is The Way', 'There's A Dead Cat On The Line', 'Snow Is On The Ground', 'Sick In Bed', 'Papa Told Mama', 'Who Was There A While Ago', 'Down In Clarksdale', 'Don't Out Me Out', 'My Home In Mississippi' and 'My Baby Told Me'.

15 Mike Batt was working for a publishing company called Metric Music. It was only later on when he went to Liberty (which became United Artists). He went on to provide the music to The Wombles' children's television program. The Wombles had many hits in the 1970s and he became famous. He still produces music, including an album in 2003 for the acclaimed singing sensation Katie Melua.

16 Michael Hasted had turned up at Andrew Lauder's office with his portfolio, only a few days before the shoot, hustling for work. He was in luck!

17 John Lee Hooker was touring with Bonnie Raitt in 1990. Tony got backstage passes from his friend, Barry Riddington, who was involved with the record company. Initially, he was disappointed because the first gig that Hooker booked at the Hammersmith Odeon on 7 July clashed with a gig Tony had in Barnstaple on that night. Shortly after announcing the first gig, they added another on 16 July. It would be no exaggeration to say that Hooker never forgot a face, just like Bob Hall. Even though Tony had changed a lot since their last meeting, Hooker recognised him without prompting and greeted his old friend with 'Hello, Mac'. They managed to speak for ten minutes. It was the last time Tony saw him.

18 The man who was usually responsible for finding Rye was Mick Hubbert. He was a friend of Jo Ann Kelly and Bob Glass. He'd be there as a fan, but later, he found himself as the Groundhogs' first roadie.

19 One of the artists included is John Lewis, who was a fine piano boogie player. In the 70s, he became Jonah Lewie and had a few hit singles, including the classic Christmas single 'Don't Stop The Cavalry'. Brett Marvin and the Thunderbolts are featured on two cuts. Brett Marvin became Terry Dactyl in the 70s and his big hit with his Dinosaurs was 'Seaside Shuffle'.

20 The Groundhog Series consisted of *Me And The Devil* (various artists), *Scratching The Surface* (Groundhogs), *Hand Me Down My Old Walking Stick* (Big Joe Williams), *If You Miss Your Connexion* (Andy Fernbach), *I Asked For Water – She Gave Me Gasoline* (various artists) and *Blues Obituary* (Groundhogs).

21 In the 21st century, Tony updated his feelings: 'In 2004, with the invasion of Iraq in full swing, increasing hostilities in Israel and growing conflicts between religious ideologies of the polarised east/west, the deterrent argument against nuclear weaponry is becoming obsolete.'

22 Alan Tanner disappeared shortly after the work for the sleeve was completed. The band wanted to use him again for *Split* but it was not to be. He was last heard of living in Wales. He later moved to Scotland, and up until recently, that's where he was last heard of.

23 Part of the promotion, written to coincide with the release, was a contribution by Martin Cerf – executive of UA in the States. It was decided to exploit the Groundhog Day connection: 'This year, to really add punch to this day we call Groundhog Day, we are dedicating the entire year to the creatures and are sending you their latest album, *Thank Christ For The Bomb*, along with an exciting anthology book on the Groundhogs. You'll quickly realise these are English compositions. These are English Groundhogs, rare in these parts. The fact is, these Groundhogs are rare – period – as you'll soon see! Enjoy.'

24 Tony Zemaitis (1935-2002) started making guitars in his spare time, but it wasn't long before he was working 12-hour days from his home in Balham, London. He was apprenticed as a Cabinet Maker after leaving school. He learned to play the guitar and played semi-pro in clubs, but he got into making guitars by stealth. He recalled in an interview at the time: 'It was over a good many years that I realised I was becoming a guitar maker. I managed to get a job that allowed me to work two or three days a week as a cabinetmaker and I used to spend the rest of the time on guitars.' His list of other clients included Donovan, Marc Bolan, Peter Green, Spencer Davies, Jo Ann Kelly, Ronnie Lane, Ronnie Wood and Greg Lake.

25 Denis Knowles joined Liberty-UA in the summer of 1969; he came from CBS. His job was to help launch new bands and to exploit ways of ensuring the trail didn't go cold with the media. When he worked at CBS, he had 52 vans at his disposal to cover the UK. However, as

he related recently, Liberty was a much smaller operation: 'Philips (distributor for Liberty) had many problems and needed to move their operation to larger premises in Romford. The move happened the week before the release of *Thank Christ For The Bomb*. They were unable to distribute any labels for over a week despite protests from Dave Betteridge MD of Island Records, for whom Philips distributed. The band had built up a strong following and demand by the release date. At the time, Liberty-UA had just five sales vans: three in London and the suburbs, one in the Midlands and one to cover Manchester and Liverpool.'

But the situation got worse the further away from London, as Knowles was keen to point out: 'One Scottish dealer in particular, Bruce Findlay's Records, had five shops spread around Edinburgh, Glasgow and Stirling etc. Bruce rang me out of desperation, as he could not get the new Groundhogs album (*Thank Christ*) and the demand in his shops was considerable. To cut a long story short, I was able to ship him large quantities overnight via Security Express. We also supplied other important dealers in the same way, all of which made returns to the album charts. The result was that the album shot in at number nine in the top 50 album charts, which, of course, gave us more publicity and increased demand.'

When the Philips contract ran out after *Split*, they signed a deal with EMI for distribution.

26 In the 1990s, *Mojo* ran a regular item called 'Last Night a Record Changed My Life'. Karl Hyde of Underworld – their 'Born Slippy' became the anthem of the hit film *Trainspotting* – cited *Split* as a seminal influence. In the article, he recalls, at the age of 14, going to the Birmingham Town Hall to see them: 'I thought it was just incredible. Tony McPhee had a fantastic voice – he reminded me of Roger Chapman of Family. But his guitar playing was brilliant. I loved and still do his sense of syncopation. I still do things that I learned from listening to Tony McPhee.' He remembers well the first time he heard the album: 'My mate's dad put these big egg-shaped headphones on me and said 'Listen to this!' It blew me away.' He was mesmerised by the pictures of the band on stage on the album cover, too: 'I wanted to be on that stage, playing all those incredible guitar licks, going into reveries of the imagination.'

27 The US release of *Split* has a different cover. It features three individual black-and-white pictures of the band members playing

their instruments. Showcased in the background of each shot are artificially produced mountain/desert scenes. The inside cover features two groundhogs standing up on a mound of earth. There are extensive sleeve notes that tell the story of *Split*. This is how it starts: 'Screaming, pulsating lead guitar riffs throw you into a rhythm track that creates enough motive for even the weakest muscle of your body to move sharply and involuntarily as if it were experiencing a spasmodic nerve attack – you have entered the first phase of *Split*.'

28 The BBC was called 'Auntie' because they had a tendency to be prim and proper, and sort of 'nanny' their audience. Tapes were wiped for a variety of reasons, including cost and the need to reuse them. They also only had a short-term use and they didn't want to archive them.

29 Tony knew Fanger as he had been the guitarist when he produced Andy Fernbach's *If You Miss Your Connexion*.

30 In spite of the acrimonious split, Tony did work with Roy Fisher again. In December 1978, he asked Tony if he'd produce a band he was managing called Pure Hell. It was a clear indication that there was no bad blood between the two men, as Roy Fisher remembers: 'I have never been a person to bear grudges, so contacting Tony to see if he would be interested in producing the session was not awkward. He accepted and the results were fun, although, due to the band's US management contract, the tapes were never released and have been in my archive box ever since. It would be good if they finally got to see the light of day.' Tony journeyed to London on his motorbike. Roy Fisher recalls the session: 'The punk band that Tony produced in 1978 was Pure Hell, a New York-based black punk band that I brought over to England to tour, with the dates being booked by Barry Dickens at the ITB agency. Tony produced three tracks – 'American', 'Hungry Eyes' and 'I Want Your Body' – at Utopia Studios, engineered by Damian Korner, who was the son of Alexis Korner.' He did the session, which only lasted a few hours, and returned to Haverhill. The journey was tortuous as it was quite cold and he had to stop a few times to warm up in the phone boxes along the route. The scene must have been bizarre, with Tony jumping up and down on the spot in such a restricted space.

31 Tony McPhee got his publishing royalties separate from performing royalties.

32 They were billed to appear at the Great Western Festival on 27 May, second on the day to The Beach Boys. But, for some reason, they didn't perform.

33 The Black Panther movement was led by the charismatic and uncompromising Malcolm X. Their aim was to achieve secure rights for black people by nonviolent and violent means. They were in direct opposition to Martin Luther King's peaceful tactics. Before the 1960s ended, both men had been assassinated.

34 This kind of intimidation was not uncommon in the US. Led Zeppelin played a gig at The Forum, Inglewood, in 1970. Robert Plant makes a reference to the police tactics on a tape of the gig: 'All those people with big sticks and we don't care.'

35 Anthony Minghella went on to become a film director. His credits include *The Talented Mr Ripley*, *The English Patient* and the recent American Civil War epic, *Cold Mountain*. He passed away in 2008.

36 Hemdale produced the very successful film *Women In Love*, starring Oliver Reed and Glenda Jackson in the early 70s. They also produced *The Terminator*, starring Arnold Schwarzenegger, which was a massive box office hit.

37 In 1995, Mick Stones, who ran the *Hogs Feedback* magazine, went to Memphis to seek out Tony's old haunt; it was not as he expected it: 'As many people know, '3744 James Road' is not just a track on the *Hogwash* album but it is an account of Tony's first impressions of America, flying and the warm reception the band received when they first arrived on US soil. It is also, of course, the address of where they stayed in Memphis.

I can remember waiting for the taxi in the hotel lounge to take me and my wife over to the address and the look on the cabbie's face almost said, 'Well there's nothing out there to see'. It was, indeed, in a remote part of Memphis, not far from the freeway, surrounded by fields but very peaceful. It was not what I expected. It looked like a building rich in history, with a long drive surrounded by deep green lawns. The one thing that stood out, in-particular, was a plaque at the gateway with the house number emblazoned on it – perfect for documenting the occasion with a photograph. The cabbie must have thought I was nuts to have come all this way to have my picture taken in a gateway in a remote suburb of Memphis. We visited Graceland and had our picture taken in the gateway there, but for me, 3744 James Road, Memphis, Tennessee is my special memory of visiting America. Unfortunately, more recent visitors report that the house has been torn down.

38 It was an eye-catching advert, with its proclamation style of delivery: 'The Groundhogs lost 18 plectrums, used eight sets of assorted 'Clifford Essex' and 'Rotosound' strings, smashed two 'Weatherking' plastic heads and 15 'Hayman C' sticks, got through 48 bottles of coke, 30 pints of Lowenbrau and assorted non-chateau-bottled wines, fiddled with 'Astronic' equalisers, Schaller wah wah's, ring modulators, ARP synthesizers and ended up with 18,500 feet of 'BASF' tape and one lump of polyvinyl chloride with added carbon black – they call it *HOGWASH*.'

39 Apart from being heavily involved in the music scene in the UK, Wilf had another less publicised life across the Atlantic. In a book based on his life, author John Pearson outlines it: 'Only two Englishmen have ever been closely involved with the American mafia ... The second was Wilf Pine ... But thanks to a chance encounter with a leading figure in the Genovese crime family in New York, Wilf became accepted as one of his own family, a trusted friend and associate of the influential godfather Joe Pagano.' The links were solid as Joe was best man at Wilf's wedding and he also became involved with John Gotti, who was boss of the Gambino family.

After the Groundhogs split, Wilf continued in management with Stray, Edgar Broughton Band and Jimmy Helms – the latter was taking up more and more of his time. When Hemdale ceased to be quoted on the stock market, Wilf's interest in WWA also ceased: 'This convinces me that the WWA bid had always been a ploy to get into Hemdale, since Hemdale had the prestige of being a publicly quoted company with a gambling license for various bookmaking operations they conducted.' After giving advice to his acts on where they could get new management, he quit the music business in 1976. Before the end of 1977, he declared himself bankrupt.

Wilf got to know Charlie Kray back in England, and before long, he was visiting his twin brothers (Reg & Ron) in prison. He was also involved in the film made about them in the late 80s, starring the Kemp brothers from Spandau Ballet. Wilf was at Charlie's side when he died in prison

Wilf met up with Tony to talk about old times in 2004 at the Bournemouth gig of the Alvin Lee/Edgar Winter tour (they have always kept in touch with each other). The gold discs of Groundhogs,

Black Sabbath and Stray still hung on the wall of Wilf's sitting room. Wilf passed away in 2018. Their whereabouts now are unknown.

40 On a short tour of Scotland, the Groundhogs played a gig on 19 October 1986 in a little place called Irvine, just outside Glasgow. It was a nice gig, small and fully seated throughout. There was an obstacle when they arrived, as there was no PA. A quick call to the promoter solved the problem. It was a good gig and they packed the gear away and put it in the van. It was parked in a compound that was fenced off as some bands had gear pinched before. They were in the bar till about 2 am and Tony got talking to a couple of locals about his precious Gibson. It had taken a lot of wear and tear by then. Tony had solved the problem of it going out of tune very quickly (that had plagued him in The Tony McPhee Band), but there were other problems, as he used to throw it down at the end of gigs, so the neck was cracking right by the pickups. Tony takes up the story: 'I joked to them that I should pension off my Gibson. I went back into the dressing room after the drink and saw the case open and the strap on the floor. The Gibson had gone. What happened was our roadie, Gonzo, had become bored and removed it from the van to play it.' It was obvious Gonzo had forgotten to put it back. Tony is convinced that the two guys he was talking to pensioned it off for him. Even though the promoter made noises that he would investigate, nothing was ever heard from him. Tony is certain that more could have been done as it was 'members-only' and there were only a few people that stayed over. But, in the end, it was too late to do anymore.

On Track Series

AC/DC – Chris Sutton 978-1-78952-307-2
Allman Brothers Band – Andrew Wild 978-1-78952-252-5
Tori Amos – Lisa Torem 978-1-78952-142-9
Aphex Twin – Beau Waddell 978-1-78952-267-9
Asia – Peter Braidis 978-1-78952-099-6
Badfinger – Robert Day-Webb 978-1-878952-176-4
Barclay James Harvest – Keith and Monica Domone 978-1-78952-067-5
Beck – Arthur Lizie 978-1-78952-258-7
The Beat, General Public, Fine Young Cannibals –
Steve Parry 978-1-78952-274-7
The Beatles – Andrew Wild 978-1-78952-009-5
The Beatles Solo 1969-1980 – Andrew Wild 978-1-78952-030-9
Blue Oyster Cult – Jacob Holm-Lupo 978-1-78952-007-1
Blur – Matt Bishop 978-178952-164-1
Marc Bolan and T.Rex – Peter Gallagher 978-1-78952-124-5
Kate Bush – Bill Thomas 978-1-78952-097-2
The Byrds – Andy McArthur 978-1-78952-280-8
Camel – Hamish Kuzminski 978-1-78952-040-8
Captain Beefheart – Opher Goodwin 978-1-78952-235-8
Caravan – Andy Boot 978-1-78952-127-6
Cardiacs – Eric Benac 978-1-78952-131-3
Wendy Carlos – Mark Marrington 978-1-78952-331-7
The Carpenters – Paul Tornbohm 978-1-78952-301-0
Nick Cave and The Bad Seeds – Dominic Sanderson 978-1-78952-240-2
Eric Clapton Solo – Andrew Wild 978-1-78952-141-2
The Clash – Nick Assirati 978-1-78952-077-4
Elvis Costello and The Attractions – Georg Purvis 978-1-78952-129-0
Crosby, Stills and Nash – Andrew Wild 978-1-78952-039-2
Creedence Clearwater Revival – Tony Thompson 978-178952-237-2
The Damned – Morgan Brown 978-1-78952-136-8
David Bowie 1964 to 1982 – Carl Ewens 978-1-78952-324-9
Deep Purple and Rainbow 1968-79 – Steve Pilkington 978-1-78952-002-6
Depeche Mode – Brian J. Robb 978-1-78952-277-8
Dire Straits – Andrew Wild 978-1-78952-044-6
The Divine Comedy – Alan Draper 978-1-78952-308-9
The Doors – Tony Thompson 978-1-78952-137-5
Dream Theater – Jordan Blum 978-1-78952-050-7

Bob Dylan 1962-1970 – Opher Goodwin 978-1-78952-275-2
Eagles – John Van der Kiste 978-1-78952-260-0
Earth, Wind and Fire – Bud Wilkins 978-1-78952-272-3
Electric Light Orchestra – Barry Delve 978-1-78952-152-8
Emerson Lake and Palmer – Mike Goode 978-1-78952-000-2
Fairport Convention – Kevan Furbank 978-1-78952-051-4
Peter Gabriel – Graeme Scarfe 978-1-78952-138-2
Genesis – Stuart MacFarlane 978-1-78952-005-7
Gentle Giant – Gary Steel 978-1-78952-058-3
Gong – Kevan Furbank 978-1-78952-082-8
Green Day – William E. Spevack 978-1-78952-261-7
Steve Hackett – Geoffrey Feakes 978-1-78952-098-9
Hall and Oates – Ian Abrahams 978-1-78952-167-2
Peter Hammill – Richard Rees Jones 978-1-78952-163-4
Roy Harper – Opher Goodwin 978-1-78952-130-6
Hawkwind (new edition) – Duncan Harris 978-1-78952-290-7
Jimi Hendrix – Emma Stott 978-1-78952-175-7
The Hollies – Andrew Darlington 978-1-78952-159-7
Horslips – Richard James 978-1-78952-263-1
The Human League and The Sheffield Scene –
Andrew Darlington 978-1-78952-186-3
Humble Pie –Robert Day-Webb 978-1-78952-2761
Ian Hunter – G. Mick Smith 978-1-78952-304-1
The Incredible String Band – Tim Moon 978-1-78952-107-8
INXS – Manny Grillo 978-1-78952-302-7
Iron Maiden – Steve Pilkington 978-1-78952-061-3
Joe Jackson – Richard James 978-1-78952-189-4
The Jam – Stan Jeffries 978-1-78952-299-0
Jefferson Airplane – Richard Butterworth 978-1-78952-143-6
Jethro Tull – Jordan Blum 978-1-78952-016-3
Elton John in the 1970s – Peter Kearns 978-1-78952-034-7
Billy Joel – Lisa Torem 978-1-78952-183-2
Judas Priest – John Tucker 978-1-78952-018-7
Kansas – Kevin Cummings 978-1-78952-057-6
Killing Joke – Nic Ransome 978-1-78952-273-0
The Kinks – Martin Hutchinson 978-1-78952-172-6
Korn – Matt Karpe 978-1-78952-153-5
Led Zeppelin – Steve Pilkington 978-1-78952-151-1

Level 42 – Matt Philips 978-1-78952-102-3
Little Feat – Georg Purvis – 978-1-78952-168-9
Magnum – Matthew Taylor – 978-1-78952-286-0
Aimee Mann – Jez Rowden 978-1-78952-036-1
Ralph McTell – Paul O. Jenkins 978-1-78952-294-5
Metallica – Barry Wood 978-1-78952-269-3
Joni Mitchell – Peter Kearns 978-1-78952-081-1
The Moody Blues – Geoffrey Feakes 978-1-78952-042-2
Motorhead – Duncan Harris 978-1-78952-173-3
Nektar – Scott Meze – 978-1-78952-257-0
New Order – Dennis Remmer – 978-1-78952-249-5
Nightwish – Simon McMurdo – 978-1-78952-270-9
Nirvana – William E. Spevack 978-1-78952-318-8
Laura Nyro – Philip Ward 978-1-78952-182-5
Oasis – Andrew Rooney 978-1-78952-300-3
Mike Oldfield – Ryan Yard 978-1-78952-060-6
Opeth – Jordan Blum 978-1-78-952-166-5
Pearl Jam – Ben L. Connor 978-1-78952-188-7
Tom Petty – Richard James 978-1-78952-128-3
Pink Floyd – Richard Butterworth 978-1-78952-242-6
The Police – Pete Braidis 978-1-78952-158-0
Porcupine Tree – Nick Holmes 978-1-78952-144-3
Procol Harum – Scott Meze 978-1-78952-315-7
Queen – Andrew Wild 978-1-78952-003-3
Radiohead – William Allen 978-1-78952-149-8
Rancid – Paul Matts 978-1-78952-187-0
Lou Reed 1972-1986 – Ethan Roy 978-1-78952-283-9
Renaissance – David Detmer 978-1-78952-062-0
REO Speedwagon – Jim Romag 978-1-78952-262-4
The Rolling Stones 1963-80 – Steve Pilkington 978-1-78952-017-0
Linda Ronstadt 1969-1989 – Daryl O. Lawrence 987-1-78952-293-8
Sensational Alex Harvey Band – Peter Gallagher 978-1-7952-289-1
The Small Faces and The Faces – Andrew Darlington 978-1-78952-316-4
The Smashing Pumpkins – Matt Karpe 978-1-7952-291-4
The Smiths and Morrissey – Tommy Gunnarsson 978-1-78952-140-5
Spirit – Rev. Keith A. Gordon – 978-1-78952- 248-8
Soft Machine – Scott Meze 978-1078952-271-6

Stackridge – Alan Draper 978-1-78952-232-7
Status Quo the Frantic Four Years – Richard James 978-1-78952-160-3
Steely Dan – Jez Rowden 978-1-78952-043-9
The Stranglers – Martin Hutchinson 978-1-78952-323-2
Talk Talk – Gary Steel 978-1-78952-284-6
Tears For Fears – Paul Clark – 978-178952-238-9
Thin Lizzy – Graeme Stroud 978-1-78952-064-4
Tool – Matt Karpe 978-1-78952-234-1
Toto – Jacob Holm-Lupo 978-1-78952-019-4
U2 – Eoghan Lyng 978-1-78952-078-1
UFO – Richard James 978-1-78952-073-6
Ultravox – Brian J. Robb 978-1-78952-330-0
Van Der Graaf Generator – Dan Coffey 978-1-78952-031-6
Van Halen – Morgan Brown – 9781-78952-256-3
Suzanne Vega – Lisa Torem 978-1-78952-281-5
Jack White And The White Stripes – Ben L. Connor 978-1-78952-303-4
The Who – Geoffrey Feakes 978-1-78952-076-7
Roy Wood and the Move – James R Turner 978-1-78952-008-8
Yes (new edition) – Stephen Lambe 978-1-78952-282-2
Neil Young 1963 to 1970 – Oper Goodwin 978-1-78952-298-3
Frank Zappa 1966 to 1979 – Eric Benac 978-1-78952-033-0
Warren Zevon – Peter Gallagher 978-1-78952-170-2
The Zombies – Emma Stott 978-1-78952-297-6
10CC – Peter Kearns 978-1-78952-054-5

Decades Series

The Bee Gees in the 1960s – Andrew Mon Hughes et al 978-1-78952-148-1
The Bee Gees in the 1970s – Andrew Mon Hughes et al 978-1-78952-179-5
Black Sabbath in the 1970s – Chris Sutton 978-1-78952-171-9
Britpop – Peter Richard Adams and Matt Pooler 978-1-78952-169-6
Phil Collins in the 1980s – Andrew Wild 978-1-78952-185-6
Alice Cooper in the 1970s – Chris Sutton 978-1-78952-104-7
Alice Cooper in the 1980s – Chris Sutton 978-1-78952-259-4
Curved Air in the 1970s – Laura Shenton 978-1-78952-069-9
Donovan in the 1960s – Jeff Fitzgerald 978-1-78952-233-4
Bob Dylan in the 1980s – Don Klees 978-1-78952-157-3
Brian Eno in the 1970s – Gary Parsons 978-1-78952-239-6
Faith No More in the 1990s – Matt Karpe 978-1-78952-250-1

Fleetwood Mac in the 1970s – Andrew Wild 978-1-78952-105-4
Fleetwood Mac in the 1980s – Don Klees 978-178952-254-9
Focus in the 1970s – Stephen Lambe 978-1-78952-079-8
Free and Bad Company in the 1970s – John Van der Kiste 978-1-78952-178-8
Genesis in the 1970s – Bill Thomas 978178952-146-7
George Harrison in the 1970s – Eoghan Lyng 978-1-78952-174-0
Kiss in the 1970s – Peter Gallagher 978-1-78952-246-4
Manfred Mann's Earth Band in the 1970s – John Van der Kiste 978178952-243-3
Marillion in the 1980s – Nathaniel Webb 978-1-78952-065-1
Van Morrison in the 1970s – Peter Childs – 978-1-78952-241-9
Mott the Hoople & Ian Hunter in the 1970s – John Van der Kiste 978-1-78-952-162-7
Pink Floyd In The 1970s – Georg Purvis 978-1-78952-072-9
Suzi Quatro in the 1970s – Darren Johnson 978-1-78952-236-5
Queen in the 1970s – James Griffiths 978-1-78952-265-5
Roxy Music in the 1970s – Dave Thompson 978-1-78952-180-1
Slade in the 1970s – Darren Johnson 978-1-78952-268-6
Status Quo in the 1980s – Greg Harper 978-1-78952-244-0
Tangerine Dream in the 1970s – Stephen Palmer 978-1-78952-161-0
The Sweet in the 1970s – Darren Johnson 978-1-78952-139-9
Uriah Heep in the 1970s – Steve Pilkington 978-1-78952-103-0
Van der Graaf Generator in the 1970s – Steve Pilkington 978-1-78952-245-7
Rick Wakeman in the 1970s – Geoffrey Feakes 978-1-78952-264-8
Yes in the 1980s – Stephen Lambe with David Watkinson 978-1-78952-125-2

Rock Classics Series

90125 by Yes – Stephen Lambe 978-1-78952-329-4
Bat Out Of Hell by Meatloaf – Geoffrey Feakes 978-1-78952-320-1
Bringing It All Back Home by Bob Dylan – Opher Goodwin 978-1-78952-314-0
Crime Of The Century by Supertramp – Steve Pilkington 978-1-78952-327-0
Let It Bleed by The Rolling Stones – John Van der Kiste 978-1-78952-309-6
Purple Rain by Prince – Matt Karpe 978-1-78952-322-5

On Screen Series

Carry On… – Stephen Lambe 978-1-78952-004-0
David Cronenberg – Patrick Chapman 978-1-78952-071-2
Doctor Who: The David Tennant Years – Jamie Hailstone 978-1-78952-066-8
James Bond – Andrew Wild 978-1-78952-010-1
Monty Python – Steve Pilkington 978-1-78952-047-7
Seinfeld Seasons 1 to 5 – Stephen Lambe 978-1-78952-012-5

Other Books

1967: A Year In Psychedelic Rock 978-1-78952-155-9
1970: A Year In Rock – John Van der Kiste 978-1-78952-147-4
1972: The Year Progressive Rock Ruled The World – Kevan Furbank 978-1-78952-288-4
1973: The Golden Year of Progressive Rock 978-1-78952-165-8
Babysitting A Band On The Rocks – G.D. Praetorius 978-1-78952-106-1
Eric Clapton Sessions – Andrew Wild 978-1-78952-177-1
Dark Horse Records – Aaron Badgley 978-1-78952-287-7
Derek Taylor: For Your Radioactive Children – Andrew Darlington 978-1-78952-038-5
The Golden Age of Easy Listening – Derek Taylor 978-1-78952-285-3
The Golden Road: The Recording History of The Grateful Dead – John Kilbride 978-1-78952-156-6
Iggy and The Stooges On Stage 1967-1974 – Per Nilsen 978-1-78952-101-6
Jon Anderson and the Warriors – the road to Yes – David Watkinson 978-1-78952-059-0
Magic: The David Paton Story – David Paton 978-1-78952-266-2
Misty: The Music of Johnny Mathis – Jakob Baekgaard 978-1-78952-247-1
Nu Metal: A Definitive Guide – Matt Karpe 978-1-78952-063-7
Remembering Live Aid – Andrew Wild 978-1-78952-328-7
Tommy Bolin: In and Out of Deep Purple – Laura Shenton 978-1-78952-070-5
Maximum Darkness – Deke Leonard 978-1-78952-048-4
The Twang Dynasty – Deke Leonard 978-1-78952-049-1

And Many More To Come!

Would you like to write for Sonicbond Publishing?

At Sonicbond Publishing we are always on the look-out for authors, particularly for our two main series:

On Track. Mixing fact with in depth analysis, the On Track series examines the work of a particular musical artist or group. All genres are considered from easy listening and jazz to 60s soul to 90s pop, via rock and metal.

On Screen. This series looks at the world of film and television. Subjects considered include directors, actors and writers, as well as entire television and film series. As with the On Track series, we balance fact with analysis.

While professional writing experience would, of course, be an advantage the most important qualification is to have real enthusiasm and knowledge of your subject. First-time authors are welcomed, but the ability to write well in English is essential.

Sonicbond Publishing has distribution throughout Europe and North America, and all books are also published in E-book form. Authors will be paid a royalty based on sales of their book.

Further details are available from www.sonicbondpublishing.co.uk. To contact us, complete the contact form there or email info@sonicbondpublishing.co.uk